Music Psychotherapy and Anxiety

SOCIAL, COMMUNITY, AND CLINICAL CONTEXTS

Rebecca Zarate

Jessica Kingsley Publishers
London and Philadelphia

First published in Great Britain in 2022 by Jessica Kingsley Publishers
An imprint of Hodder & Stoughton Ltd
An Hachette Company

2

ISBN 978 1 78775 597 0
eISBN 978 1 78775 598 7

Printed and bound in Great Britain by CPI Group UK

Jessica Kingsley Publishers
Carmelite House
50 Victoria Embankment
London EC4Y 0DZ

www.jkp.com

For Luis,
My love, light and inspiration. Your unwavering
support keeps me creative and courageous.
For my family,
You have shared me with my passion for music
therapy in ways that are immeasurable.
Without you all believing in me and the beautiful work
of music therapy, this book would not exist.

Acknowledgements

First and foremost, I want to acknowledge my clients because without their bravery to be in the work and the vulnerability and trust that entails, none of this work would exist. I remain humble and honored to have been witness to their process and transformation. I have been lucky enough to have incredible mentors in my life. This book would also not be possible without them, and whose music wisdom I bring with me every day to the work. I cannot name everyone, but you all know who you are. You have nourished me and provided me with the conditions to be the person I am today. My family mentors, my friend mentors, my professional mentors, I carry a deep gratitude for you all.

Thank you to my music therapy and creative arts therapy community both national and international friends and colleagues. Particularly to my dear friends in our Flow-er Power Change Process Research group!

Deepest gratitude to Barbara Hesser for your constant support and guidance.

My sincere gratitude to my Lesley community and the incredible amount of support I have received for doing this book, from the idea through to the finished product. Particularly to my fabulous colleagues in the Expressive Therapies Department. I am truly humbled and warmed by your professional and personal generosity of time and care for me and this piece of work.

It takes a village, and I could not have done this project without the support of our home community, especially while my husband and I were extremely ill with covid in early 2020 through to 2021. Thanks to Bob, Terry, Nancy, Patrick, Nick, Emily, Julia, McKenna, David, Jimmy and Nancy for being the best, caring neighbors, friends, and supporters.

Last, but certainly not least, a loving shout out to my goldendoodle pups and writing buddies, Shea Shea and Logi, who constantly reminded me that naps do help! They brightened up my day when I couldn't write a single word by just being cute and fluffy.

Contents

Part IV: Applied Dimensions

Preface

Introduction to the dimensions of anxiety model

Concerns about anxiety and the devastating impact it can have on people's lives and community infrastructures have been increasing over the past several years. Particular attention has been placed on the relationship of anxiety to the increase of burnout and fatigue in healthcare professionals, cyberbullying behaviors, social hostility, and random or surprise acts of violence in various settings, including community gatherings and education campuses. More recently, the concerns for other manifestations of anxious and stressed behaviors in people have increased as the world has been experiencing a global pandemic. It has taken a hold on individual, collective, and systemic functioning in all aspects of human life, including families, politics, and racial inequality.

Anxiety can be a debilitating illness that impacts an individual on multiple levels. This includes the social, cultural, and economic systems that are connected to that individual. For example, Chisholm and colleagues expressed concern that when treatment of anxiety is not scaled up to fit the rate of its prevalence, "more than 12 billion days of lost productivity (equivalent of more than 50 million years of work) are attributable to depression and anxiety disorders every year, at an estimated cost of US$925 billion" (2016, p.419). The authors also discuss the global cost, which is in the region of $1–15 trillion. In America, for example, anxiety disorders are the most common mental illness, affecting 40 million people over the age of 18 per year. It can be undiagnosed or misdiagnosed for ten years before it is treated adequately (Anxiety and Depression Association of America, 2017). The result of this statistic means that close to one in ten people live with anxiety. Primary care physicians are the first step to potential screening and referrals for alternative and complementary treatment of such individuals. In 2014, Combs and Markman found that close to 20 percent of patients surveyed from a total of 965 had at least one anxiety disorder (p.1007). The major problem, however, is the consistent history in the anxiety literature that most people with identified anxiety disorders fail to obtain evidence-based psychotherapies for their condition (Goisman *et al.*, 1993; Goisman, War-shaw, & Keller, 1999). Furthermore, a large portion of our communities have a population that is living with medium to high stress, in repeated cycles and exposures, long before any anxiety or other physiological or psychological consequence is manifested.

In 2018, Lily Martin and colleagues provided a systematic review on creative arts interventions for stress management. They revealed that in Germany over the past 15 years there has been a "drastic" increase in stress-induced absenteeism at work (p.1), and they described stress as a preparation to act, and "the most widespread disease of the modern age" (2018, p.2).

Music therapy and music-informed healthcare for anxiety offers cost-effective and sustainable health benefits that target the root of the symptom. With rising reports from the major mental health association (Anxiety and Depression Association of America, 2017) of children and particularly teenagers who experience anxiety, particularly related to social media, relationships, identity, and self-esteem formation, the stakes are too high in the current social psyche and culture to not address the convergence of anxiety being experienced across all ages and in a variety of cultural and social contexts.

I hope to offer new knowledge that supports the sustainability of the mental health of individuals and communities through careful and informed use of music, music psychotherapy practice, and a clinically informed approach that may assist in avoiding the overuse and abuse of anti-anxiety medications. Key topics addressed in the book include: the presence and meaning of anxiety in current culture; how to consider and work with the interpersonal roots of the individual's *story* of anxiety (a contemporary and current trend to shape methods that capture client voices in mental healthcare); the role of music and sustainable musical environments and anxiety; and methods and techniques of working with anxiety in music therapy (clinical improvisation, specifically).

During my career, I have noticed the way in which anxiety is used in various fields and contexts. In some, it is dissected into pieces of specific knowledge on the brain that can support the use and treatment of medi-cations. In others, it has been used so generally that it has no real meaning attached to it. In the field of music therapy, while there is certainly interest in anxiety, I have noticed the same trajectory happening. We know it is there, and present in any music therapy study or treatment approach, but we do not have consolidated or unified understanding of or language for the presence and meaning of the stress–anxiety continuum in our clients' lives. How is it possible that we can approach anxiety with a level of confidence within musical creations together, as well as outside the music (in our verbal exchanges about the music that is shared), if we don't have the information or research to guide us? The motivations for this book stem from this question, and I attempt to bring together some large but vital topics on stress and anxiety in an effort to consolidate and expand current practice and thinking on anxiety, music, and music therapy. I draw from my experience as a mental health professional who works from a cultural, collective lens and trauma-informed perspective. I offer *a way of improvisation* to contribute to clinical, educational, sustainable, and transformational practices of music therapy as a treatment of choice for anxiety in mental healthcare. It is aimed at clinicians, educators, and consumers of music therapy, as well as individuals, looking for helpful ways to integrate healthcare that support de-stress techniques using music improvisational work. It is also intended to educate policy-makers and organizations interested in supporting employee health and well-being, alongside productivity. I've included some ideas on how to conceptualize areas of corporate social responsibility and sustainable approaches using musical environments that are shaped by music therapy-informed and direct music therapy care and services in workspaces and community lives.

The dimensions of anxiety in music psychotherapy

I explain a way of considering anxiety as a multifaceted phenomenon that can be approached and worked with from a deeply creative, caring, empathic, clinically informed, and socio-cultural way. It is aimed to empower readers in a way that allows for an expanded understanding of exactly what anxiety and stress look like in our everyday lives, and how we can work on them either ourselves or in our practice or our classes. I offer a model that I have been deeply interested in and developing for my 20+ years of working in mental health and music, and music psychotherapy. It encapsulates what I consider to be the *dimensions* of anxiety and stress. Each dimension accounts for a certain lens from which to look at anxiety and stress. In each dimension, I offer relevant and prevailing *themes* and in those themes are *expressions* of anxiety that people may see, or experience, on a daily level. You see, in this way, we all get to decode what is really happening in our brains and our bodies. When we harness our musical creativity in our daily lives in order to tackle living within these dimensions, we can break away from the learned concepts and dis-empowering moments that shape the cycles of stress that lead to anxiety. I am completely fascinated with stress and anxiety and the immediate effect music shows us on the themes and expressions within these dimensions. When my team and I from the Music and Mental Health Lab realized that music therapy and arts-based, improvisation techniques would shape a completely different experience and understanding of this complex thing we call anxiety, it was time to get this into a book to reach the wider public.

Part I: Theoretical Dimensions (collective anxiety, the social architecture of anxiety, and shared values for sustained mental health and wellness)

The Social Architecture of Anxiety is the theoretical framework for the whole concept of the dimensions of anxiety because it begins with the outside world first, as opposed to the approach taken by typical clinical books which begin with the details first and expand out. It is purposeful and poignant, and can be related to any socio-cultural situation at any given time. Its corresponding themes include the presence and meaning of anxiety in our lives, the collective impact of anxiety, and its embedded expressions of cultural projections and their economic impact. Dimension 1 is explained and discussed in Chapters 1, 2, and 3.

Part II: Psychological Dimensions (the psychological-physiological architecture of anxiety)

Within the structures of this dimension, I provide a detailed explanation of why we conceptualize and think about anxiety in certain ways, as explained by psychotherapy, social psychology, and neuropsychology research on attachment, bonding, relationships, and our brains. Part II connects the first dimension to the second through a series of threads, informed from each area's literature and research in the field. The corresponding themes include the neurologic function of stress and anxiety, and attachment systems and how we bond. The expressions of these themes are explained as emotional-physiological constructs in the brain and the body, and the role they play in everyday life and in people's environments and contexts. These topics are explained and presented in Chapters 4, 5, and 6.

Part III: Music and Music Therapy Dimensions (the musical architecture of anxiety)

This is where I explain the combined forces of what we know as music, as part of a greater creativity mechanism that causes change. I explain how the neurological, psychological, physiological, creative ingredients of music interact with humans on multiple sound levels. The themes that correspond with this include your physio-psychology of music, and the accompanying expressions of this, which are musical representations of our anxiousness; for instance, our rhythms, tempos, and daily structures that are represented in sound, and how dimension one and dimension two interact with these expressions. Music therapy and technique are explained in the theory of critical social aesthetics within the framework of critical improvisation and its applied method of clinical listening–cultural listening. In critical improvising, expressions of anxiety are discussed through the lens of boundaries (in and out of the music) and in-musical behaviors such as anxious musical transitions. I explain about these ideas in Chapters 7, 8, and 9.

Part IV: Applied Dimensions (applications in action)

I take you through my professional architecture of experience, breathing life into these concepts of the model in clinical, community/collective, educational, and arts-based research contexts. I explain how I use and operationalize clinical improvisation creatively in music psychotherapy and music therapy-informed ways. At its core, it is rooted in sustainable, socio-cultural, reflexive, accessible, and health-promoting approaches. The expressions of the sounds of anxiety are presented through a community women's human rights chorus on collective and shared social anxieties, an arts-based research framework, and finally a teaching example. This section covers methods for teaching anxiety in social and clinical contexts, with an example of an arts-based action research project utilizing the method of critical improvisation.

PART I

THEORETICAL DIMENSIONS

CHAPTER 1

Introduction: Music Psychotherapy and the Way of Improvisation

Defining music psychotherapy

Just like psychotherapy, music psychotherapy explores matters of the psyche and the psychic life of individuals in their personal and group/community contexts by evaluating and treating behaviors and their patterns related to previous relationships, such as possible attachment trauma and fearfully avoidant or fearfully ambivalent repeated anxious behaviors. These patterns are understood as sitting somewhere in an individual's experience of consciousness (individual and collective unconscious, preconscious, or conscious states). Unless treated and addressed, they can come out sideways in adapted patterns and distorted perceptions that cause havoc and harm in someone's life.

Music psychotherapy is an action-oriented, experiential-based psychotherapy that uses music in either a receptive or expressive/active approach as the primary mode of communication within the therapeutic alliance. Interpersonal processes (musical and non-musical) within the alliance are used to facilitate the client's change process, with advanced clinical musicianship skills and techniques. A music psychotherapist is trained at master's level and post-master's levels of education in theories of personality, psychopathology, and clinical assessment, from American Music Therapy Association-approved programs. There are four identified levels to approach music psychotherapy: music as psychotherapy, music-centered psychotherapy, music in psychotherapy, and verbal psychotherapy with music (Bruscia, 1998).

Bruscia identifies the experiential-based forms of music psychotherapy as transformative therapy, which, as he explains, is the "music experience itself that leads to change" (1998, p.4). The musical process is the client's process. It is expressed symbolically and creatively through interaction of the client's world and their issues, and, in the case of stress and anxiety, the symptoms and their stories. As Brusica highlights, "The premises for this are that the musical process is in fact the client's personal process when interacting with the world, that the musical outcome is the desired therapeutic outcome and that the process and outcome are inseparable" (1998, p.4). This is the music-centered transformative model from which my work is derived. It is a blended approach between the first two levels and the second two, mentioned above, depending on individual or group contexts, age, the population needs, and goals. In individual anxiety contexts, the client engages with me in a creative verbal warm-up, co-created music, and verbal processing and articulation of the clinical-musical data created. It acts as a means of translating insights from the symbolic work into verbal articulations and gaining insights into symptoms, associated emotional processes, and any socio-cultural contexts. In children's and teens' anxiety group contexts, music-centered warm-ups may be more necessary. In essence, I have a hybrid, eclectic music psychotherapy framework where I use all of the forms: a verbal/creative check-in and warm-up, a music-centered co-constructed process of improvised music, followed by breathwork and verbal processing before the session ends.

I was trained in the Wolberg (1967) model of psychotherapy, which integrated the music psychotherapy levels into improvisation-based music in/as therapy, mainly from analytical music therapy (Eschen, 2002) and free-improvisation techniques (Alvin, 1977; Bruscia, 1987) in the framework of the continuum of treatment levels. Those levels are the supportive level, the re-educative level, and the deeper personality work in the reconstructive level. The supportive level's purpose provides symptom relief, and supports and strengthens the client's personality structure. The use of resourcing techniques and focusing on the strengths of the client is the goal. Hesser explains, "The therapist is generally active, authoritative, directive and supportive. The therapist is a sympathetic and uncritical listener. Positive transference is encouraged. The therapist most often decides what activity the session will contain" (1979, p.10). Playing or singing *about* the symptom would be an example of this level. Re-educative music psychotherapy involves looking at the client's behaviors, relationships, and conditioned responses to relationships related to self and other dynamics (including individual, group, and community contexts). It involves mainly here-and-now, self-actualization (Rogers' theory), and examination of current intimate and social attachments. Playing or singing *to* the anxiety symptom would be an example of this stage. Reconstructive music psychotherapy is advanced post-master's training work, such as vocal psychotherapy (Austin, 2008).

The purpose is to help clients re-calibrate developmental wounds in their personality and reclaim capacity for intimacy, creativity, vitality, and a sense of self via interpersonal processes (Stern, 1985). In her improvisation approach called artistic music therapy, Albornoz describes this recalibration as harnessing clients':

> artistic power to mold what has been invented within and to use that creative power to work on the unawareness, destructive confusion, and suffering that prevent his personal growth. Transforming the individual's destructive patterns into creative ones is more critical than normalization or reaching a standardized set of achievements. (2016, p.47)

From the music-centered therapist's point of view, Aigen (1990) writes, "subjective data of this type is not merely complementary to a scientific account, but it is instead an essential component of adequate scientific description" (p.47). He is suggesting that the experience of the therapist is just as important in the music therapy process as documenting how the client is. It is an important feature to include when dealing and working with music, because how a client "is" from a therapist's point of view may or may not be distorted exactly by the therapist's viewpoint, or rather the experience. This gives rise to the consideration of where boundaries meet, or merge, or separate within the music therapy relationship with people who have attachment trauma and presenting anxiousness.

Psychodynamic improvisation involves using methods and techniques to reconstruct and repair attachment trauma and other complexes or split parts of the personality in a post-traumatic growth context. Playing or singing *as* the anxiety symptom would be an example of working in a reconstructive way. Just as there are several psychotherapy domains (Freudian, ego, object relations, self-psychology, and Jungian), music psychotherapists will typically be drawn to one of these domains as a core base for theory and practice (Hadley, 2003). Core clinical concerns of music psychotherapy practice are grounded in psychotherapy constructs of transference and countertransference, projection, projective identification, personality defenses, and resistances. Core musical, clinical skills required for sound music psychotherapy practice are concerned with how music is operationalized and manipulated to respond to, steer, and guide clinical musical discourse via methods and techniques. Those are primarily related to musical projection techniques, aesthetics and transference, musical transference and countertransference, and induced musical and vocal (or song) recall. From a transformative philosophy for social change, the critical-social aesthetics theory of critical improvisation in music psychotherapy influences the methods and techniques. I combine attachment theory and anxiety and Jungian theory in my practice, within a change process understanding of the musical alliance's function, here-and-now, and creativity. I operationalize a combination of aesthetics (Lecourt, 1998) and projection (Alvin, 1977) constructs in my clinical listening–cultural listening method as a way of understanding how to create a projective musical object from which both therapist and client can work. Once the musical object emerges, an anxiety symptom, clinical issue, or topic can explore the dynamics (emotional, creative, and psychological) and processes of both the therapist's and client's associations and responses to that object (an anxiety symptom or clinical, social issue, or topic). I approach analysis of the unfolding of the stories behind anxiety via therapist–client relationship from a developmental boundary perspective. I ask questions about the psychological meaning of transitions as they appear in the music and as related to historical developmental transitions and interruptions associated with anxiety. The whole approach includes the critical improvisation framework—the theory, method, and techniques grounded in the transformative music psychotherapy approach to treating stress and anxiety in clinical, socio-cultural, and community contexts.

Within the music psychotherapy community, there is a body of knowledge represented in various clinical and research contexts. There has been dialogue on the approach since the 1960s (see Hadley, 2003 for a detailed historical and in-depth description). Three pivotal books, initially written in English, have influenced my philosophy and practice: *Dynamics of Music Psychotherapy*, edited by Bruscia (1998), *Psychodynamic Music Therapy*, edited by Hadley (2003), and *The Music in Music Therapy. Psychodynamic Music Therapy in Europe: Clinical, Theoretical, and Research Approaches*, edited by Backer and Sutton (2014). All three books offer a collection of robust case studies that explore the clinical and musical-clinical concerns of personality, psychosis, mood, states, and emotions in mental health and well-being. Though written a while ago and in company with more cutting-edge critical work being discussed in this book, this collection of clinical material continues to be relevant and influences my core practice and thinking. Other practicing clinicians offer various case and theory examples in areas of personhood and change (Hannibal, 2003), bereaved teenagers (McFerran-Skewes, 2000), general introduction and overviews (Isenberg, 2015; Kim, 2016; Metzner, 2016), training considerations (Sobey & Woodcock, 1999), and early abandonment (Walsh Stewart & Stewart, 2002).

Psychodynamic improvisation

There are clinical contexts and applied community contexts in psychodynamic improvisation. Some of the most exciting research occurring is in its efficacy to change mental health states of depression and anxiety and affect regulation (Aalbers *et al.*, 2019, 2020; Erkkílä *et al.*, 2012; Erkkílä, 2014; Erkkilä *et al.*, 2019; Zarate, 2016a) and showing important change factors within psychodynamic improvisation. We are finding decreases and sustained low levels in scores for depression and anxiety. My focus is mainly on the unfolding processes of specific sounds of anxiety symptoms and their accompanying interpersonal/intersubjective stories.

Other colleagues are exploring issues related to self-organization processes for neurological rehabilitation (Schmid, 2014); methods with anxious autistic children (Zarafshandardaky, 2019); applications in medical settings (Lee & Clements-Cortes, 2014); aesthetic, artistic, and interpersonal dimensions (Hartmut, 2007; Metzner, 2005, 2016); meaning-making and experiences of self (Austin, 1996; Gilbertson, 2013; McCaffrey, 2013; Smeijsters, 2005; Weymann, 2000); single-session (Chen, 2019) and musical performance anxiety (Kim, 2016; Kim, 2008); and critical perspectives (Sajnani *et al.*, 2017).

Regardless of the approach, there are general guiding principles for the music therapist to apply. Those are, as Wigram (2004) explains, to "start with a simple idea; listen carefully to one's music; practice techniques and specific skills; master skills one at a time before attempting to combine and integrate a number of skills" (p.12). He continues to highlight an important skill—and I think the foundation of clinical improvisation—which is listening. He writes, "Above all, I believe the most important and vital element for anybody learning improvisation is to listen to what you are doing and enjoy the experience of doing it" (Wigram, 2004, p.12). Listening to what is being played and evaluating in the here-and-now from a creative, cultural, and clinical perspective can be daunting for initial exposure to improvisation. Wigram's basic introductory steps are a manageable approach, which I use when teaching and which have helped me to develop my framework of critical improvisation over the collection of clinical experiences in my 20 years of experience as a music therapist. Guiding principles for how I also approach improvisation focus on creativity and creative expression to explore ruptures and distortions in relationships and experiences that impact changes in pleasure, engagement, control, and trust.

Listening for the past and present in the realms of consciousness
A psychodynamic approach requires understanding that the present and the past are brought into each session. All consciousness levels concerning the mind and body are present and elicited in the multisensory musical play encounter. Neurophysiological, neurobiological, and psychophysiological sciences inform music psychotherapy practice more than ever in terms of how the body stores and remembers experience (Porges, 2017; Schore *et al.*, 2021; Siegel & Solomon, 2020; van der Kolk, 2015). Music

physiology and consciousness in altered state contexts also inform practice (Aldridge & Fachner, 2006; Battles, 2018; Schneck, 2015; Schneck & Berger, 2006). It is helpful to understand consciousness in music therapy processes using Ken Wilber's model of the spectrum of consciousness. Wilber (1977) addresses the different levels at which a human being can experience consciousness. Level one includes the all-inclusive, non-dualistic reality, where we are at one with the universe. Level two is the total organism, whereby a movement from the first level to the second means we can identify with the human organism, the body/mind area. The third level is called the ego level. This is where the body and mind split, where we can say, "I exist in the body, but not as the body. Our body is now with self-image, only a mental reflection of the total organism" (Rugenstein, 1996, p.15). The fourth level is the persona level, where any undesired facets of the ego are disowned and projected outwards onto other people. Rugenstein comments, "At this level, we are left with a narrow, inaccurate, impoverished self-image or persona" (p.16). Altered states and transcendent experiences happen in improvisation contexts. The consciousness model operationalizes theories and research associated with the collective unconscious (Jung's theory), artistic expression, and psychophysiology perspectives. For evaluation of these levels of consciousness in the analysis of the music's points of interest (where there is an aspect(s) of the physical, interpersonal, artistic, psychological, and spectrum of consciousness actions that stands out), skills in countertransference and projection centered in musical language and models in music therapy are needed. The presence of intentional versus unintentional motifs and patterns would be an example of using the spectrum of consciousness to analyze levels of consciousness within the clinical musical data.

Listening for transitions

I view transitions in psychodynamic improvisation as a sign of psychological and emotional shifts. A key point to remember is whether the transition is an abrupt or fluid one within any given point of interest occurring in the music. Transitions are critical because they represent the stored, cellular memories of developmental transitions and symbolic, artistic transitions representing such memories and, therefore, the client's process. A number of music therapists are interested in the role and function of transitions in music improvisation. For example, in his work, Turry (2012) refers to the importance of the therapist's use of major and minor harmonies as a "vital component" of the idea of transitions as representations of psychological processes (p.127). Once identified, a deeper analysis of the quality of the transition can occur. Wigram (2004) names several of these qualities as seductive, limbo, overlapping transitions, which the therapist can apply in the improvisation realm. In my work, I view the transitions that show up in exploring anxiety symptoms as representations of psychic activation moments. The improvisation process may cause these moments to express or voice possible attachment trauma, past or current neglect or abuse, or a significant moment related to the symptom story. They can come from the past or the present or act concurrently and recur in active memory, or recall a current pattern of fear or panic responses. The responses will be associated with the symptom and its personal, social, and community impacts and contexts, giving an opportunity to shape further clinical discourse.

Listening for cultural-musical projections

Past and present occur in the spectrum of consciousness in the musical relational space. Stories we have been told about others and the stories we tell ourselves of others are also occurring. Transgenerational and intergenerational transmission of those stories also happens in the improvisational world. The interpersonal dimensions of the socio-cultural environment are just as important as any other dynamics. Stapleton refers to this context as needing to apply improvisational responsibility (Stapleton, 2013). Such contexts require acknowledgment and receptive musical presence for growth (to use Siegel's concept and the act of receptive presence as a response to panic) (Siegel, n.d.) of our personal and cultural stories. They are what makes the work so rich and help us find meaning-making of our worlds and each other. The psychodynamics of this aspect of improvising are present in every encounter. It takes an astute and culturally empathic music psychotherapist to allow cultural identity to be voiced in the process. For example, if I played in a modal framework to engage in an initial exploration about the anxiety symptom, I would need to make sure that I had considered my client's cultural meaning and preferences. I would need to do this in my planning and the here-and-now decisions for the discourse for the improvisation, including any pre-planned instrumentation and song usage. When a cultural projection might happen, the therapist and client's musical impressions and expressions of unconscious musical responses to frameworks and mediums would be considered within the music. If I felt confident about playing a certain medium outside my cultural heritage and realized that I was projecting my perceptions of what I think the music should sound like based on the client's cultural background, this would be an example of me projecting cultural musical images onto my client. If my client began singing in an English accent, that would be their cultural musical projections towards me. Projections are protection and incredibly powerful in developing the alliance and gleaning more information about the client's story.

Listening for musical countertransference in the aesthetics

Scheiby defines musical countertransference as:

> sound patterns that reflect or evoke feelings, thoughts, images, attitudes, opinions, and physical reactions originating in and generated by the music therapist, as unconscious or preconscious reactions to the client and his or her transference. The medium through which these countertransferences are conveyed is the music played in the session. (1998, p.214)

Musical countertransference happens when the interpersonal musical and non-musical psychodynamics are active in the improvisation. A song or piece of music comes into the therapist's psyche due to musical transferences from the client. It is so powerful to use; I can still recall my first example of consciously recognizing this and trusting the process enough to use it as an intervention from an internship in a men's trauma group in inpatient psychiatry.

I was lucky enough to be taught by some of the leaders in theory and practice. Benedikte Scheiby was the person who ushered me through honing that specific skill of psychodynamic improvising. To this day, it is one of my inspirational memories of practicing music therapy. This is how I explained it back then on a moment of interest exploring death anxiety in response to a young adult group member losing a family member. The relationship enabled shadow behaviors and had distorted relationship patterns. He was processing the meaning of the death within the young adult group context:

> Suddenly, I spontaneously introduced a hymn that I had sung at primary school when I was about five or six years old! I say introduce because it felt like a fade-in, or mix, from one record to another. I was completely aware of what was happening. I knew the melody that my fingers were beginning to play, and I was singing the words in my head but did not sing them out loud. I checked in with myself, wondering what was going on, and asking myself whether this was coming from me or someone else, as well as questioning whether I should go with it. I decided to go with it, and it had an amazing effect on the group's music. The clients became more animated in the music, they played stronger, lifted their heads, and the tempo became slightly faster. What interested me was that the song's tempo, rhythm, and chord structure were nearly the same as those of the first song. I also underwent a change in my artistic and state responses to the music, emotion, and feeling, from sad and heavy, to a sense of resolution. After listening to the session's recording, attempting to map all of the territories with the boundary model, and asking my supervisors what their opinions of this event were, I concluded that what

had happened was indeed musical countertransference. It was some form of a healing message coming through in the form of a song that had been accessed via all of the dynamics circulating in the therapy room. It felt as if it had come from way out in the realms of what Wilber (2001) would call "unity consciousness," and brought forth into the present situation.

Musical countertransference for me represents a doorway into a deeper understanding of the client's and my associations with the story. It serves to enhance an experience of agency and reflexivity via the intersubjective, interpersonal, intra-musical, and inter-musical processes—for both therapist and client on all aspects of the "clinical" problem being addressed. The group showed symbolic (musical) and actual (behavioral) signs of what Ahonen-Eerikäinen (2007) highlights as musical altruism in the analytical group music therapy process. Musical countertransference expresses the multisensory dynamics and the story's emotion in a creative, artistic way. The act of artistic expression by the therapist of the musical countertransference provides an opportunity for psychological process and integration from a deeply aesthetic sense and perception of the emerging co-constructed musical objects and their meanings. Lecourt grounds her work on four aesthetic assumptions: "That music is a transformational (or transitional) object, that it is a 'relief art,' that it is a process of pain 'aestheticization,' and it is a form of sublimation therapy" (1998, p.139). In her view, there are aspects of aesthetic factors, and particularly on a couple of important factors that consider aesthetic biases and their potential for creating distortions in the therapeutic relationship, and how music can be a separate object in itself. It can provide a medium within which the therapist and patient can separate, or it can be a shared object wherein the patient and therapist fuse through acts of seduction or intrusion. These opportunities for creating distance or intimacy are evident in many of our clinical and aesthetic assumptions.

In my view, aesthetic factors in musical countertransference also function as dual, concurrent moderators with creativity. They deepen the change factor of the *musical alliance* in the therapeutic alliance and ultimately influence growth in the therapeutic process. Musical countertransference is a vital skill to practice. As Wigram suggests, specific practice is part of getting good at improvising. I continue to spend specific, focused practice and evaluation time on this skill alone.

Listening for resistance, regression, and defense in attachment system responses

Austin and Dvorkin write: "Because music can facilitate regression and call forth younger aspects of one's personality, the client experiences the threat of revealing those parts of the self that have never been accepted" (1998, p.125). Symbols of stress and anxiety patterns can emerge as projections during the musical processes and be defense actions of the self. They may be described as an ice block, or, in one client's case, "the iceman" or a wall, or some form of barrier. Instruments and songs are used to project these images and play with them. The "iceman" found a song, "Raindrops Keep Falling on my Head," and this showed the beginning of the healing and discovery process of melting the ice or peeling back the layers of resistance. The ice was changing into water or melting. A way to stay in the therapeutic relationship when these layers of resistance, regression, and defense come up is via the act of a receptive musical presence (I see you, I hear you, I'm with you). Austin and Dvorkin (1998) explain:

> Resistance can be observed as clients consistently choose or avoid using particular instruments. This can be due to an identification with an instrument and a resulting vulnerability. The self is too exposed because the person is merged with the instrument, and therefore one's whole sense of self-worth is riding on the performance. Resistance can also be due to projecting an aspect of oneself onto a certain instrument (the shadow, for example, the angry child projected onto the drum). Both these resistances become more intense when the instrument is the voice. (p.126)

The voice is connected to our whole being and functions as the mediator of change because of all the connections to our psychophysiological, biological self. The vagus nerve, for example, is one of those essential physiological evolutionary linkages. It responds to infants' and caregivers' early vocal sounds and is responsible for our social-emotional connections and needs. When we activate the psyche via music and voice interventions, we activate the whole body and its cellular, unconscious, pre-conscious, and conscious memory, contexts, and associations.

Psychodynamic work includes various techniques and methods that can either induce or regress. For example, in the evidence-based method of induced song recall by Diaz de Chumaceiro, she describes the use of songs and their associations as "a psychotherapeutic tool that facilitates access to feelings and thoughts that are out of immediate awareness. It is particularly useful for clarifying and resolving impasse cases when inevitable 'blind,' 'dumb,' 'bright' or 'dim' spots may be preventing progress in treatment" (1998, p.366). Songs and their contexts are the musical symbols of the client's psychic life but can be used as supportive intervention levels, such as conscious coping tools for affect regulation during times of stress. Diaz de Chumaceiro also researched film music and evocative states using induced song recall. These are typical techniques that I will use in sessions because people associate songs with films, memories of anniversary events or days, and, most importantly, they are grounded in the intermusical actions of improvising.

Working through musical and non-musical processes of remembering lyrics, melody, memories, and so on with a client, or when a client (or therapist) forgets specific lyrics to familiar and meaningful songs, is an example of where the therapist can begin to work with resistance processes and patterns.

Listening for the themes

As with any improvisation, thematic development is the core of how the anxiety story is told and expanded. Within the process of unfolding, I work within certain musical frameworks. Frameworks are critical in approaching psychodynamic improvisation because of the containment and alignment needed in shaping the musical structure to work within. I use the method of frameworking significantly in my work. Wigram (2004) defines frameworks as "the creation of some appropriate musical structure to enable a client to engage, or in response to a client's music" (p.117). He goes on to describe the function of the tool: "A framework might have the function of inspiring and encouraging, or it might equally have the function of stabilizing and containing" (p.118). Various techniques are applied within these structures. Techniques are described in detail by Bruscia (1987) and Wigram (2004), and these are valuable resources. I use Austin's vocal holding and free-associative singing method to explore the symptom's story and create a dialogue with the client from my vocal psychotherapy work. I apply the technique of experimenting as a guiding pillar to most of my free-improvisation interventions. Pure forms and hybrid versions of approaches are equally important to me. For example, suppose I do not use vocal psychotherapy. In that case, I apply psychodynamic vocal work with aspects of the voice (the authentic voice, for example), informed from Baker and Uhlig (2011), and expand instrumental-based work at the piano with clients, which is deeply informed by the creative music therapy approaches from Nordoff-Robbins (2007). Improvised play and songwriting are particularly beneficial with anxious children.

In any session, the practical matters of place, space, and procedure need to be considered, such as the acoustic environment and instruments being used (Nordoff-Robbins, 2007, p.175). The piano is my principal instrument, and so all of my work is grounded in piano-informed improvisation. See Nordoff-Robbins (2007) for details on other practical requirements and clinical musicianship details.

I like to apply matching and attuning techniques to each musical and non-musical *quality* and *characteristic* of a client's sounds, using receptive musical-cultural presence in my intention, typically as a form of alliance-building and as an in-session, ongoing evaluation of the client's state. Mirroring and reflecting the sounds' melodic qualities, I send the message through the music of "I see you, I'm with you, I hear you," in the act of empathic intention. Grounding is a technique that I tend to use frequently, especially with clients who have more physiological, psychological response systems related to panic. A particular intervention that I've noticed works is octaves and grounding, with textured yet simple harmonic structures accompanying vocalizing, singing, or instrumental melodic development. When the anxiety story's themes begin to unfold in more advanced work, I use dialoguing techniques alongside mirroring with musical amplification of motifs or patterns that emerge, representing deeper layers to the anxiety story. Extemporizing and expanding the story via the musical narrative is a method where I'm able to activate and utilize the concepts discussed in this chapter in and through the music and musical alliance. Examples of how I bring all of these ingredients together can be found in Part III.

A model of affect regulation and developmental repair of anxiety symptoms

The model explains how I understand each intervention as a function to move a client from aroused stress responses and anxious states to a state of affect regulation and a sense of well-being through the concept of flow. It is an adapted version of Elliot's model informed by the model of flow (Csikszentmihalyi, 1975), and offers a balanced and client-aligned, action-oriented experience or *action opportunities and challenges* in the form of music therapy interventions and *action capabilities* through the functions of *creativity* in the therapeutic alliance and process.

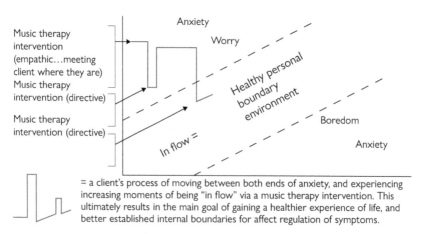

= a client's process of moving between both ends of anxiety, and experiencing increasing moments of being "in flow" via a music therapy intervention. This ultimately results in the main goal of gaining a healthier experience of life, and better established internal boundaries for affect regulation of symptoms.

Figure 1.1: Adapted model of flow state

28

CHAPTER 2

The Collective Impact of Anxiety

Issues in mental health care and anxiety

Data from the Global Burden of Disease Study conducted by the Institute for Health Metrics and Evaluation (IHME) showed that 792 million people were suffering from any given mental disorder in 2017, or 10.7 percent of the world's population, which was at 7.6 billion, according to the United Nations (UN) annual population prospects report (United Nations Department of Economic and Social Affairs, 2017). Of the total number, 284 million people, or a 3.8 percent share of our global population, had experienced an anxiety disorder, ranking anxiety as the top-rated mental health disorder across all mental health categories and above that of depression. The number for depression comes in at a close second with 264 million people, 3.4 percent (Dattani *et al.*, 2018). In the same report, the United States (US) revealed 20.9 million people having an anxiety disorder in a population of 325 million.

As a stark difference from the US, the United Kingdom (UK), my native country, showed 2.96 million reports from a population of 66 million (55.6 million, England) (Office of National Statistics, 2017). Reported cases of anxiety have remained steady in UK numbers since 1990, with barely any increase. However, there has been almost a systematic increase of five million cases in the US since 2014. Possible reasons are stigma and culture, and potential strategies for profit-making from various stakeholders in medicine. Since 2000, certain global groups and institutions have come together to solve the overall continuum of mental health (from prevention and treatment to long-term care) across the globe. It has involved multiple stakeholders and ideas, representing the vastness of cultural, economic, and social strengths and challenges of all involved nations. The UN has been a leader in cultivating conversations and convening opportunities to shape strategy. These efforts have had various iterations of projects and initiatives to support and treat global mental health. More recently, in the past ten years, there has been a shift and movement towards a more comprehensive and integrative strategy for global mental health that stretches beyond the traditional walls of different countries' health sector strategies. In 2013, at its 66th meeting, with the endorsement of its 194 ministers, the World Health Organization (WHO) launched its *Comprehensive Mental Health Action Plan 2013–2020*, which dovetailed into its millennial health goals. The plan rested on four central pillars: leadership and governance in mental health; integrated, responsive, community-based mental healthcare and social care services; strategies for promoting mental health awareness; and preventing mental health issues and crises.

In *The Lancet*'s commission, Patel and colleagues (2018) explain the four areas that have primarily been considered within global mental health reform and transformation strategies: the social determinants of mental disorders, the global burden of disease attributed to mental health, the inadequate investments in global mental health, and the near absence of access to quality care globally. The categories have come to articulation as a result of a series of initiatives over time. Institutions and organizations that have been drivers in that movement have been calling to tackle the systemic issues in a real-world way. For example, solutions need to address links with mental health to social, collective, and sustainable health in all cultures and societies. Other interested stakeholders have also joined in to shape the movement to form clinical, organizational responses to this exponential rise in mental health issues. The Royal Foundation of the Duke and Duchess of Cambridge is worth a specific mention on this. In 2016, its Heads Together initiative was launched to respond to the UK's unique systemic mental health problems.

The initiative illuminates a range of social, cultural, and economic issues related to mental health (Royal Foundation of the Duke and Duchess of Cambridge, 2021). The pattern of increases in mental health issues in the UK and US is a pattern that is repeated worldwide. Furthermore, the connection to the healing and transformative power of the arts and mental health has been highlighted by the Royal Foundation, with various projects, such as Full Effect, initiated in 2013 by HRH Prince Harry and the Duchess of Sussex, Meghan Markle.

Globalization, sustainability, and collective mental health
During the 2018 semi-annual Chief Executives Board meeting of the UN, leaders convened a roundtable on global mental health to discuss concerns. These concerns addressed the context of the updated millennial goals to the Sustainable Development Goals (SDGs) initiative. Mental health falls in goal number three: Good Health and Well-being (United Nations., n.d.). The roundtable, chaired by the UN Secretary-General António Guterres, also featured his Deputy Secretary-General Amina J. Mohammed, the WHO Director-General Tedros Adhanom Ghebreyesus, the United Nations

International Children's Fund (UNICEF) Executive Director Henrietta Fore, and 20 other representatives from academia, government, and stakeholders in society. The discussion's general sentiment shows a deep concern that inadequate health does not happen in a vacuum, that societal and environmental factors are involved, and a united message of *no health without mental health.* Mohammed, in particular, has called for a more significant cross-sectional investment (beyond the health sector) in mental health that considers equality and fundamental individual human rights.

In 2018, the Lancet Commission on Global Health and Sustainable Development released a detailed update on the new SDGs to prevent and treat mental health disorders (Patel *et al.*, 2018). The group reframed the strategy to decrease the disease's global burden into four significant pillars and six actions. The four pillars are:

1. Mental health is a global public good and is relevant to sustainable development in all countries.
2. Mental health problems exist along a continuum from mild, time-limited distress to a chronic, progressive, and severely disabling condition.
3. The mental health of each individual is the unique product of social and environmental influences.
4. Mental health is a fundamental human right for all people that requires a rights-based approach (Patel *et al.*, 2018, p.1553).

The six actions named in the same executive summary by Patel and company are:

1. Integrate and scale up mental health services into the global response of other health priorities.
2. Address the barriers that threaten mental health across sectors, such as lack of awareness, attention, promotion, and protection.
3. Address the constraints caused by stigma and discrimination.
4. Act on threats to mental health due to global climate change.
5. Decrease inequality and disparities in access to care, epidemics, and pandemics, including the Covid-19 pandemic which began in 2019.
6. Update policies and development efforts.

Protecting mental health through policies and developmental efforts includes an interdisciplinary range of community stakeholders, which are mentioned in the report: education, workplaces, social welfare, gender empowerment, child and youth services, criminal justice and development, humanitarian assistance (Patel *et al.*, 2018, p.1554). It is an approach that speaks to the need to look at the care of mental health as it is related to social and environmental "determinants that have a crucial influence on the mental health of developmentally sensitive periods, particularly in childhood and adolescence" (Patel *et al.*, 2018, p.1554). The new direction offers new opportunities and an approach that trains non-specialist individuals in the community for greater reach and assistance. It also includes investments in digital technology, carving out access for the employment continuum to mobilize multiple voices in the care continuum. Substantial and additional investments will support the economy and health of nations severely damaged due to the lack of global resources and strategies. Efficiency and effectiveness of treatment alongside care methods with local and existing resources are also part of the plan, as are re-allocation of current funding, specific investments in research and novel approaches informed from diverse disciplines. Genomics, neuroscience, health services, clinical and social sciences are all included sectors, "both for implementation research on scaling up mental health interventions and for discovery research to advance understanding of causes and mechanisms of mental disorders and develop effective interventions to prevent and treat them" (Patel *et al.*, 2018, p.1554).

Access to mental health services

The impact of the costs of globalization on mental health and sustainability is in our everyday lives. Whether we are impacted directly by it or a by-product flits through our daily routines and interactions, it is present. The health and mental health ecosystem is off-balance, and people's lives are at stake because of it. If such strategies to solve this problem have been put into place by those responsible for global mental health, why is access remaining a significant determinant of lack of progress? A critical perspective is important. On the one hand, there is a big business behind the anxious mental health condition, and on the other, there is no general business to manage public health. As the data shows, mental health gets less than 3 percent of national and international health costs per fiscal year (Patel *et al.*, 2018). When we critique this situation, the lack of success in this global strategy is obvious from the stark differences across cultures and nations.

The current opioid crisis is the single most corrupt act in health care of modern-day times. While this has been causing so much harm and destruction, particularly in the US, there has been a similar trajectory in the increase of anxiety medications in mental health care. Bachhuber and colleagues (2016) collected data on benzodiazepine use on prescriptions, and overdose mortality in the US. Their findings showed that close to 9000 deaths occurred, and 13.9 million people were filling a benzodiazepine (an anti-anxiety medication) prescription. According to the authors, the deaths from benzodiazepine overdoses "rose at a faster rate than did the percentage of individuals filling benzodiazepine prescriptions" (Bachuber *et al.*, 2016, p.687). Furthermore, anxiety and opioid addiction are two interconnected clinical-social issues in today's contemporary culture. This doesn't help us gain a clearer understanding of anxiety, medication, or pain, because of the co-occurring associated combinations that compound this stark situation. Two significant mental health crises are occurring here—the pharmaceutical treatment of anxiety in the US is also a product of capitalist philosophy and a four-billion-dollar industry (Bachhuber *et al.*, 2016). The pattern of access via capitalistic gains from product creation to product dissemination and product usage is an issue of governmental and societal responsibility, with the need to regulate and educate about access, use, and recovery strategies.

Stigma, mental health, and anxiety

One of the more prominent barriers to gaining and providing access to services is the attached stigma around mental health, particularly within societies that have built their social and cultural structures around individualism, ableism, and elitism. Reflecting on the comparison data between the US and UK, and the little to no rise in *reported* anxiety disorders, is one way of looking at that, as it is related to stigma issues. If the data isn't reflecting the accurate representation of a phenomenon, then it is all the easier not to provide funding for services for that phenomenon. It is not just happening the UK (England particularly). There is a lack of data in collectivist cultures that have certain moral expectations to the collective and these cultures are also at risk of the same plight—no treatment or a lack of treatment that is informed and that works. In my own experiences of working with anxious individuals, I have seen a complete demoralization of a sense of agency and vitality. Progressively, the stressors that cause anxiety disorders become too much to be able to manage. Consequently, individuals retreat and isolate themselves from family, work, and community, or simply break down due to the unbearable load of constant worry that keeps them up at night. These cycles become continuous, with no beginning or end. It is heartbreaking. Immediate and strategic attention is needed to assess, treat, and, more importantly, prevent the constant worry and fear that shape the internal and external narrative of people's lives via these structural and systemic mechanisms.

Reducing the treatment gap

Reducing the treatment gap as a focused strategy on this global health concern means a paradigm and philosophical shift in the way in which mental health is perceived. As suggested above, a comprehensive model of social, environmental, and biological factors is needed. The shift is moving towards an understanding of universal factors contributing towards good health and mental health, and creating a system that supports economic stability and social stability. Within these initiatives and organization around mental health prevention, treatment, and recovery, it must be recognized that anxiety is a social, systemic, and cultural problem, which is caused by the various local and global community and political systems. Given the obvious need for more access to services, music therapy for mental health can make some very important strides in theory, practice, and research. Let's begin with a theoretical idea on the power of a socially relevant lens offered in Chapter 3.

Permission has been granted to re-publish this chapter in this book. The original publication can be found in the open access journal *Voices: A World Forum of Music Therapy* (2016), volume 16, issue 1.

CHAPTER 3

The Social Architecture of Anxiety and the Potential Role of Music Therapy

Clinicians currently understand anxiety as a blanket term for a complicated bundle of clinically defined symptoms. However, in the US, anxiety presents itself as an operationalized social construct, historically embedded in the social fabric in the form of a work ethic from the 1950s and sometimes referred to as *the emblem of struggle* (Tone, 2009). The social roots and the multisensory, intersubjective, relational, embodied presence of anxiety—in other words, the social architecture of anxiety—in the US is not sufficiently recognized as an important component that informs clinical practice, theory development, or research in music therapy.

Music therapists work with a wide variety of clients who are experiencing stress and anxiety, yet the relational and subjective experience of these conditions has not received sufficient attention in music therapy literature. This chapter starts from the premise that social pressures, to be successful in Western society, are linked to anxiety. Those social pressures have formed a social architecture of anxiety that is embedded within certain inherited power relationships and manifests in an intersubjective, embodied context. It is within this context that music therapy may be useful in the treatment of anxiety, may contribute towards decreasing its prevalence, and help to increase the wellness and productivity of individuals and their roles within their communities.

Personal and professional context of the author

Differences in culture (i.e. education, employment, and use of music) have always intrigued me. I am a White Cornish straight woman from the UK, who has been privileged with an education from the UK and trained as a music therapist in the US, and currently lives in the US. As a practicing clinician and professor of music therapy, I am constantly cross-referencing my cultural boundaries and my trans-cultural identity because they will always be complicated, intriguing, and different from those of many colleagues and clients in the US. Yet, wherever I have lived or worked, certain community and collective phenomena and events have moved me to provide service in my field from within a trauma-informed approach. I have a passion and a privilege to use my craft to support vulnerable voices whose lives have been impacted by social hostility and to explore the relationship between social hostility and cultural/collective anxiety from a critical, reflective, and reflexive stance.

I am curious to explore the cultural and collective unconscious motivations that are apparent in a social model of anxiety. Major events in my career, taking place in a variety of settings and countries, have shaped my current theoretical perspective and have forged my motivation to continue a trauma-informed approach to my music therapy practice and pedagogy. Those experiences included practicing in quintessential rural English communities, where mental health care services seemed to use the absence of empathy and professionalism as a psychological shadow tool to oppress a split part of the community psyche. I have also witnessed the terror of life bestowed on children and young people in Romania in the wake of Nicolae Ceauşescu's regime. In more recent years, I worked as a new Master of Music Therapy in the mental health hospital system in New York City through the 9/11 air attacks, and later through Superstorm Sandy, and the Boston Marathon bombings as a seasoned clinician and educator, while also living in the affected communities. The deep social influence of these kind of events and their relationship to anxiety is an area that I consider necessary for the field of music therapy to explore. I continue to be inspired to use my experiences and observations to look more closely at the cultural context of anxiety and the mechanism of collective anxiety from a humanitarian, psychoanalytic, anthropologic, and social justice perspective. My research is grounded in the US, but it also applies more broadly to the global context. Using a cultural lens, I hope to bridge the clinical-social gap in research on music therapy and anxiety.

The cultural and collective context of anxiety

According to the World Health Organization (n.d.), anxiety has become a serious international threat to global health, productivity, and sensibility. When a person suffers from anxiety, it impacts all aspects of their well-being, as well as people close to them. Productivity, lifestyle, work, ability to maintain relationships with loved ones, and even the ability to do basic errands such as grocery shopping can be negatively impacted by anxiety. When the lens is widened and individual impacts on relationships become community or even trans-cultural issues, the cultural and collective impact of anxiety can be a menacing social construct that requires inquiry and action. The presence and meaning of anxiety is different in all cultures; in certain countries, there are very few reports of anxiety episodes, while in others, such as the US, anxiety is more prevalent. There is a rooted social history of anxiety in the US that is directly linked to balancing success with a fear of failure. This history has created a widely accepted narrative of how the country has shaped itself culturally, including a clinical discourse that has, in turn, become an opportune landscape for pharmaceutical companies to explore how anti-anxiety medications can prevail over potential alternatives.

Although fairly broad in terms of history and etiology, anxiety has been addressed in the literature primarily in terms of clinical treatment rather than the experience of anxiety from a social and cultural perspective. Certain authors, such as Rollo May (1996), Karen Horney (1992), Andrea Tone (2009), and Howard F. Stein (2004), have infused their psychological and medical research on anxiety with social theory, but, by and large, the clinical field of anxiety has remained separate from social and cultural studies,

Whereas assessment criteria in the clinical field of anxiety have remained focused on pathology—see the *Diagnostic and Statistical Manual of Mental Disorders, 5th edition (DSM–5)* (American Psychiatric Association, 2013)— other disciplines are also involved in the broader conversation on anxiety and culture, namely sociology and psychology. Since the 1970s, certain social psychologists, such as Rollo May and Karen Horney, have commented on and theorized about anxiety as a social phenomenon stemming from modernist sensibilities. Both Horney (1992) and May (1996) drew their ideas from contemporary sociologists who questioned humanity's relationship with anxiety. Karen Horney (1992) identified the environment as a critical factor in personality development. Her writing also touched on the notion of social hostility that has permeated the interpersonal environment with the emergence of competitive individualism. Social hostility and basic anxiety provide an overarching mechanism to further understand anxiety as a larger cultural phenomenon. Particular social themes that Horney addressed in addition to social hostility are anxiety as a cultural experience, economics of modern society and competitive individualism, and structures in cultural processes and their relationship to the structure of neurosis. May (1996) addressed the maintenance of self as a personality and the notion of threat and fear as main characteristics that challenge personal and collective adequacy and value.

One author whose work may be helpful in further bridging the gap between the clinical and social body of knowledge on anxiety is Iain

Wilkinson (2001). Wilkinson is a seminal author in sociology and anxiety who presented the notion that society is more "risk conscious" in contemporary culture and that this impacts the social dynamics of modern society. This construct is generally understood as a definition of cause of anxiety or an expression of anxiety. Wilkinson (2001) theorized that it is risk consciousness that perpetuates anxiety in society. His ideas move us towards an understanding of how and why anxiety appears on the collective level, and complement those from the psychology world and add to the growing need for an understanding of social impacts in anxiety theory.

Stein (2004) presented a view similar to Wilkinson's by addressing the unconscious motivations behind certain behaviors that seem to create a collective anxiety, as well as addressing behaviors that deliberately create hostility towards others. His refreshing critical perspective on unconscious desires to soothe collective anxieties has prevailed through building on the psychoanalytical construct of the shadow part of the personality structure and the mechanism of "othering" through the creation of the "evil" other. Stein (2004) develops this idea through a psychoanalytic anthropology lens by asserting that the air attacks in New York and Washington in 2001 left a "free floating anxiety" (p.8) that has permeated the consciousness of America. He further stated that this incident left US culture in a "vicious cycle of anxiety and defense" (p.14). In brief, Stein (2004) theorized that the 9/11 attacks were a psychological de-masculinization of iconic American symbols and a double projective identification situation that was ultimately representative of rage towards parents. Stein further stated that the reaction to the attacks was one of humiliation and rage. The rage resulted in another cycle of projections towards a split part of the collective psyche. The anxiety literature on social and cultural context, such as the work of Wilkinson and Stein, points towards an overarching, highly charged, intersubjective, interactive theme and therefore positions anxiety as a relational concept.

Attempts to conceptualize the intersections of anxiety, culture, and diversity have been presented by a number of fields of inquiry. The Oxford Handbook of Anxiety and Related Disorders provides a current perspective of anxiety and culture through a multi-modal clinical and anthropological approach (Asmal & Stein, 2009). Other studies have investigated the impact of anxiety with college students (Abbassi, 1999), acculturation and ethno-cultural issues (Bissiri, 1999; Vandervoort et al., 1999), organizational healthcare (Hinshelwood & Skogstad, 2000), diagnostic patterns of anxiety, globalization and cross-cultural issues (DeCoteau et al., 2003; Horowitz, 2006; Mak, 2001; Rego, 2009; Salman et al., 1997; Salzman, 2001; Takriti & Ahmad, 2000), religion, post-traumatic stress disorder (PTSD), and urban violence (Bressan et al., 2009).

There is a small yet growing discussion of the social experience of dissonance for those who are treated for anxiety in the US and who have certain religious or non-Western medical perspectives. For example, in some cultures certain letters and grammatical tools are perceived as symbols of negative higher powers. If acted on, however, these perceptions are also representative of symptoms that meet the clinical criteria for obsessive-compulsive disorder (OCD) (American Psychiatric Association, 2013; DiTomasso & Gosch, 2007). Similarly, a study by Yorulmaz and colleagues (2009) suggested a connection between compulsive behavior and extreme religious behavior (also known as "religiosity") and that such behavior is shaped from a psychosocial perspective at a multicultural level. Studies such as these illuminate the need for caution in the treatment of anxiety in an increasingly culturally diverse country like the US and in the age of globalization and convergence. It is a reminder of the potential to exacerbate the dichotomy between traditional Western medical models and other models that offer diverse means of treatment for anxiety. A literature that reflects this range of beliefs and practices could help to redefine how anxiety is viewed in relation to culture in diagnostic assessment and treatment-based forums.

The lack of a trans-cultural perspective may stem from the historical context of anxiety which is deeply grounded in state and trait theoretical explorations from the 1970s. One such theorist who began the conversation was Peter Lang. In 1971, Lang presented a model of anxiety that became known as the three-part response channels: a) cognitive-anxious predictions, assumptions, beliefs, and information processing biases; b) behavioral-avoidance, compulsions, distractions, and overprotective behaviors; c) physiological-physical sensations, palpitations, dizziness, and sweating. The emergence of this model brought forth various theoretical and research discussions that moved anxiety into empirical research and scholarly discussions from the 1970s through to the 1990s (this is discussed further in Chapter 5).

Two particular theoretical models have been prevalent in producing such movements. These theories are social learning theory and state-trait anxiety theory. Social learning theory (SLT) is based on the premise that individuals learn new behavior from observing their social environment. Albert Bandura (1977) is associated with formulating this theory. The state-trait anxiety theory was developed by Michael Eysenck (1997) and is based on the premise that there is a relationship between state-only anxiety, which could be a short-term internal response to a threatening situation, and trait-only anxiety, which implicates part of an individual's personality and genetic structure in response to threatening situations.

This chapter supports the more contemporary construction of anxiety through Matt Ridley's (2003) concept that builds from, and combines, both of these particular theories of state via trait. Ridley's work suggested that clinical practice could better integrate causes and effects of anxiety. It complements both state-trait theory and SLT, while challenging current Western clinical culture and perspectives towards anxiety.

In the early to mid-1990s, Antony and Barlow (1996) and Clark and Watson (1991) provided new working definitions of anxiety. They established two unique core elements: the emotion associated with anxiety is fear, and anxiety is a future-oriented cognitive and emotional process that includes a highly charged negative affect, difficulty concentrating, a tendency to worry, and a heightened sense of lack of control over a situation. Both research papers found that the fear factor included an alarm reaction and an intense motivation to escape from perceived danger. In addition, accompanying physiological symptoms of heart-racing, sweating, and shaking were found to be more predominant in those suffering from anxiety. These landmark studies added to the growing body of literature about anxiety and launched theoretical exploration and treatment of anxiety into a new realm.

There is an important body of literature that directly connects anxiety to relationships. Originally formulated by John Bowlby in 1969, and later updated in 1982, attachment theory has influenced clinical and theoretical approaches in the field of developmental and social psychology. Bowlby postulated two key components of attachment theory: anxious and disorganized attachment in children and fearful-avoidant attachment in adults. More recent research based on working with individuals who experience fear and avoidance or anxiety in relationships is from a couple perspective (Previti & Amato, 2004) and a transgenerational perspective (Hesse & Main, 2000; Lieberman et al., 2005) and highlights two important psychodynamic and biological mechanisms: a) adult fearful-avoidant attachment as a developmental disorder born out of primary caregiver experiences occurring in childhood; and b) acknowledgement that both environmental and genetic factors are involved in shaping generational familial patterns of anxious and benevolent behavior. Beck (2010) expanded this foundational social research in anxiety by addressing the unique processes that compound issues of anxiety in the interpersonal environment. He approached this through the lens of relational theories of friendship formation, cyclical interaction patterns between parents and children, biological influences, social experiences, and the impact of anxiety disorders. Beck's work has also increased awareness of the contribution of early bullying to adult social anxiety. Beck (2010) also was influenced by the main principles of three seminal interpersonal theories of anxiety: the aforementioned attachment theory (Bowlby, 1982), along with the interpersonal circumplex theory by Donald Kiesler (1996), and the relational theories of friendship formation from the works of Harry Reis and Philip Shaver (1988). All of these theories focus on: a) developmental approaches and early social processes; b) self-schemas built around others' reactions to the individual; and c) stored information about significant others.

Some of the newer and less-researched approaches to anxiety are in the cognitive and biopsychological fields. In the cognitive group, one theory appears frequently in juried searches: attentional control theory. This theory has been tested in a growing number of studies by Coombes and colleagues (2009) and Eysenck and colleagues (2007). While they represent a small body of knowledge, these studies generate thought-provoking ideas and reveal that state and trait anxiety reduces attention. This is similar to social learning theory which predicts that the reaction to a task is slower when anxiety is present (Powers *et al.*, 2010; Rescoria & Wagner, 1972). The idea that a person's ability to carry out simple tasks is debilitated by high levels of anxiety suggests potentially significant problems in society at large.

Intergenerational transmission of anxiety is also being discussed in the current literature. Some of the pioneers of that line of inquiry are Erik Hesse and Mary Main (2000), Evelyn Fox Keller (2010), and Matt Ridley (2003). These authors have pushed forward the exploration of links between learned patterns of anxiety and intergenerational transmission through extra-genetic influences on DNA. (See Chapter 8 for more on this topic.) It seems fitting to integrate the idea of nature via nurture as previously presented in the work of Ridley (2003) and also in the work of Keller (2010). Keller's findings in epigenetics research suggest that anxiety may be passed down through generations. This kind of work theorized that anxiety may not necessarily be hardwired into genes, and therefore that the anxiety state could be influenced through non-pharmaceutical approaches.

As noted above and so far, the WHO (2009) has stated that anxiety has become a global economic concern. The connection of anxiety to relational and lived experience may contribute to intergenerational anxiety where a pattern of fear response to triggering events among individuals and certain groups or populations is passed down. The growing awareness of violence and global discord and links to community anxiety is reflected in the related theories of Bozo and colleagues (2009). These studies have further opened the conversation and assisted efforts to bridge the gap in understanding between clinical and social impacts of anxiety. They bring us into close and intimate proximity with many perspectives on anxiety, albeit with one underlying rationale: to expose and explore the impact of the relational and psycho-cultural and socio-cultural function of anxiety.

41

The need for a critical social theory of music therapy and anxiety

The way in which the field of music therapy currently conceptualizes anxiety suggests that more studies are needed to specifically target the larger relational and social contexts of anxiety. Music therapists currently treat and discuss anxiety in vast array of clinical contexts (Kim, 2008; Lata & Dwivedi, 2001; Smith, 2008), including terminal illness (Clark *et al.*, 2006; Ferrer, 2007; Grocke, 2008); state anxiety (Gadberry, 2011); neurobehavioural disorders (Hitchen *et al.*, 2010); transplants and music listening (Akombo, 2007); pregnancy and delivery (Chang *et al.*, 2008); root canal operations (Lai *et al.*, 2008); pre-operative anxiety (Miluk-Kolasa *et al.*, 2002); Alzheimer's (Guétin *et al.*, 2009); intimate partner violence (Hernández-Ruiz, 2005; Teague *et al.*, 2006); students and stress (Wu, 2002); and inpatient psychiatry (Choi *et al.*, 2008).

Almost all of the above examples address clinical interventions in either group work or individual inpatient issues during or after treatment for other diagnoses and disorders where anxiety becomes a prevalent secondary factor. Although Smith (2008) reflected on a movement towards contributing to defining anxiety from the perspective of stress in the workplace, the field of music therapy is far from presenting a comprehensive view of the treatment of anxiety based on empirical evidence. There is some recent discussion about the relationship between neuroscience, music, psychoanalytic anthropology, and anxiety that may support the theoretical development of music therapy that combines these fields as well as including the more known fields of music psychology and psychology. There is, however, a growing presence of the notion of social medicine in resource- and recovery-focused approaches in music therapy and mental health that is currently active in Europe with the work of Randi Rolvsjord (2010), in particular. Rolvsjord's perspective complements the pragmatist-constructivist position of this chapter on how collective anxiety is developed in the relational environment and how the relational-musical environment can work towards transforming those constructed meanings.

Pertinent and related literature in the musical, clinical, medical, and philosophical scholarly discussions of Karen Estrella and Michele Forinash (2007), Gemma Fiumara (2001), Mitchell Kossak (2015), Melissa Smith (2008), and Peter Vuust and Morten Kringelbach (2010) supports the notion of a vibrant multisensory environment that can be harnessed through creative inquiry. Fostering such an environment allows therapists to better appreciate the kind of relationship that is built between client and therapist in music therapy. The unique interpersonal environment of music therapy provides a space to inquire about and acquire a clearer approach towards

42

working with the relational, multisensory aspects of anxiety. Creating a sense of internal and external safety for a person experiencing anxiety is an important factor in treating that anxiety. The most reasonable way to create such safety is through an interdisciplinary approach because simply attempting to soothe anxiety as a one-dimensional operating symptom that is not in relationship to someone or something is a misrepresentation of the complex causes and impacts of anxiety. Exploring the relational connections between anxiety arousal sequences and music therapy arousal/intervention sequences from such a multisensory perspective may shed light on the inter-subjectivity of anxiety within the music therapy context.

The famous quote from the play *The Mourning Bride* by William Congreve claims: "Music hath charms to soothe a savage breast, to soften rocks, or bend a knotted oak" (Congreve, 1703). This often-misinterpreted quote ("breast" being replaced by "beast") exemplifies the power of music to break down barriers and change the structure of things thought to be immutable. The replacement of breast with beast over time suggests that music soothes rather than re-structures, as the original quote intended. The same stance can be applied in this chapter. Anxiety has many shapes, forms, and structures, and soothing certain clinical symptoms is only one part of a complicated whole. There are other voices of anxiety that require a platform for expression.

In my work with clinical improvisation and anxiety, I have witnessed the impact of the learned power dynamics in my clients' relationships with others. This has been an important practice-based observation that has contributed to my theoretical development. The links revealed from the sound symbols and themes that have emerged through this work have helped to uncover roots of early caregiver relationship ruptures, complicated grief, ethnic and cultural difference, and a general sense of loss and disempowerment in certain clients' relationships. I have learned through my research that these ruptures can manifest in circumstantial situations that cause unique responses to fear of something or someone, an inability to relax, and nervousness.

In a study carried out from 2010 to 2012, I explored this concept using psychodynamically informed improvisation methods and vocal psycho-therapy methods. Three main "sounds" emerged, which were associated with the most frequently reported symptoms of anxiety: inability to relax, nervousness, and a fear of the worst happening. These symptoms found voice in each individual clients' improvisations through specific thematic discourse, which led clients to find root, relational, and embodied causes for their anxiety experiences, not just alleviate the symptom in the present moment. The individuals in the study who showed the most significant decrease in anxiety over time were those who suffered with generalized and social anxiety; these clients reported improved sense of wellness and productivity and increased behaviors of empowerment.

I have come to use the term *behaviors of empowerment* because clients reported experiencing transformations in the way they walked in the world: how they self-advocated in situations that were once perceived as disempowering, often with people of authority (e.g. bosses, teachers, parents, or siblings) and how they resolved complicated grief losses that had debilitating impacts on social functioning. Clients reported that real-life enactments of relational shame and perceived danger (either physical or emotional) had eased away, and were replaced with productive engagement and participation in each individual's social circles. In other words, the participants had regained a sense of transformed identity, and what I now consider the concept of *productive power*.

Implications for a theory and model of anxiety in music therapy

Based on the above literature review, anxiety is best described as a relational, embodied phenomenon that is a lived, multisensory experience on an individual level and in social circles. Engaging in the music therapy process is also a relational, embodied, and multisensory experience. I argue that the way in which music therapists organize ourselves through the creative process of active music engagement with the purpose of facilitating transformation makes music therapy a valuable approach for working with the larger phenomenon that we call anxiety. My intention is to take this approach beyond the walls of the clinic and into community practice. To do so will require working with groups from various backgrounds and contexts to find the "group" or "community" anxiety sound or sounds, and dialoguing with that group/community to seek relationships to fears and move towards productive group power. As described below, there are certain qualities to the musical experience in this context that would provide a vital role in the application of this approach. The music experience is multisensory as it entails relationship, supports the process of creating and providing safety, and provides an encounter with perfectionism, performance, and flow.

Anxiety as a multisensory, embodied experience. Given the array of options for anxiety treatment presented in the literature, there is surprisingly little discussion of the importance of visceral and multisensory memory and its relationship to anxiety. The trauma literature, however, does acknowledge the multisensory environment (Lieberman *et al.*, 2005; Pender *et al.*, 2007), as does neuroscience, with the emerging understanding of the neurological structures of music expectation and sensation of predictability (discussed below) (Vuust & Kringelbach, 2010). As argued above, the literature on anxiety reflects an interest in the effect of behavioral changes on symptoms but has not addressed other ways of working with the relational etiology of stress, whether from genetic or environmental sources, that leads to anxious behaviors. However, the overall climate of scholarly discussion suggests that a movement towards learning more about the brain's functioning in times of stress and anxiety has begun. Such a body of knowledge may allow for the discovery of how anxiety is experienced on cognitive, behavioral, emotional, social, biological, and spiritual levels, rather than from a single perspective. There are certain authors who have contributed to foundational work in this discussion. Estrella and Forinash provided insights into the multisensory environment from a narrative inquiry perspective, and Fiumara (2001) exposed the idea of the mind's affective life from a philosophical and theoretical perspective. Vurst and Kringelbach (2010) brought forth new knowledge in neuroscience regarding the mechanism of music expectation and how that mechanism is activated when the music is internally processed through the imagination or externally through a recorded or live musical sample. Kossak (2015) discusses a need for a deeper understanding of attunement as a healing agent that is foundationally bio-physical and organized through relationships between humans, sound rhythm, and certain frequencies.

Safety, relationship, and transformation. There are a wide range of ideas within the areas of safety, relationship, and transformation for music therapists to consider. As discussed above, music therapists have a respect for and deep knowledge of the lived experience and the unique capacity for deep transformations to occur within the music therapy relationship. According to Beck (2010), Keller (2010), and Ridley (2003), anxiety is an interpersonal phenomenon that is activated through a learned conscious or intergenerational fear response pattern to perceived danger. The unique interpersonal environment is an area from which theoretical inquiry into a clearer approach towards working with the relational aspects of anxiety can begin. Creating a sense of internal and external safety for a person experiencing anxiety is a foundational first step.

For example, Benedikte Scheiby (2005) illustrated the uniqueness of the music therapeutic relationship, describing it as a more "mutual relationship than the typical relationship in verbal psychotherapy. Because the music therapist also plays music in the work [and] in order for transformation to take place, the music therapist and the client must go on a musical journey together" (p.10). Baker and Wigram (2005) stated: "The process of creating, notating, and/or recording lyrics and music by the client or clients and therapist within a therapeutic relationship [is used] to address psychosocial, emotional, cognitive, and communication needs of the client" (p.67). Working from a multicultural perspective, Shapiro (2005) shared that "appreciating, learning about participating in another person's musical culture, and encouraging them to share it with others can be influential in forming therapeutic relationships, especially with people who cannot speak the dominant language" (p.29). Oldfield (2006) also placed emphasis on the intrinsic interactive qualities of the therapeutic alliance in music therapy.

According to Mitchell Kossak (2009, 2015), attunement is the fundamental ingredient required for healing to occur in the therapeutic alliance. When this attunement is shared through sound, it is amplified, and the unique experience of playing music together matches the constant flux of stem cells in the brain to work in syncopation in real time. Kossak postulates that this is where the physical transforms into the emotional state, and the therapeutic relationship allows for a change in perception of such states. Kossak's theory suggests a potential perspective of applying attunement as an active mechanism from a critical social improvisation perspective—one that supports the idea of cultural difference and anxiety as being held in real time in improvisation. This consideration offers an opportunity to demystify and dismantle the learned or conditioned lived experience of difference and consider a broader conversation around trans-cultural healing of collective anxiety between communities.

Perfectionism, performance, and flow

There cannot be a full discussion of anxiety and music without spotlighting core concepts of performance anxiety and their impact on an individual and group sense of productivity and purpose. Performance anxiety is similar to a more general "fear of the worst," which is a frequently cited problem for many individuals (Zarate, 2012).

The major studies in music therapy research on performance anxiety lean towards behavioral psychology in design and approach, and address cognitive responses (Elliott *et al.*, 2011; Kim, 2008; Orman, 2004; Silverman, 2010), music listening and neurophysiological responses (Krout, 2007), live music-making in the workplace (Smith, 2008), the effect of live music-making on performance anxiety with musicians (Kim, 2008), and performance wellness that works with the "polarizing perfectionist"(Montello, 2002, 2005, 2010, p.112). The performance wellness model aims to transform the polarizing elements in the musical themes through a variety of improvisational techniques, such as musical self-statements and group music improvisation. It has been the predominant relational and improvisational-based music therapy model used to treat performance anxiety, with musicians specifically. In the field of music psychology, however, Kirchner and colleagues (2008) have investigated the experiences of performance in terms of a sense of relaxation or a sense of flow. This is an area that music therapy theory and practice could draw on to address the social contexts of anxiety for musicians and non-musicians. The researchers' work with musicians highlighted certain areas of experience, such as: a) relaxed/feel-good/enjoyment, b) emotional expression, c) loss of awareness of time/pain/sound, d) reaching goals/getting the right feel effortlessly, e) being absorbed/immersed/focused, f) transcension/dissociation, and g) not having to think. Such areas are similar to qualities of empowerment and presence with self and other that may benefit a broader group of people (i.e. non-musicians).

Exploring the broader impact: Music and productive power

Music is a global resource that can be harnessed to strive for social sustainability and social agency in villages, towns, or cities. A recent compendium released by the United Nations, *Music as a Global Resource* (Heinemann & Hesser, 2011), reported a number of different studies and projects that have used music in education, as art, and as therapy. Those studies and projects collectively revealed positive outcomes in quality of life in various communities throughout the world. Specifically, a sense of social agency gained through music in the community is seen in the work of musicologists and music therapists, who have established this paradigm and begun critical conversations on and action-oriented direction of individual and collective movements (DeNora, 2004; Hadley, 2013; Hahna, 2013; Kenny, 2006; Navaro-Wagner, 2015; Pavlicevic & Ansdell, 2004; Ruud, 2010; Stige, 2002). The discussion I put forward in this chapter highlights anxiety as an embodied, relational, intersubjective social construct with rapidly growing transgenerational and trans-cultural components. Music therapists hold a unique expertise in and knowledge of how to transform and transcend such an omnipresent construct. An anxiety and music therapy theory has potential to better identify and define anxiety within our convergent current culture.

To conclude, the way we think about anxiety in the creative process of music-making is key to understanding the broader negative impacts of anxiety in communities. Engaging and participating in the conversation about anxiety from a multisensory, psychoanalytic anthropology and humanitarian perspective supports the idea of a social architecture of anxiety and music therapy theory. New areas of our work may emerge by harnessing the qualities of the multisensory environment and relational characteristics in our music-making with others. More poignantly, this theory could address key symptoms of anxiety by analyzing their impact on individual and group empowerment and sense of productive power. It is difficult to form a theoretical structure around a topic that is, as Pearson (2008) pointed out, simultaneously "unbearably vivid yet insanely abstract" (p.11). I have presented an idea that challenges our own music therapy culture on how we define and locate anxiety. I am eager to engage with those who would like to continue the discussion and are moved to approach the work through this lens.

CHAPTER 4

Shared Values of Mental Health, Music Therapy, and Sustainable Practices

Strategies and actions for healthy collective mental health

I see a path forwards in facilitating behaviors of empowerment and avenues for productive power by striving to solve the active and harmful ways healthcare and political systems intersect. Organized programs that reflect a philosophy of social responsibility represent one of these harmful ways. Corporate social responsibility (CSR) is an area of deep interest for me because of the potential for structural change that includes music therapy and an approach that fits this gap. CSR concerns the role of business in society. There are many references to what that means and its function "being captioned under many names, including strategic philanthropy, corporate citizenship, social responsibility, and other monikers" (Rangan *et al.*, 2012, p.1). In their working paper from 2012 for Harvard Business School, Rangan and colleagues describe CSR as centered around the dominant paradigm on the idea of creating "shared value" and action of unification and bridging differences from what historically has been conflicting perspectives and thoughts on CSR. It is an effort to capture the diverse investments of any given business and how it supports the community and how the community can support the company. The authors present a practical framework that I consider applicable to higher education and institutions where mental health services are available. The framework presents three *theatres* of a CSR program, which I find particularly synonymous with the creative arts therapies and arts in health language. Theatre one represents charitable instincts. Theatre two represents CSR activities that are "symbiotic and intended to benefit the company's bottom line, as well as the environment or social impacts of one or more of their value chain partners, including the supply chain, distribution channels, or production operations" (Rangan *et al.*, 2012, p.5). Finally, theatre three represents programs that are designed to transform business models and fundamentally change the company's ecosystem to "enhance the company's long term business position, but frequently entails short-term risks in order to create societal value" (2012, p.5). While these "theatres" capture the frameworks of an overall CSR program, the authors are quick to point out that a company does not need to undertake all of them at once, sequentially, or even all of them. In fact, what makes this framework practical to consider for mental health training and services in community and cultural contexts is its flexibility and accessibility. These are two pivotal points that can make or break a solid CSR program in mental health contexts.

Music therapy as a CSR factor: A solution for global and social mental health

The idea that music therapy can operate as part of a CSR initiative is not so far-fetched with regard to reducing the global gap for the treatment of stress and anxiety and mental health. If the model of Rangen and colleagues is conceived within a music therapy context, there are many connections to the *shared benefit* and *shared goals* of CSR. Music therapy is a field that has been known to bring out and activate charitable and philanthropic actions in its consumers. Models and approaches already exist that support this notion. For example, in the group models that exist in music therapy, the research points towards increases in a sense of altruism when doing music together in group contexts (Ahonen-Eerikäinen, 2007; Ahonen-Eerikäinen *et al.*, 2007; Carr *et al.*, 2012; Gardstrom & Diestelkamp, 2013). The feelings are also shared between the therapist and the client in certain studies (Chen, 2019). These kinds of findings and anecdotal stories from the field suggest a strong and effective use of music therapy as a means of elaborating on whatever is already present in the current workforce of the company.

To recap the components of theatre two, the company will have activities that are "symbiotic and intended to benefit the company's bottom line as well as the environment of social impacts of one or more of their value chain partners, including the supply chain, distribution channels, or production operations" (Rangan *et al.*, 2012, p.5). Let's pause for a moment on this, because you are probably thinking, how did we jump from music therapy practice ideas to supply chain and distribution channels? The answer is that there has only been one person in the music therapy instrument supply industry who has been able to: a) connect with the right supplies to make the right kind of durable, effective, green, animal-free skin material for the percussion instruments used in music therapy practice, b) create a supply chain to provide the relevant stores, clinics, hospitals, institutions, and company structure, and c) become and remain a trusted provider of music therapy (and other music disciplines such as special education). My point is that if one person can accomplish it for percussion in music therapy, another can accomplish it for guitars, keyboards, and other beloved tools of the trade that music therapists require to practice with. The demand for supplies is on the up, mainly due to increased demand for training, education, and services, leading to the rise in demand for sustainable supplies and global affordable sustainable supply chains. Having supplies that have the right material for the right needs in cultural music therapy contexts is a critical direction the field needs to take. It is critical because two areas for any kind of enterprise need to be considered: the supply chain and the value chain of the company.

The third domain, or theatre, is described as "emblematic of wide scale and disruptive change to a corporation's business model that puts the priority first on crafting a solution to a societal problem, which would then lead to financial returns in the long run" (Rangan *et al.*, 2012, p.9). "The company attempts to create societal value by significantly addressing a critical social or environmental need that is within its business reach, but that may not return immediate benefits" (Rangan *et al.*, 2012). It is a radical move for any company to change its ecosystem. It requires commitment and clarity from the highest executive through to community stakeholders. In the music therapy ecosystem of training to practice, music therapists are involved in a variety of business ecosystems that are impacted by what they do in all their roles and hats that they wear. For instance, the business model of any professional organization is responsible for the representation of its membership, and for the growth of its membership, and the sustenance and growth of the field. When patients and clients only get treated by a limited diversity of music therapists who may not represent the wider community and its cultural needs, there is a critical social problem that is a source of stress on many levels. I speak from my international perspective on this topic. How can music therapists and music therapy organizational and educational institutions lead a CSR enterprise that specifically targets low morale during the global pandemic? How can we update business models and draw on the current creative arts therapies and music therapy change process research to solve issues of employer morale and work stress? On the other hand, the field has high burnout and attrition rates, and how would a CSR strategy from the organizations through to educational settings support burnout prevention embedded in the business models? On the topic of mental health, stress, and anxiety, as a field, music therapy is equipped to provide programs and people that support CSR strategy in companies and across ecosystems, but some business models of those systems require good actors to work in this theatre, in this domain of radical transformation.

While there is no current involvement in formal CSR strategies, music therapists are looking towards how and what can be considered with regard to sustainability.

Music therapy as a sustainable treatment for mental health and well-being

There is a body of knowledge in a variety of approaches and models in music therapy that can be connected to the three proposed theatres of the CSR model discussed earlier.

In the past ten years, for example, attention has been paid to music therapy and sustainability in an effort to guide the evolution of the field in meaningful, ecological ways. Carolyn Kenny's model, the field of play, has been the most established theoretical framework that integrates the individual and collective by way of an ecology of being model. Kenny's theory is deeply connected to her Indigenous identity and experience. A key feature of her theory is the ongoing interconnections she stresses between the individual, the relationship, and the environment (Kenny, 2006). Gary Ansdell has also offered an ecological model of music therapy which expands the ideas of what clinical practice usually presents itself as, and instead inquires about the other, expanded possibilities of music therapy and its uses in community and community environments (Ansdell & DeNora, 2016). Linking sustainability practice as a critical discourse of empowerment has also been established in areas of cross-cultural musical reflexiveness (Whitehead-Pleaux & Tan, 2016). More recently, between 2015 and 2020, there has been an upsurge in concerns about sustainability and how it intersects and informs international development, cost effectiveness, and practice and environmental crisis. From an international perspective, Bolger and McFerran (2013) propose that a definition for a "sustainable orientation to music therapy involves prioritizing and planning for the ongoing impact of a program beyond the life of the music therapist's direct involvement."

In 2015, Lioara Popa presented findings on the social and economic effects of music therapy from a Romanian and US perspective (Popa, 2015). From the US case study, based in San Francisco Bay Hospice, the time spent in treatment and the frequency of treatments decreased, and the costs on expenditure for patient care for those in music therapy and those in standard treatment differed. Popa notes that "the average daily cost per patient decreased by 24.4 percent from $12.85 to $9.71" (Popa, 2015, p.32). Let's pause for a moment and think on larger scales with this information. If there was analysis of the number of beds in a hospital and the average frequency of stay for a 3000-bed institution that struggled with movement of patients, causing excess usage in infrastructure and materials and resources, the savings created by having the time-effective music therapy as the treatment would actually make way for more patients to be seen, and move both hospital and community to better ecosystem and health-related outcomes, particularly on the global mental health level. Two major hurdles would be accomplished—time taken for treatment and cost of treatment—both of which are critical performance and production points for healthcare settings.

In 2020, several studies emerged which focused on sustainability as a cultural, clinical, and environmental concern. Deborah Seabrook offered the first presentation, in the journal *The Arts in Psychotherapy,* of a direct concern towards climate change, music therapy, and mental health. Seabrook names her emerging approach as eco music therapy, which, she says, "can be understood as the intersection between the discipline and practice of music therapy and the climate crisis including political, environmental, and cultural elements" (Seabrook, 2020, p.6).

Within this context, Seabrook explicitly lifts out the current knowledge on levels of pervasive worry and anxiety that impact mental health in individuals. Referring to a presentation (Clayton *et al.*, 2017) on the implications of climate change on mental health, and Albrecht's coined term *eco-anxiety* (Albrecht, 2011), she urges professional organizations, institutions, and individuals to consider critical and transformative best practices that specifically concern climate-related mental health or the eco-anxiety of clients and ourselves as music therapists. In the same year, Lucy Bolger and Katrina McFerran, provided information from a scoping review for the World Federation of Music Therapy which inquired into the current practices and considerations for international development music therapy, published in *Voices: A World Forum for Music Therapy.* They shared sustainability measures and complex ethical considerations as high priorities for international music therapist respondents. In this case, they mentioned that sustainability measures "refer to aspects of a music therapy project intended to offer continued benefit or support to communities beyond the scope of a fixed-term project" (Bolger & McFerran, 2020, p.3). In light of current conversations that are emerging in the field on what is musical appropriation and what is musical creativity and vitality, these findings from scoping the tone and sentiment of our international community are vital for a sense of organizational and corporate social responsibility practices in training, education and research. More importantly, the way in which this information can be used can also inform how the field interprets and considers sustainable strategies so that we leave the field in better, more equitable hands for future generations.

Practical and ethical considerations were also shared, which ranged from understanding the political landscapes, having the time to build relationships, observe, and listen to people (also mentioned in Bolger's 2012 case study of a women's music group (Foxell, 2015) in rural Bangladesh and India, and Bolger and McFerran's 2013 study, and Rachel Foxell's (2015) field report on program set-up), giving consideration to resources and equipment, having universal positive regard, and, most relevant to a broader potential CSR program, having an exchange approach rather than a help approach. In the community setting with the daily care of people with dementia and their spouses, Ayelet Dassa, Michal Rosenbach, and Avi Gilboa found that music therapy in-home services were sustainable for the mental health of the caregiver-spouse, in particular (Dassa *et al.*, 2020). Caregiver health and well-being is also growing in the area of music therapy and dementia from the research of Dassa and colleagues (Clark *et al.*, 2018; Dassa *et al.*, 2020). In other areas of community work, intergenerational singing has shown to increase self-expression, provide a sense of accomplishment, and improve respiration and feelings of general well-being (Vaillancourt *et al.*, 2018). Guylaine Vaillancourt and colleagues worked from a community music therapy (CoMT) model for ten weeks with a range of people aged from 20 to 65 years old. The participants lived in a lower-income neighborhood in a large Canadian city. The researchers shared the complications of this kind of work as well, with the challenges around multilingual repertoire, and the general limitations of sustainability (such as the ones mentioned above) with equipment and personnel, and the capacity for commitment by internal and external stakeholders.

Therapeutic music cultures in communities

Creating music cultures using CoMT theories and practices in schools was also offered by Daphne Rickson and Katrina McFerran in their book, as a means of supporting any music specialist who works in the school setting to promote community well-being and connectedness in the classroom and greater school community (Rickson & McFerran, 2014). Other music therapists have reported similar results from their field reports, research, and practice. From the angle of applied practice and clinical musicianship, there is also an argument for more robust and conscious integration of music technology as a sustainable practice (Crooke, 2018).

Given this building interest and need to progress the field in a responsive and responsible way, a CSR agenda has the potential to inform music therapy leadership and program decision-making as a practice, and one that can also support the use of music within all levels and structures of any company, institution, or organization that already has music therapy in it, or aspires to have music and health programs that are informed by music therapy. For example, in higher education, where I am currently located, an organized CSR agenda using music, creativity, and music therapy-informed research and practice would benefit the individual as well as the collective. Let's say the implementation of music and a creative culture that uses wellness musical groups, such as community chorus, to support stress responses during high-pressure and high-stress times for students, faculty, and staff, in exam weeks. Furthermore, if there is already an established arts performance program in a college or university, music therapy and music therapy-informed community activities could decrease stress surrounding performance anxiety processes for the lead-up, immediate pre-performance, and post-performance strategies. The Performance Wellness Model discussed in Chapter 2 would be one to consider here. A study on music and sustainable mental health practices that came out of my lab recently, pre-Covid era, interviewed 20 stakeholders across my university, and my question was about whether we could gather information that showed us how people's stress transferred into the workplace, with a particular focus on active shooters in schools and universities in the US. As an international scholar and educator, it has been a significant cultural "norm," and I say that with the utmost caution, that has impacted my work and thinking in trauma work over the years. I wanted to shift the needle from reactive-based trauma work to preventative-based trauma work, on collective scales, and in organized, evidence-based ways. I figured that I would start at my home institution in Cambridge, Massachusetts. The findings from this study are still in the works, but are showing profound connections between the neuropsychology of anxiety, the physiology of music, the brain and its function with emotions, and the intersections between culture—community events—and gender roles.

For example, familiar music, particularly from an individual's teenage years, emerged as a characteristic of coping with stress, along with the brain's predictive functions with situational contexts, and the fight/flight modes. Nature sounds in these contexts were not clear for some individuals, and clearly unpopular for others, and in some participants were found to be unpredictable, or to cause arousal that led to stress, reflecting current neuroscience literature on the brain and emotions (Feldman Barrett, 2017). The findings showed that an informed composed set of music, or live intentional improvised music in certain spaces at certain times of the academic year, or during cultural events, may lead to a reduction in actual and perceived stress. If this occurred, the action of doing this kind of work would perhaps slow down and even prevent the onset of anxiety attacks and disorders that go far beyond any given one-off stressful moment.

The big picture is important. The environments in which we work are important. Mental health and well-being in those environments is important for the whole ecosystem. Leadership in music therapy, research in music therapy, education in music therapy, business and management in music therapy, and the practice of music therapy are all areas that can contribute to good mental health.

PART II

PSYCHOLOGICAL DIMENSIONS

CHAPTER 5

Anxiety in Clinical Contexts

Defining anxiety

The word *anxiety* comes from the Latin word *anxietatum* or *ango*, meaning distress or trouble. The Merriam-Webster dictionary defines anxiety as "an apprehensive uneasiness or nervousness usually over an impending or anticipated ill." Below is a brief description of the trailblazers who began the investigations in the field of anxiety. I highlight their significant findings, which shifted our understanding and provided the clinical foundation for approaching music therapy treatment approaches.

The three-part response channel

In his model, briefly discussed in Chapter 3, Lang (1971) presented what became known as the three-part response channels: a) cognitive, b) behavioral, and c) physiological. Table 5.1 displays the three-part response model. The emergence of the model prompted various theoretical and research discussions on whether the three items were correlated.

Table 5.1: Lang's anxiety three-part response channels

Cognitive	Behavioral	Physiological
Anxious predictions, assumptions, beliefs, and information-processing biases	Avoidance, compulsions, distractions, overprotective behaviors	Physical sensations, palpitations, dizziness, and sweating

Two studies showed evidence that the response items from Lang's model were not highly correlated but highly interrelated (Rachman, 1990; Rachman & Hodgson, 1974). In their 1982 investigation, Lehrer and Woolfolk pointed out the importance of measuring the response items separately. The studies by Rachman and Hodgson (1974), Rachman (1990), and Lehrer and Woolfolk (1982) kindled a scholarly dialogue that led to theories that emphasized the importance of context, multi-systemic, and individual experience.

Fear and future

In the early to the mid-1990s, Antony and Barlow (1996) and Clark and Watson (1991) provided new working definitions of anxiety. They established two core elements that were unique to anxiety. One was that the emotion associated with anxiety is fear, and the second was that anxiety is a future-oriented cognitive and emotional process. They found that this process included a highly charged negative affect, difficulty concentrating, a tendency to worry, and a heightened sense of no control over a situation. The fear factor had an alarm reaction and an intense motivation to escape from perceived danger. The accompanying physiological symptoms of heart racing, sweating, and shaking were predominant in those suffering from anxiety. These landmark studies added to the growing body of literature about anxiety and launched the exploration and treatment of anxiety into a new realm, including connections to anxiety's subjective-emotional experience.

Current treatment of anxiety

Anxiety presents and translates differently across ethnicities and cultures and has a broad range of social responses to it, from intense stigmatism through to not taken as psychologically seriously as it needs to be and used as a free-floating word for being within a normal range of stress. Equally, however, the impact is isolating and debilitating on all areas of human functioning. The term and definition are widely used, yet a specific understanding of the word is still lacking in the music therapy community and its wider creative arts therapies community.

Anxiety: An intersubjective and interpersonal experience

Anxiety is the intersubjective and interpersonal experience of our life stories. The seminal literature that informs this principle includes the research which connects anxiety to relationships. And as the data shows, those relationships are connected to every aspect of our lives. Previti and Amato (2004) highlighted the couple therapy perspective that acknowledges adult fearful-avoidant attachment as a developmental disorder born out of primary caregiver experiences occurring in childhood. A conversation that is important to mention concerns the ongoing dialogue on anxiety and adult attachment. For example, adult separation anxiety and adult fearful-avoidant anxiety are worthy of note as potential contributing factors for stress and pressure. Also, the transgenerational perspective of Hesse and Main (2000) and Lieberman and colleagues (2005) acknowledges that both environmental and genetic factors are involved in shaping generational familial patterns with anxious and benevolent behavior. More pertinent to the psychodynamic music therapy approaches are epigenetics and intergenerational transmission (Keller, 2010). These studies imply that a critical feature of anxiety is that it is an interpersonal phenomenon of learned patterns. There may also be specific changes in genetic structures based on the general concept of intergenerational transmission (Hesse & Main, 2000; Keller, 2010; Ridley, 2003).

On a closer look at more contemporary theories, mentioned in Chapter 2, Aaron Beck (2010) addressed the unique processes that compound issues of the interpersonal environment and the impact of anxiety disorders. The chapters of Beck's book are noteworthy and highlight the essential topic of understanding the social impact of anxiety disorder. They include the relational theories of friendship formation, cyclical interaction patterns between parents and children, biological influences, and social experiences. Beck (2010) also increases awareness of the impact of early bullying on adult social anxiety and the more contemporary concept of state via trait theories. He also points out the three seminal interpersonal ideas and their main principles that are helpful with this topic: attachment theory (Bowlby, 1982), interpersonal circumplex theory (Kiesler, 1996), and the relational theories of friendship formation (Reis & Shaver, 1988). A more recent psychotherapy theory that aligns with an interpersonal and intersubjective approach to anxiety and music therapy is interpersonal reconstructive therapy (IRT), developed by Lorna Smith Benjamin. According to the IRT theory, "maladaptive lessons from attachment figures about safety and threat are a major cause of pathological versions of anxiety" (Benjamin, 2018, p.175). These interpersonal and relational theories focus on: a) developmental approach and early social processes; b) self-schemas built around others' reactions to individuals; c) stored information about significant others. (Chapter 6 continues the exploration of this with a focus on attachment theory.)

Some of the newer and less researched approaches are cognitive and biopsychological. In the cognitive group, one theory frequently appears in juried searches, called attentional control theory. This theory appears in a growing number of studies by Coombes and colleagues (2009) and Eysenck and colleagues (2007). The studies revealed that state and trait anxiety reduces attention. Like social learning theory, it predicts a person's task reaction time as slower when stress is present (Powers *et al.*, 2010; Rescoria & Wagner, 1972). A person's ability to carry out simple tasks is reduced due to high anxiety levels, suggesting potentially more significant problems in society. Remember the data explained in Chapter 1? The connection between intergenerational patterns of fear-response triggering events and the need for swift intervention supports the UN and the WHO's concerns about this situation's seriousness. The fields of biopsychology, neuroscience, experimental psychiatry (Buckarov & Knyazev, 2011; Lange *et al.*, 2011), and psychological medicine (Palm *et al.*, 2010) have been uncovering mechanistic features of the brain that activate and regulate certain elements connected to anxiety. In their study, Palm and colleagues (2010) explored the relationship between blood oxygen level dependence (BOLD) and the prefrontal cortex. Their findings suggested that potentially altered balances may occur in emotional and cognitive processes in externally and internally directed responses to facial expressions in individuals who reported generalized anxiety disorder (GAD).

Anxiety as a multisensory experience

The theory that has shifted the needle in our understanding of stress response and the connections between the psychophysiological, interpersonal, relational environment is the polyvagal theory and the social engagement system developed by Stephen Porges (2001). Since 2001, this theory, informed by a combination of phylogenetics and the psychological, behavioral, and physiological processes in the stress response system, has been affirming and re-defining how I treat and think about anxiety and clinical applications of music in music therapy. More on this in the following chapter, but it is worth mentioning here. Regarding the potential for change on a multisensory level, this body of knowledge may discover how anxiety experiences affect cognitive, behavioral, emotional, social, biological, and spiritual levels.

Comorbidity

It is often unclear what is co-occurring with anxiety and when or how that comorbidity emerged, making it difficult to treat. From what we do know, the disorders that often co-occur with anxiety disorders are other anxiety, personality, and mood disorders (Dreessen & Arntz, 1998). More recent authors have inquired into the relationship between social anxiety and the suppression of anger in perceived rejection (Breen & Kashdan, 2011), body dysmorphic concerns, and rejection sensitivity (Fang *et al.*, 2011), attention alterations (Pacheco-Unguetti *et al.*, 2011), anorexia nervosa (Thornton *et al.*, 2011), and bipolar disorder (Okan & Caykoylu, 2011).

Current assessment of anxiety

There are currently numerous measures and models available to assess the variety and breadth of anxiety disorders; however, the first element in the assessment process is the diagnostic criteria. In their book, Martin and Orsillo (2001) reported 38 internally and externally valid measures designed to assess and screen generalized anxiety from a cognitive, emotional, and behavioral perspective. Two of the most established tests are the Beck Anxiety Inventory (Beck & Steer, 1993) and the Anxiety State-Trait Inventory (Spielberger et al., 1970). The most recent addition to the list is the Anxiety Attitude and Belief Scale (Brown et al., 2000), which assesses psychological vulnerability to anxiety symptoms. All examples show a movement towards the subjective experience and an increase in multi-dimensional designs which capture the unique and individual anxiety experience.

There are just as many measures for the assessment of anxiety. In their book, Antony, Orsillo, and Roemer (2001) provided an extensive review of available tests and anxiety measures. A measure from this source includes the Looming Maladaptive Style Questionnaire-Revised, in which vignettes explore participants' anxious reactions. The use of certain qualities of state, trait, and perception is the focus of the Endler Multidimensional Anxiety Scale. The Mood Anxiety Symptom Questionnaire is an established measure that references a combination of mood states with anxiety symptoms to cross-check for the presence of comorbidity. These measures provide a helpful overview of specific physiological, situational, perceived, and emotional symptoms that predict more specific anxiety symptoms that meet the typical diagnosis requirements for generalized anxiety disorder. Most of the children, youth, and adults I treat present with symptoms related to GAD.

Qualities unique to GAD

GAD is one of the most prevalent anxiety disorders in current times. It does present with a set of unique qualities that are important to highlight and help to distinguish it from other types of anxiety. For example, the *DSM-5* describes individuals who experience GAD as being able to function in everyday activities and having an absence of phobic avoidance. Also, DiTomasso and Gosch (2007) discuss that emotional avoidance is a significant factor in assessing GAD because it manifests excessive worry about more than one thing. The fear of adverse outcomes highlights the intense subjective (Beck et al., 2005; Beck, 2010) and psychobiological essence of this disorder (American Psychiatric Association, 2013; Antony & Barlow, 1996; Buckarov & Knyazev, 2011; Clark & Watson, 1991; Palm et al., 2010).

Furthermore, most important, and according to DiTomasso & Gosch (2007), a sound assessment aids the treatment planning process for anxiety.

Treating anxiety
Psychopharmacology
Treatment of anxiety typically occurs with two evidence-based treatments: cognitive behavioral therapy and psychopharmacology. As highlighted in Chapter 1, the co-occurring illness of anxiety is depression which is the leading cause of disability in the US. Prescription medications will typically be anti-anxiety medications known as benzodiazepines, as well as antidepressants, or selective serotonin reuptake inhibitors (SSRIs), serotonin and norepinephrine reuptake inhibitors (SNRIs), monoamine oxidase inhibitors (MAOIs), bupropion, and tricyclics, and in some instances beta-blockers. The rise of risk factors for abuse associated with anti-anxiety medications has influenced some physicians in the last ten years or so to prescribe anti-psychotics because they can specifically block the arousal system associated with anxiety and limit the risk of abuse (Comer *et al.*, 2011).

Cognitive behavioral therapy (CBT)
Beck, Emery, and Greenberg (2005) describe the basic premise of CBT as identifying current working core thoughts, beliefs, and behavior patterns that contribute to anxiety symptoms. CBT designs help individuals to find alternative, healthier means of functioning in these three core areas. It is a blended approach that combines behavioral therapy and cognitive therapy. The use of this integrated system has informed practice for the past 50 years, and empirical studies show that it effectively deals with anxiety (Beck *et al.*, 2005; DiTomasso & Gosch, 2007). Exposure therapy is an area within CBT that has shown positive outcomes for OCD and panic-related anxiety disorders. Recent studies have suggested, however, that this well-known manual-based approach may be too specific to treat anxiety because of the growing awareness of the interaction of anxiety with comorbidity and co-occurring conditions (Ledley *et al.*, 2005; Weertman *et al.*, 2005; Westen *et al.*, 2004).

Other treatments for anxiety
Although the predominant approaches that treat anxiety are CBT and psychopharmacology, it appears that there is not a one-size-fits-all approach. Whether for a symptom containment and management strategy or a more profound, process-oriented reconstructive psychotherapy approach, various treatments are available for anxiety. DiTomasso and Gosch (2007)

found a way to synthesize the vast array of clinical methods known in the treatment of anxiety in their descriptions of the following: psychodynamic psychotherapy (PPT), person-centered therapy (PCT), interpersonal psychotherapy (IPT), supportive-expressive therapy (SEP), Adlerian therapy (AT), contextual family therapy (CFT), context-centered therapy (CCT), and acceptance and commitment therapy (ACT). There are many more, but it is apparent that all of the above consist of core elements of assessment, treatment formulation, and treatment processes. In their writing, DiTomasso and Gosch (2007) offer key components for discussing holistic considerations of treating anxiety.

Treatment outcomes in clinical research

Clinical experimental research is of great importance because of the applications for addressing the multi-systemic experience of anxiety. It seems that a paradigm shift is occurring and moving towards a *real-life* perspective and a flexible, dynamic approach to research. In the past ten years or so, more information on outcomes has been gleaned. In 2010, Olatunji and colleagues carried out a meta-analysis that showed the impact of specific comorbidities had higher levels of anxiety in post-treatment evaluation (Olatunji *et al.*, 2010).

The nuances of the timing of treatment often skew the representation of treatment success, due to how people report and feel their symptoms alleviated at the beginning of treatment. This is the case in music therapy where collecting more data in post-treatment follow-up and longitudinal experimental studies for symptom relief is needed.

CHAPTER 6

Attachment Systems and Anxiety

Attachment in contexts
The safe haven and cycle of attachment

Attachment is grounded in the premise that individuals need a *safe haven* in relationships. A safe haven means that intentional non-toxic, non-harmful, emotionally focused, attuned, predictable behaviors are being practiced in the home and life of the individual that shape an experience of a *felt security* and *good enough* attachments. When separation and loss of an attached figure in infancy and early childhood of the primary caregiver occurs, there are essential strategies that are activated and operationalized. These strategies serve the purpose of emotion regulation. Once a sense of safety is established, they are deactivated, and the cycle continues with each interaction between caregiver and child. Bowlby and Ainsworth called this separation and loss of an attached figure *maternal deprivation* (1976). The attachment bonding process is vital for survival and a sense of predictability, security, and comfort (Siegel, 2020). When bonding processes occur healthily (e.g. an infant has an available attachment figure when help is needed or a response from proximity-seeking behaviors such as crying, smiling, or moving towards the attachment figure), a secure attachment style is known to exist. When they do not (e.g. calls for help are ignored or the caregiver represents comfort and danger at the same time), the patterns of attachment are disrupted and ruptures are created in the bonding process.

The different ways infants neurologically, affectively, and psychologically respond and react to caregivers are ultimately shaping other styles that the infant adapts as a means of survival amid adversity. Those typical styles have been named anxious-ambivalent, dismissive-avoidant, and fearful-avoidant (Ainsworth, 1979; Bowlby, 1969) and, in cases of highly severe abuse, disorganized attachment (Main & Solomon, 1986).

Main and Solomon discovered this fourth attachment style from reviews of tapes of Ainsworth's Strange Situation observations. Main and Solomon

(1990) added the fourth category and procedures of assessment to the attachment styles, where individuals showed "awkward behavior and unusual fluctuations between anxiety and avoidance" (Mikulincer & Shaver, 2018, p.23). An essential component of any attachment style is that the stress response system will always be ready to turn on in relational, environmental contexts of threat or perceived danger. The level and type of reaction to such a threat depend on what the infant or child has experienced and internalized from their primary caregiver. This begins to shape that style's lifelong journey and translates into individuals learning those attachment patterns and bonding in other relationships. However, current research in interdisciplinary approaches in psychotherapy and related disciplines shows the potential for transforming attachment styles in adolescence and adulthood. We know now that there is an opportunity to change these internalized models of attachment and their associated behaviors (Kohut, 1984; Stamoulis *et al.*, 2017).

A brief history of attachment

Attachment theory is grounded in inquiring about the impact of early environmental experiences on healthy child development, influenced by Bowlby's early volunteer years at a school for disenfranchised youth, his work as an army psychiatrist during World War II, a six-month consultancy for the World Health Organization in 1953, and his work with families at the Tavistock Clinic. Attachment theory was developed by John Bowlby and Mary Ainsworth in the 1950s, and their work continued into the 1990s.

Since the early 1940s, the clinical community has been interested in how human beings bond and attach in our developmental journeys, from Bender and Yarnell's (1941) nursery observations, Levy's (1937) work on the concepts of primary *affect hunger*, Spitz's (1945) enquiry into *hospitalism* and the beginnings of psychiatric conditions in early childhood, to Bowlby's and Goldfarb's early work with institutionalized teenagers and the impact on their development (Bowlby, 1944; Goldfarb, 1943b). It is notable that the surge in interest in this field occurred as people experienced immense loss and separation from the unhinging of communities during World War II. This was also when music as a treatment was used, particularly for veterans recovering in hospitals, which eventually led to the formalization of music therapy's clinical practice.

Post-war attachment and relationships research

In the early post-war years, during the 1950s, Bowlby, a British psychoanalyst and psychiatrist, provided a unique, original theory of attachment that was deeply relational and evolutionary. It was an initial interdisciplinary-focused framework that blended several approaches, including object-relations views, post-Darwinian ethology, and cognitive-developmental psychology, and challenged areas in the current psychological thinking on the established Freudian drive theory. Ainsworth, a clinical psychologist who began working with Bowlby in London in the early 1950s, contributed towards the theoretical, international literature on the concept of attachment style in her longitudinal research on the Strange Situation Test (SST). The test was published in 1967 and provided empirical research and applied psychometrics to attachment theory. Ainsworth is most known for articulating the attachment patterns that are known as the significant attachment styles. Findings from her in-depth empirical observations of mothers and their infants in the first year, in Uganda, Africa, Baltimore, and the US, were presented in her book in 1978. She provided countless observations and case studies that revealed four "styles" of attachment (secure, anxious-ambivalent, dismissive-avoidant, and fearful-avoidant). Between them, Bowlby and Ainsworth also named dependent and co-dependent attachment styles. From a more global attachment perspective, one of the discoveries from Ainsworth's research was how her findings revealed a difference in the quality of the communication between secure and insecure attachment. She identified attunement as the factor related to this (Sroufe & Seigel, 2011). In his book *A Secure Base*, Bowlby describes this as:

> attachment behaviour that results in a person attaining or maintaining proximity to some other identified individual who is conceived as better able to cope with the world. It is most obvious whenever the person is frightened, fatigued, or sick, and is assuaged by comforting and caregiving. (Bowlby, 1988, p.27)

Bowlby authored several books that are known as the *Attachment and Loss* trilogy. They outlined the essential principles and tenets of attachment theory. *Attachment. Attachment and Loss* (volume 1) was published in 1969 and again in 1999 (Bowlby, 1969); *Separation: Anxiety & Anger. Attachment and Loss* (volume 2) (Bowlby, 1973); and *Loss: Sadness & Depression. Attachment and Loss* (volume 3) (Bowlby, 1980).

The late mid- to late 1970s continued to see a movement into more relational-based object-relations thinking in psychoanalysis, with the development of attachment theory and self-psychology with Heinz Kohut (1984) and Donald Winnicott (1971). By the 1980s, interest continued with attachment theory and its expansion into the area of attachment in adulthood. Prominent experimental researchers and theorists interested in this area include Mary Main (one of Ainsworth's students), Philip Shaver, and Mario Mikulincer.

Main was interested in the role and function of imagination and narrative discourse to understand historical contexts and relevance of the parental relationship history of parents of children. Using the attachment theory premises, she designed an interview that included questions about attachment, loss, rejection, and separation: the Adult Attachment Interview (AAI) (Main *et al.*, 2005; Main & Goldwyn, 1988).

Mikulincer and Shaver (2018) shared an interest in research on existing issues in psychology (Shaver: self-awareness and fear of success; Mikulincer: stress and learned helplessness), and were keenly interested in psychoanalysis as Bowlby published his books on attachment and loss. Cindy Hazan, one of Shaver's doctoral students, used attachment theory to conceptualize and connect specific areas of investigation and attachment patterns, such as loneliness and romantic love, and her research offered the field a new direction. Before Mikulincer and Shaver began working together, they noticed these connections in the areas in which they were studying. In particular, Mikulincer saw similarities between certain forms of helplessness in adulthood and the effects of parental unavailability in infancy, intrusive images and emotions in the case of PTSD, and the anxious attachment pattern described by Main (Hazan & Shaver, 1987; Hesse & Main, 2000; Main, 1990) and avoidant strategies for coping with stress disorder and the anxious attachment pattern (Hazan & Shaver, 1987; Mikulincer & Shaver, 2018, p.5).

The stories that bonding and attachment experiences shape, and how we express these stories, manifest in our environments with others and with the world. It is one of the most critical areas of human life. While Bowlby and the other early researchers evolved attachment theory in a culture and time, scholars criticized it for not representing the general public in various cultural and community contexts. The more recent studies have shifted the discourse into more inclusive and diverse ideas. The ongoing inquiry is required to fully represent the complex nature of human attachment systems, the attachment psychodynamics between therapist and patient, and the impact of critical systemic global problems such as war, poverty, and the need for access to equitable healthcare practices.

Attachment working models

Attachment models are a way of organizing memories and mental representations of individuals and caregivers in attached relationships to attain and sustain the experience of a felt sense of security. Strategies to get to that are engaged and operationalized within the dynamic context of the self and the other's experiences with specific interactions in specific proximity-seeking contexts. A child develops models related to interpersonal experiences of proximity-seeking outcomes that have either been successful or failed due to the interconnected behaviors (conscious and unconscious and intergenerational transmission) between the child and the individual or caregiver. They are subjective and intrinsically held biases. Mikulincer and Shaver offer this perspective as it translates into adulthood, in that "working models of self and others reflect only in part how the person and a partner actually behaved in a given interaction. They also reflect the underlying regulatory actions of attachment strategies, which can shape cognition, emotions, and behaviors" (Mikulincer & Shaver, 2018, p.21). They name these instances "blends of accurate representations of what actually happened in a relationship" (Mikulincer & Shaver, 2018, p.21). From a psychodynamic music therapy perspective, it is a fitting description because this is what happens in music-centered contexts. There is a blending of multiple levels of artistic, conscious, and unconscious musical symbolic representations that occur in and out of the action of playing music together. This is a vital construct to remember with attachment psychodynamics and musical work.

Multidisciplinary perspectives on attachment, stress, and anxiety

How do the brain and body connect in attachment, relationships and anxiousness? The science of developmental bonding requires a multidisciplinary approach. I attempt to understand this by looking at the active mechanisms that work in music psychotherapy and attachment systems concerning insecure, anxious attachment and its consequences. Neuroscience is critical to our understanding of interpersonal science and what causes these active mechanisms, for example the musical alliance, to work. While awareness of the influence of neuroscience in rehabilitation increases, the field has yet to delve deeper to connect the current research on anxiety and the role of attachment across the lifespan with music psychotherapy research and practice.

The rate at which neuroscience, psychophysiology, and neurochemistry inform the clinical psychology and psychotherapy world is increasing rapidly. It can notably support attachment theory concepts and the associated measures used, such as the SST and AAI. It informs music therapy practice, as it assists with the other understanding constructs in music and the brain. The ones that seem to be essential are prediction, expectation, and preference mechanisms; the role of oxytocin, also known as the cuddle hormone; and the vagus nerve within the specific context of music therapy, stress, and anxious attachment systems. While there is much to learn, bridge, and meld in this area, I feel it is essential to address some current research relevant to the topic.

The neurobiology of attachment

In his book *Attachment in Psychotherapy*, David Wallin offers a perspective on neuroanatomy and attachment by explaining that "psychological patterns are also patterns of neural organization" (2007, p.69). He further relates this explanation by linking to Siegel's description that what registers in the mind and body as *experience* corresponds at the neural level to patterns in the firing or activation of brain cells. These neuronal firing patterns establish synaptic connections in the brain that determine the nature of its structure and functioning. Paraphrasing the neuroanatomist Donald Hebb, Seigel writes, "neurons that fire together wire together" (Seigel, 1999, p.26, in Wallin, 2007, p.69). With this fundamental understanding, our neuroanatomy is at the center of our relational and environmental learning from in utero. Wallin continues to illuminate this point by explaining that our brains are "built to learn from older brains, and attachment relationships are the setting in which most of this learning originally occurs" (Wallin, 2007, p.70). Attachment and anxiety inform the phylogenetic, psychophysiological stance towards social engagement (person-environment and social transactions). Think about it from the perspective of sound, frequency, and music having an essential role in informing transformative practices in music therapy, shaping *safe musical environments* and *safe soundscapes*, and the operational use of music as a self-help tool for anxiety and environment.

The vagus nerve and attachment

The vagus nerve, also known as the wandering nerve, got its name because it is the longest cranial nerve which begins in the brainstem and *wanders* through various organs in the neck, thorax, and abdomen. It shapes human experiences of safety, danger, or threats to life. There are two branches to the vagus, the new (myelinated ventral vagus) and the old (unmyelinated dorsal vagus). The medical, psychological, physiological, and psychophysiological fields research the theory. In a general database search, I retrieved over 9000 articles on the subject. Studies emerged concerning PTSD, anxiety, larynx, and breath. These interconnections speak to the connections between music and mind/body-psychological social systems (attachment) and inform potential new directions for music therapy and the stress response system.

Polyvagal theory

This was developed by Dr. Stephen Porges, with the first publication released in 1995. The polyvagal theory illuminates the "phylogenetic origins of brain structures that regulate social and adaptive survival-oriented defensive behaviors" (Porges, 2001, p.126). It is rooted in evolution and that the "most basic human need or motive is safety" (Lucas *et al.*, 2018, p.8). The theory assumes processes that include psychological, behavioral, and physiological, which are associated with emotional regulation and social behavior (Porges, 2001, p.126). It also shows that the mammalian nervous system's adaptive strategies are responsible for behavioral and autonomic responses linked to emotional regulation and social behavior (Porges, 2001, p.126).

The assumptions are that evolution has modified the structures of the autonomic nervous system:

> The autonomic nervous system retains older parts and functions of the system, emotional regulation and social behavior functional derivatives of structural changes in the autonomic nervous system due to evolutionary processes; the response strategy has a hierarchical function, and starts with the newest part first, and reverts to the oldest, most ancient structural system when all else fails, and finally, that the phylogenetic stage of the autonomic nervous system determines affective states and the range of social behaviour. (Porges, 2001, p.126)

The social engagement system

Key features of the polyvagal theory pertinent to understanding stress responses and anxious attachment styles come from the social engagement system. This includes how heart–brain connections facilitate and shape safety. The social engagement system involves regulating the muscles of the face and head and the heart through the motor fibers of five cranial nerves (special visceral efferent pathways) that originate in the brainstem. This system enables emotional communication through facial expressions. It gets even more exciting for music work when we think of how prosodic vocalizations enhance, listen to voices, and calm the physiological and behavioral state by increasing the vagal influence to the heart through a branch of the vagus originating in the nucleus ambiguous. Functionally, the collective description of the social engagement system is known as the ventral vagal complex.

In the absence of safety, the second most basic human need is to reduce threat; however, removing danger is not sufficient to trigger the neural circuits that support connectedness and health, growth, and restoration. Porges explains that:

> specifically, the Social Engagement System includes the regulation of the eyelids through the orbicularis oculi (e.g., social gaze and gesture), muscles of facial expression (e.g., emotional expression), middle ear muscles (e.g.,

extracting human voice from background sounds), muscles of mastication (e.g., ingestion, sucking), laryngeal and pharyngeal muscles (e.g., vocalizing, swallowing, breathing) and muscles of head-turning and tilting (e.g., social gesture and orientation). Collectively, these muscles act as filters for social stimuli (i.e., observing others' facial expressions and the detection of prosody in human voice), and they allow the expression of the motor behaviors necessary for engagement with the social environment. (Porges, 2011, p.7)

Polyvagal theory and attachment
In their clinical research with group therapy, Flores and Porges share that:

> since many features of attachment theory are implicitly dependent on the neurophysiological mechanisms described in polyvagal theory, the infusion of polyvagal theory helps shift the perspective of attachment from a strictly psychological theory to a more integrated biobehavioral theory. Further, polyvagal theory provides a conceptual bridge between scientific inquiry and practical clinical application by offering a new paradigm to explain the biobehavioral intricacies of social behaviors that occur during child development and are expressed as adult attachment. (Flores & Porges, 2017, p.203)

As Flores and Porges (2017) point out, it's a paradigm shift in how we operationalize our psychological theories into practice. Their case study revealed that the social processes and cues that accompanied the therapeutic group process enhanced trust and safety with members.

While there has been ongoing research and reviews on the vagus nerve in the medical and psychological community, there has been little interest in the topic of music therapy. As of 2020, there was one study from creative arts therapies, in dance/movement therapy (Wagner & McGinn Hurst, 2018) and none (yet) in music therapy. A couple of studies have connected mindfulness and breathing and yoga practice, which show promising interests for team science development between neurophysiological and creative arts therapies fields (Lucas *et al.*, 2018; Sullivan *et al.*, 2018).

The vagal brake
The autonomic mechanism is identified as the ultimate regulator for managing both fight/flight and social interactive behavior with flexibility and adaptability. According to Porges and Furman:

> The mammalian nervous system did not develop solely to survive in dangerous and life-threatening contexts but also to promote social interactions

and social bonds in safe environments. To accomplish this new adaptive flexibility, a new neural strategy requiring safe environments emerged, while the more primitive neural circuits to regulate defensive strategies were retained. To accommodate both fight-flight and social engagement behaviors, the new mammalian vagus evolved to enable rapid, adaptive shifts in the autonomic state. The myelinated vagus functions as an active vagal brake (Porges, Doussard-Roosevelt, Portales & Greenspan, 1996) in which inhibition and recovery of the vagal tone to the heart can rapidly mobilize or calm an individual. (Porges & Furman, 2011, p.109)

Oxytocin, "the cuddle hormone"

Alison Heru is a professor of psychiatry based at the University of Colorado and follows a multidisciplinary approach (Heru, 2020). She describes research, conducted by Stamoulis and colleagues and published in 2017, which revealed the neuroscience of attachment. The detailed study on children abandoned in Romanian orphanages before the 1989 revolution was called the Bucharest Early Intervention Project. They found certain abnormalities in "two aberrantly connected brain networks: a hyperconnected pareto-occipital network and a hypoconnected network between left temporal and distributed bilateral regions." The study provided "the first evidence of the adverse effects of early psychosocial neglect on the wiring of the developing brain" (Heru, 2020, p.2). These findings support the longitudinal research by Chisholm from 1998, where she conducted a three-year follow-up of attachment and indiscriminate friendliness in children adopted from Romanian orphanages. Her results show the potentially irreversible impacts of internalized attachment ruptures (and therefore potential harm in physiological and neurological functioning) to infants aged six months or older.

There has been a lot of interest in oxytocin, "the cuddle hormone," on the promotion of attachment, because it is stimulated in mothers to promote bonding in their infant. Many studies have claimed that intranasal oxytocin's introduction increases bonding and trust with others, but recent meta-analyses challenge those findings. Nevertheless, the process of bonding and attachment is thought to engage the mesocorticolimbic system (the pathway in the brain that regulates incentives and motivations, and other cognitive responses); the nigrostriatal dopaminergic system (one of the main pathways involving movement and other functions); and the oxytocinergic system (a main anti-stress system, linked to the parasympathetic nervous system, and which stimulates restorative processes and social interactions). Topps (2014) proposed that oxytocin facilitates a shift from ventral striatal "novelty processing" towards dorsal striatal "familiarity processing." This shift to familiarity is thought to create secure internal working models (p.9).

Heru connects attachment and familiarity processing and predictive modeling using a combination of models. The inference process continuously updates the information we have on the world around us. She explains that "as more evidence becomes available, we update our internal models of the world. Any new sensory input compares our old model to our current model, and if they do not match, our internal model of the world is updated and revised" (Heru, 2020, p.9). It is, by nature, an iterative process and supports the same processes that occur in musical and non-musical exchanges in music psychotherapy.

For example, a child who has experienced neglect and abuse will experience a lack of reciprocity and attunement. Those patterns shape the expectation and predictive pathways of understanding the lack of availability, inputs, and symbols of both caregiver and danger in the internalized working model. These in-going messages will shape the mental representations that lead towards an inability to understand or experience intimacy in relationships—ultimately creating avoidant or fearful, or anxiety attachment systems throughout all the developmental phases. A true sense of being and feeling safe within these working models is also adjusted.

The predictive model is a practical offering that further understands the specific pathways and neurotransmitters that support bonding and attachment. It brings us additionally to knowing how internalized models can be programmed or uploaded in childhood and can be re-programmed and transformed via the work that occurs within the therapeutic alliance.

Bringing this together, I began to think about early infancy and attachment ruptures and the predictive model, as related to the vagus nerve. Porges and colleagues found in 2001, in their study on the development of the infant's brain, that the vagus nerve is not developed. So the infant exposed to danger, threat, and adversity will need to rely on the older system, and this possibly impacts the attachment and bonding process, making them more susceptible to developing more intense and chronic anxious behaviors. I began to wonder about music and the physiological effects on the music therapy relationship and regressive techniques that we use in music psychotherapy practice.

Key characteristics of anxious childhood attachment

Sroufe describes the peril of the infant who is faced with surviving inadequate constancy and caring attachment: "where care is chaotic, notably inconsistent, neglectful, or rejecting, or where caregiver behaves in frightening or incoherent ways towards the infant, an anxious attachment relationship will evolve" (2000, p.70). He also discusses the body of research carried out on longitudinal studies that show the lasting impact of such experiences in infancy and childhood through to adulthood. Children with an insecure attachment system will most likely have more socio-emotional and economic-based needs because they will be living with potentially more emotional problems in childhood and are more at risk of developing psychopathology in childhood and beyond. This is particularly the case with teenagers who have had to live in social care for prolonged amounts of time and systems that do not adequately address their specific attachment needs. The compounding personal and professional losses and the ripple effects of those losses, over time, are irreversible for many people.

The key characteristics of anxious attachment systems across the lifespan are listed below:

Anxious-ambivalent: This child will present with a set of behaviors that may indicate anxiousness combined with ambivalence in their struggle for attention and survival. Behaviors will show up as preoccupation with the primary caregiver's location, difficulties with exploring their proximal environment, and distress with the characteristic of helplessness when separated. The key behavior that points to the anxious-ambivalent dynamic is the reunification with the caregiver. This can show up as a continued preoccupation with the *location* and *proximity* of the caregiver rather than being *comforted* by the return of the caregiver themselves.

Ambivalent angry or anxious resistant: This child will also be preoccupied with the primary caregiver's location. The key characteristic is with the high level of explicitly external expressions of distress when there is a separation. There will be a painful moment where the child will attempt to connect with their caregiver on reunion, and then move into a state of anger and rage with another explicit expression of rejection that can range from mild behaviors such as turning away from the caregiver through to major episodes of emotional outbursts. There are some evolving discussions in child development that hysteric and/or histrionic expressions and response behaviors are linked to this particular system, but more needs to be investigated to have a clearer idea about it.

Dismissive-avoidant: This child will present in a very different way when faced with separation and reunification with the primary caregiver. When this system is activated, the child will not present as expressing any kind of external, explicit distress. But, from earlier research by Ainsworth and company, the heart rates of these individuals will possibly be really elevated. Ainsworth actually called this a "superficial indifference" (Ainsworth, 1979), because of the apparent lack of behavioral distress, and the high impact on the physiological distress. Caregiver attempts to reunify with the child will not come to anything, and the child literally appears to have shut down from any form of relational connection. This kind of attachment system can be linked to certain behavioral and response patterns with children who show schizoid, obsessional, and narcissistic tendencies, or who have a clear diagnosis of a disorder related to one or more of those.

Fearful-avoidant: This child will hover between a constant dilemma of wanting to connect and needing to avoid and disconnect. This causes a very hard, confusing, and frustrating relational dynamic between primary caregiver and the child, because there is always a push-pull feeling in the relationship. Behaviorally, the dynamic can manifest in different ways, but can be linked to more aggressiveness and conduct issues that can come out in the see-saw of closeness, then rejection, and the same with the emotional dynamic. Mainly, though, there will be a pattern of emotional disconnection and appearing to be emotionally unavailable (Sroufe, 2000).

Disorganized attachment: Disorganized attachment was lifted out from the research of Mary Main, where she discovered a specific strategy from the infant in the Strange Situation Test. Main and Solomon discuss how on reunion with their caregiver, the child backs away from the caregiver, freezes, collapses, or goes into a trance-like state (Main & Solomon, 1990). This child is in a potentially constant state of terror and responses may occur when the carer is both a source of danger and a haven—categorized from families burdened by systematic poverty, psychiatric illness, or substance abuse (Wallin, 2007). These responses have been documented in the trauma literature since their original discovery. I have worked with children who have demonstrated these responses, and made some important clinical discoveries from using psychodynamic improvisation-based music therapy, both with them individually and with their primary caregiver who has had a history or current experiences of trauma and/or abuse. There is some thought around possible connections with people with the diagnosis of Borderline Personality Disorder and having histories of disorganized attachment. This has become one of my more focused areas of interest as a sub-field of study, as it is minimally understood in the field of music therapy.

Key characteristics of adult anxious attachment

Over the past 15–20 years, there has been movement in understanding the two significant dimensions of adult attachment and anxiety. One such dimension is anxiety about separation, abandonment, or not enough love; the other is avoidance—avoidance of intimacy with others in close relationships, dependency (co-dependency), and an emotional expressiveness with a reactive-like tone. Specific scales such as the Anxiety and Aging Scale (AAS), the Acceptance and Action Questionnaire (AAQ), and the Anxiety Symptoms Questionnaire (ASQ) have led to this understanding. By 1990, this understanding shifted once more. In 1990, Kim Bartholomew, a leading scholar in adult attachment, moved to close the gap between the body of knowledge in child attachment and adult attachment by integrating Bowlby's ideas of internal models and Main's research on the AAI and disorganized attachment style. Bartholomew presented a conceptual framework for her interpretation of the two dimensions (Bartholomew, 1990). The two transformative new ideas were: a) that the two dimensions now included a fourth behavioral pattern from the established three (secure, anxious, and avoidant (Hazan & Shaver, 1987), which was named "preoccupied" and was influenced by the AAI Enmeshed and Preoccupied category; and b) that each dimension represented models of self (anxiety) and models of others (avoidance). The four category prototypes were described as secure, fearful, preoccupied, and dismissing. In 1991, Bartholomew and Horowitz created a peer attachment interview to assess where people landed in the four categories and the Relationship Questionnaire (RQ) (Bartholomew & Horowitz, 1991). Hazan and Shaver's measurement influenced the prototypes, which consisted of a multi-sentence prototype of the four types. Respondents chose the type that characterized them most accurately. It has become one of the standard ways of understanding and testing adult attachment, and is one that I also find to be relevant to music therapy improvisation-based practice, as it relates to the framework of the four quadrants of creative music therapy generated from the Nordoff-Robbins approach (Nordoff & Robbins, 2007). Below is a description of the characteristics of the four prototypes developed by Bartholomew and Horowitz's groundbreaking prototype framework from 1991. (See Chapters 15 and 16 for my interpretation of the methods and operation of the prototype.)

Adult attachment patterns in the two-dimensions of self and other

Characteristics of the four prototypes

Secure: The secure individual can be close with others and wants to be close with others; they have capacity for interdependent and reciprocal behaviors of dependence for self and others. Does not have any fear or anxiety to be alone, and does not worry about others not accepting them.

Fearful: The fearful individual is not comfortable with closeness to others. They want to be in emotionally close relationships but have difficulty trusting or depending on others. They also worry about getting hurt in relationships.

Preoccupied: The preoccupied individual wants to be close and intimate in relationships and finds that others show reluctance to get as close as they would like them to. They are uncomfortable being without close relationships. They worry that others do not value them as they value others. From the AAI: they are not coherent in their discourse and are too preoccupied with past experiences. They give lengthy descriptions, do not make much sense, and often have angry or ambivalent representations of their past.

Unresolved/disorganized: The unresolved/disorganized individual has trauma from loss or abuse. They find it hard to follow discourse, and lack reason. They show prolonged periods of silence.

Dismissing: The dismissing individual is comfortable not being involved or having close emotional relationships, emphasizing independence and self-sufficiency. They have a preference for not depending on others or having others depend on them. From the AAI: they may have a lack of memory for childhood experiences and may minimize any negative aspects of behaviors, being in denial. They also over-generalize and normalize descriptions. Their discourse is considered defensive in the AAI (Bartholomew, 1990; Bartholomew & Horowitz, 1991; Bartholomew & Victor, 2004).

Another good model to refer to for individual, couple, and family approaches is emotionally focused therapy (EFT) (Johnson, 2019), which focuses on the core principles of treatment as a source of change in reconstructing relationships.

Linking the developmental story together

The AAI results in connecting internal representations of attachment beyond childhood. The Child Attachment Interview (CAI) assessment (6–12 years old) is patterned after the AAI. Also based on the AAI, the Berkeley Longitudinal Study of Attachment tested 42 participants at age one with the SST, and again at age six with the CAI, and at 19 with the AAI. The study found that behavior, symbolic, linguistic processes from infancy to six and then to age 19 all correlated (Main *et al.*, 2005).

Loneliness

In some instances, there are similarities between chronic loneliness patterns in adults and adolescents (see Rubenstein & Shaver, 1982; Shaver & Hazan, 1984) and the insecure attachment patterns observed by Ainsworth and colleagues (1969).

Romantic attachment

Cindy Hazan named the romantic attachment in the 1980s, and the first article to highlight this as a concept in attachment theory was published in 1987 by Hazan and Shaver.

Learned helplessness, PTSD

Similarities have been found between certain forms of learned helplessness in adults and the effects of parental or caregiver unavailability in infancy. In some people, the presence and/or emergence of intrusive images and emotions associated with PTSD has a connection to anxious attachment patterns described by Ainsworth and colleagues (1979) and Hazan and Shaver (1987). Other mechanisms to manage stress include avoidant coping strategies and their possible connection to the avoidant attachment pattern defined by the same authors.

Death anxiety

Mikulincer, Florian, and Tolmacz (1990) published research on attachment patterns and death anxiety, which was one of the first studies to use Hazan and Shaver's (1987) self-report measure of adult attachment and the first to show its connections with unconscious mental processes. It is a growing area of clinical concern in music therapy, which needs further attention.

Attachment psychodynamics and bonding in music therapy: A multidisciplinary perspective

When I initially came across the evidence in the Romanian study, it profoundly impacted me because I was volunteering as a therapeutic music provider in one of those orphanages for six weeks in 1996. I wondered why this affected me, out of all of the possible studies that I would come across for this chapter. What was it that I needed to reflect on? Indeed, attachment experiences and attachment *are* an iterative process, even when the imagination is the mechanism to connect back to the moments. As I learned more about this study and Professor Heru's work relating to Bowlby, Kohut, and Friston, it became clear. I didn't need to reflect but to remember the memory from the multidimensional perspective, including Friston's framework of iteration and data collection and storage of attachment experiences. As I wrote the initial memory, I took my senses back to the time and the moment when I felt intimately connected and attuned to a boy I worked with. The visualization, visceral sensations of the music, and intentional engagement were happening as if they were simultaneous. My imagination and neuro networks were bringing back the emotional learning and experience from that time. I was in an imaginal, iterative process.

The neuroscience evidence and my observations and experiences of the children I worked with were in agreement, and here is my story of that moment.

I found books on the Nordoff-Robbins approach to music therapy. Given that I intended to move into the field, I began to follow the instructions for clinical improvisation methodology through songwriting, play, and repetition—yes, repetition, mirroring, and holding techniques. I was able to speak basic Romanian, and with the wall above my bed covered in words and phrases, I began to craft my own translated songs and music to use in my work with the children. We used the music and arts to bond and create a sense of predictability and security through the active use of the arts and the structure of daily programming with the staff.

I was 19, a certified healthcare assistant with a couple of years' experience in mental and medical healthcare settings, but it was my first experience of going into a designated music/therapeutic music room with children with profound psychological, physical, social, and emotional injuries. Initially, I did not want to do it because I had no identity with this age group or population. I was highly resistant to going because I did not trust my capacity or my skillsets to do any *good.* It was a decision that shaped what was to become my career path, and I have never looked back! I witnessed children speaking for the first time through repetitive and structured singing and songs, but it wasn't just because of the music, it was because of the bonding process that also occurred in concurrence with the music's intentional use. The trust and the restructuring of attachment *reciprocity* processes were also responsible for this.

Under the supervision of the director, I also followed supportive music therapy techniques and intentionally used mirroring, matching, and holding techniques that I carefully and lovingly integrated into the musical activities. As the children began to bond with me, so I bonded with them—all day, every day for six weeks. The "lahs" in a teenage boy who could vocalize but not speak or sing his language turned into vowels, and the vowels progressed to sung words of the Hello song. Simultaneously, the beat was slow and steady, and the vocal quality was soft and matched with his soft falsetto, child-like vocalizations. The day that I heard him sing his name, it felt like a shared, secure, musical base that had a lullaby-like quality to it. There was a deep connection and attunement in the relationship, a constant soft yet strong communicative affect through the contact of our eyes. There was also rocking and an intentional solid presence. I felt attuned, and I felt that he was, too. I kept thinking to myself that this was the first time that he had said his name in his whole life. What was happening in the music, in me, in him, and in our body–mind and brains?!

From the psychological perspective, taking Kohut's theory, I felt a mirroring-transference occurring from the boy (and my mothering counter-transference in the whole operation). I translated that into the musical framework of a lullaby. I intentionally used the various music therapy-based holding, matching, and mirroring techniques to create a predictable and repetitive environment that harnessed music to ground and secure the child. From the neurochemistry perspective, our brains were firing up the oxytocin hormone to support the three systems of activation and engagement (mesocorticolimbic, nigrostriatal dopaminergic, and oxtocinergic). It lifted the brain chemistry into the familiarity processing named by Topps and colleagues (2014), which is thought to create secure internal working models. A secure and predictable environment in the music is important for shaping opportunities for iterative processes. This, in turn, minimizes any surprises and builds on expectation, and therefore provides a framework for consistent, predictable sensory input. My work with the teenage boy is a good example of how certain modeling approaches can be applied, as in Heru's comparison research.

The early intervention study revealed this important part of the equation for me, and for my practice of music psychotherapy in my quest to understand the many complex dimensions of anxiety.

CHAPTER 7

The Broader Picture: *Collective Anxiety as a Cultural Complex*

The notion of collective psychology is not new to the world. Across the globe, there are many frameworks grounded in collectivism and collective-based philosophies that range from sociological and psychological, to cultural, religious, and political. Intergenerational transmission of cellular biological make-up is, in its essence, part of a collective—part of nature and the ecosystems that are shaped. From the psychological perspective, the Western world has been able to lean into Jungian psychology and the theory of the collective unconscious. Human existence dances in and around the continuum of consciousness, from the individual to the collective, with various life mediators that shape our sense of personhood and sense of community and cultural well-being. In her model of an *ultimate state of cultural well-being*, Seung-A Kim presents this idea with a three-part core: the individual, the collective, and the universal representations and manifestations of culture. She comments on the individual level that "no one person on Earth is exactly like another, everyone can be understood on his or her own terms and in reference to his or her own self" (2021, p.19). In this sense, she highlights the uniqueness of us in the context of music therapists' acceptance of this. Uniqueness, though, must truly embody music therapy practice from these multifaceted cultural lenses to include individuals' cultural dynamics within the therapeutic alliance and musical communication. From the collective lens, Kim describes all human beings as "innately social beings" (p.19), aligning with polyvagal theory and the phylogenetic perspective on mammalian social behaviors. She describes the social framework as beginning from the family, and writes:

> every human being is born into a society and belongs to a family as a microcosm of that society. At the very moment we are born, the relationship between at least two human beings begins: we immediately have a mother or primary caretaker. Clients can therefore be understood in that context.

As they grow, their social affiliations expand. Each individual collective culture has its own norms and expectations. (Kim, 2021, p.19)

I might add that different norms and expectations can come from within communities (grassroots) or be imposed on individuals, depending on the dominant narrative, population, or ethnicity, and so on. In those situations where choice is not afforded to someone or a group of people, a ripple effect of anxiety may occur. Its impact may show up in different contexts, from individual to social and collective, and can literally spread into communities and manifest in all kinds of anxious attachment and behavioral norms. From the universal lens of her model, Kim suggests: "Regardless of one's ethnic background, an individual goes through similar life events and emotions. For example, music is a universal phenomenon that people of all ages and cultures experience" (2020, p.20). The idea of universality, music, and group process is grounded in Yalom's theory and group psychotherapy practice (Yalom, 1995). Kim uses it as an example of how it can shape and impact the experience of not feeling alone because it helps us with common life concerns. Simultaneously, universality is an important area of concern to consider with the utmost caution and critique. Not all experiences of universality are the same. Sadness, for example, is a function and operation of the body and mind. Sadness, while a "universal mechanism" of the brain's signaling to the body to feel, is not a universal feeling because of each individual's sense and perception of whatever is making them feel sad. Sadness is a result of the individual to collective impact. The back and forth between the individual, collective, universal system is an ongoing theoretical concept, and one that needs further conversation. The model that Kim provides is extremely helpful in understanding a framework from which culture operates and lives within each of us. Of particular importance are the areas she discusses in the framework around cultural identity and the need for a *fluidity of consciousness* that leads towards expanded consciousness and an ultimate state of cultural well-being. Music is central to all of these layers and relationships within the model. As Kim describes, "music brings out the growth of our cultural self…using music, we express a way of living, who we are, and where we come from [and has] …a multidimensional energy, which moves us holistically through mind, body, and even spirit" (2021, p.20).

I first thought about the presence and meaning of what "a collective" meant during my early childhood years. Generations of family members would all have a role and function, the elders being taken care of by the middle-agers (my parents were included in that), and the younger siblings (my aunts and uncle) taking care of me as I was a child. The reverse also happened—the elders would help and assist with daily household functioning and chores while everyone was at work or school. We had a collective—an ecosystem. I was a creative, intuitive, and outspoken child. I also noticed how certain collective traits or inherited behaviors *spread* within and through the family, both positively and negatively. These experiences and life observations led me to explore my beginnings of cultural and sociological interests in my familial microcosm through imagination, music, dance, drama, and play. To reference Kim (2020), the sense and perception of an individual-collective-universal relationship became my main fascination with my own—and others'—life experiences and my/their/our relationship to stress responses and use of the arts, of music. Life experiences led me to investigate fight/flight responses in individual and collective cultural contexts and the role of music, imagination, and creativity.

Defining collective anxiety

Collective anxiety can be defined as "The presence of extreme fearfulness of a real or perceived dangerous situation related to hostile group behavior where risk assessment and risk behavior is disseminated within and across socio-cultural landscapes." As Benjamin explains, it can be felt and experienced as "the unrelenting perception of threat" (2018, p.179).

The term *collective anxiety* has been mentioned in psychological and sociological fields since the mid- to late 1980s through to the early twenty-first century. There are several versions of the general term of collective anxiety. There is "collective social anxiety," "collective political anxiety," and "collective anxiety attack" (Bartholomew & Victor, 2004; LaBar, 2014), whereby a focus on being in an age of terrorism and epidemics such as Ebola influences risk-assessment behaviors. More recent projects and initiatives have shown a greater interest in the concept. For example, in 2018, Alex Evans and colleagues began the Collective Psychology Project in response to a variety of social and political issues and because, as they say, "if we want to fix outer crises, we need to attend to the inner ones" (Evans, 2020).

As part of the project, Evans and colleagues name *status anxiety* as a current social issue in need of attention.

My lens on collective psychology comes from an integrated consideration of psychological, socio-cultural, anthropological, psychophysiological, and creative perspectives. It is grounded in the theory that there is a collective consciousness, and that cellular activity passes through generations. The generated energy is activated in any interaction with another human being. That which can pass along (the idea of anxiety being transmissible) creates social constructs of consensual definitions leading to panic-based behaviors. An example would be how toilet paper flew off supermarket shelves during the first wave of the Covid-19 pandemic. It is important to remember to keep fear responses related to panic (fight, freeze) and anxiety (the answer to the avoidable—risk assessment, behavioral, and inhibition) separate. The toilet paper was panic-related. Collective anxiety is far deeper in its social and cultural implications related to othering practice and social hostility, such as collective political anxiety (more detail is provided in Chapter 2 on the social architecture of anxiety and the role of music therapy).

The social communication of fear

LeBar frames collective anxiety within an exciting take on the contagious nature of anxiety in society (2014), with a special warning about balance related to various media forms. He writes:

> Media outlets are an effective way to widely disseminate information about social threats. But a bombardment of fear through traditional and social media unnecessarily ramps up anxiety levels that can paralyze a nation, even when a majority of the audience is not at direct risk. (LaBar, 2014)

Media outlets creating collective impact and "fear threats" for national security are not the only concerns here. The threat to mental health and well-being via social media outlets, I argue, is an international emergency that is spreading more quickly than any pandemic and becoming an inter-generational anxiety problem.

Cultural expressions of anxiety

As highlighted in Chapter 2 on the social architecture of anxiety, the frame-work is concerned with individuals' lives in groups within lived contexts. What happens when the lines are blurred or unclear between individuation processes of health and mental health (anxiety as a construct), and arche-typal, collective over-identification occurs (pharmaceutical remedies to be "normal" and "able"; "the evil other"), leading to the activation of cultural complexes (disenfranchised identification with the self and its relationship to anxiety; binary identifications of good versus bad social practices)? Using Jung's model of the psyche as a guide, it would mean that this is occurring at all layers of individuation. A by-passing occurs and creates collateral. In that structure, there is a chain of events that causes both individual and cul-tural damage because the process of individuation on a large-scale complex perspective (i.e. collective complexes resulting in a generalized, heightened sense of arousal, fear of others, the nervousness of certain life forces, an inability to be restful or relax, or a sense of feeling frozen and unable to "move" in any given life direction) has been arrested and disrupted.

The cultural complex

Complex theory is a signature of Jung's theory of the structure of the psyche. It concerns the inner and outer experiences of people. These are initially considered as part of the psychic whole, but as a result of trauma, or some form of, as Jungian analyst Fanny Brewster describes, *emotional shock* (Brewster, 2020), they become split away, disconnected from the archetype of self, from the whole, and eventually develop as a complex. This moral conflict remains in the unconscious psyche and is no longer part of the conscious and grounded ego. A complex functions as a means of understanding something that has energy in our lives, but we are unaware of its mechanism or value and worth and it is not an integrated part of our personality system. Complexes do not exist in vacuums—they can exist simultaneously, concurrently, and in multiple instances, and mediate between the unconscious and conscious continuum of the psyche. Location of complexes requires analytical and reflective inner work, and there are some areas where it/they are located. The shadow, theoretically understood as an area of the unconscious part of the psyche, can be an area of location of complexes that is part of the realm of an individual's "personal unconscious" and can make us aware of the energetic pulls when an active complex is in our lives. In her description of the nature of complexes, Brewster (2020) describes the operations in the conscious–unconscious continuum of the psyche relationship between the ego and complexes:

> A major part of the ego's psychological work is defending itself against acquiring knowledge of its limitations. There is a need for it to believe that it knows everything or can know everything. The realization that it has limitations can cause great anxiety and distress. These limitations can be in any area of human life that is touched upon by ego. The relationship between ego consciousness and complexes can become intensified when the former feels it is entering a place of unfamiliarity as is often the case when complexes become activated. The ego seeks to have the comfort of knowing where it is located in time and space. Complexes change the inner psychic landscape and usually trigger a shift in consciousness that is uncomfortable for the grounded ego. It is like the rumblings of an earthquake. Since complexes do not act in isolation, it is quite possible that two or more complexes will be activated at the same time thereby applying more pressure on the ego as it tries to defend itself against whatever the complexes are trying to reveal. (p.9)

How can this framework of complexes within the personal consciousness live and exist within any kind of group or collective-based theory? The social architecture of anxiety theory explains this from the anthropological risk-assessment perspective and the idea of a collective unconscious, another signature of Jung's view of the psyche. Singer and Kimbles approached the topic to bridge historical and theoretical gaps in the theory. In their book *The Cultural Complex*, Singer and Kimbles (2004) brought, for the first time, Jung's complex theory into the role of the cultural life of the psyche and the collective group.

According to the authors, this notion is:

> a synthesis of two potent words—"cultural" and "complex"—each carrying a long and important history of research speculation, and multileveled meaning. The notion of a "cultural complex" is a synthetic idea, i.e., it springs from particular tradition—analytical psychology—and draws on different strands of that tradition to build a new idea for the purpose of understanding the psychology of group conflict. (p.2)

In group psychotherapy theory, there are five stages of group development: the forming phase (stage one), the storming phase (stage two), the norming phase (stage three), the working phase (stage four), and finally the adjourning, termination phase (stage five) (Yalom, 1995). Stage two of the group process represents the transition phase that brings up anxiety, ambiguity, and interpersonal, intersubjective conflicts. It's the stage that sits between the two structures of group productivity and unknown territory. It can feel painful and unbearable for group members, and all kinds of boundary testing and acting-out behaviors can occur in this stage, before it moves into the more cohesive, alliance-building phase.

In this regard, group conflict addresses several different contexts of personal consciousness represented in the broader, community, collective unconscious via biological, psychological, historical, and social intergenerational transmission. In its essence, it is the phenomenon that we walk the world with and ultimately carry with us (individually and collectively) into our everyday actions in community, and in therapy sessions—as therapists, clients, teachers, and trainers. It is such a crucial part of our relational contexts that it requires scrutiny and deep internal examination of oneself.

The racial complex and the collective other

Negative uses of the concept of the other shape binary practices, reinforcing interpersonally and international, social, hostile behavior. They also represent group conflict in this broader sense of group identity and group process, and no more so than the toxic and devastating economic idea of racism. Grounded in Jung's theory of opposites, Brewster (2020) develops

Jung's concept from the argument that it has unintentionally promoted and perpetuated American racism in particular. She describes this with personal and precise analytical care:

> Our American collective has struggled with finding its identity in terms of how we will, and must be treated, because of skin color differences, and all that goes along with the cultural meaning of such a circumstance. The psychological trauma of being Other has its impact on people of color. We can be Other, but a part of our consciousness makes the Other—the white person and another. One of the aspects of white privilege and its cultural white racial complex is that it perceived itself as the only thing that can confer qualities such as "otherness." In the case of African Americans, these qualities, both consciously and unconsciously in the shadow, would have us be "primitive" and not rational minded or reasonable human beings. We would be unintelligent and slow to learn. These beliefs come from racial complexes that have lived unexplored within shadow for many centuries since the arrival of the slaves in the 1600s. (p.21).

An example is the history of public health in the southern US states in the 1600s through to the 1800s and the prevalence of hookworm. One of the significant symptoms of hookworm is severe fatigue. Someone asked the right question to clear up a collective problem that became a contagious, transmitted psychological shadow. In our clinical and personal work, we all need to ask the right questions about the reasons why we think about specific people, communities, and cultures. I found Fanny Brewster's work through the Salome Institute that focuses on socially relevant psychology. It is an excellent institute that provides current and working concepts and interpretations of Jungian psychology. When we are grappling with a racial revolution, the importance of our identity politics and relationship to such cultural traumas is never more critical. In summary, "Collective cultural trauma shows itself as having a cultural racial complex that has been formed and nurtured by first slavery, and down through deceased the racist aspects of American life" (Brewster, 2020, p.20). Trauma theory highlights, in times of mass harm, the need for communities to heal, integrate psychic trauma, reintegrate, and transform the suffering into practice for post-traumatic growth. Attachment traumas from intergenerational harm require relational and interpersonal practices for that growth. If the abuse and neglect continue and are perpetuated in individual and systemic ways, the complex is given a landscape to shape the devious and painful path of racism's existence. How, then, do we shift into a transformative state of relational healing and interpersonal insight to engage in behaviors of empowerment and productive power?

Collective wisdom as an anti-anxiety construct

Collective wisdom, or group wisdom, is shared knowledge of multiple intelligences and experiences. To be wise is to have a sound judgment and actions related to knowledge. Collective wisdom aggregates knowledge from principles, traditions, and societies. In the case of a true integration of cultural, racial, and collective complexes, society needs a group wisdom approach. Think about the second stage of the group process, and the painful ambiguity and anxiety it causes. Now think about systemic and group-based ways the process can be altered and moved into a cohesive and working stage. A group-based approach on broader collective levels can transform the meaning and presence of anxiety as it is expressed via the complexes present in our current societies.

A collective affect

The humanitarian notion of a *collective affect* of attunement to relationships, and the co-construction of ideas and growth-supporting sustainable relationships, is the ultimate idea of transformation and a concept of group affect regulation. It's not such a far-fetched idea, if we consider ourselves and each other in the way that Patricia Arah Ann Taylor describes, as a legacy of *enough* or "together reaching" in our stories and in our ways of being (2017, p.40).

CHAPTER 8

Our Bodies and Minds in the Affective Life of Anxiety

Themes, expressions, and symptoms of anxiety

The presence and permeability of anxiety manifest in the various individual, group, and collective contexts shows itself through expressions relevant to those contexts. In those expressions are specific themes, expressions, and symptoms. These themes and symptoms guide treatment decisions. Because of the multifaceted nature of anxiety via cognitive, physiological, and psychological processes, evolutions, and linkages in the body, it is essential to spend some focused time on them as a means of understanding their functioning. Major themes associated with stress responses, our bodies, and anxiety include fear and loss; heightened arousal; anger and moving through space; expressions of test anxiety and environment; noise irritation/annoyance and environment. This chapter describes the physiological and neurological nature of anxiety and its trajectory and purpose in human affective life.

The stress response system

In her interpersonal reconstructive approach (IRT), Benjamin (2018) argues that:

> perception of conditions of threat and safety are fundamental to affective expressions that appear as symptoms of anger, anxiety, or depression. Because a threat is stress, studies of stress during development are quintessentially relevant to understanding the development of affective symptoms of anger, anxiety, and depression. (p.178)

While traditionally associated with depression, anger, in this case, is directly related to the continuum of the stress response, offering a more logical and holistic opportunity to consider its clinical implications in music psychotherapy practice.

When a person is *stressed out*, there is a concurrent physiological and emotional (*affective*) response to the stressful situation. There is an interplay between the person who is stressed out and the *person, group, place*, or *thing*, or the *perceived* person, group, place, or thing, causing the stress, also known as a *stressor*. It can be in real-time such as work, political, educational, or social settings. There is a general knowledge in the field that fear-based responses come back after certain treatments. That fear is translated into stress responses. When the stress cannot be shaken off, past interpersonal, cultural, intergenerational, or transgenerational trauma (e.g. caregiver attachment ruptures, cellular memory) could be the culprit. Symptoms progress into serious chronic health problems such as high blood pressure, heart conditions, and state anxiety. This connection between brain, body, and past attachment has become more prominent in anxiety research across clinical paradigms. Stress research has been building since the 1920s, and has, as Porges points out, occurred not by plan but by default on the significant premises from arousal theory (2001, p.125). Benjamin (2018) offers a contemporary, relational lens that advances models such as Selye's (1950) general adaptation syndrome (GAS) which links adaptive theory and physiological response systems to resultant pathology such as psychosomatic responses created from chronic stress. There are three stages in the GAS: 1) the alarm stage, which kicks off the adrenal system and the surge, 2) the survival instincts to resist or adapt, and 3) exhaustion. In her book, Benjamin discusses how her IRT approach parallels this response to stress in functional analysis of anxiety and depression. She writes:

> first are the stages of alarm plus resistance, and they are associated with anxiety (generalized fear) and anger (resistance). Depression is a passive defense of last resort. Demobilization and the behaviors of withdrawal and hiding seem comparable to the stage of exhaustion as the end point of GAS. (2018, p.178)

Furthermore, she argues that the "connections to behavior in the face of threat are interrelated, with anger sponsoring transitive action in relation to the threat, depression reflects intransitive retreat while anxiety is an amobilized state poised between those two options" (2018, p.178). I see this in clients' musical dialogues to their responses, highlighted in Chapters 16 and 17.

Taking a phylogenetic approach to stress response evolution also helps us to understand and contextualize the meaning and presence of stress and anxiety in current contexts. Consider the role and function of music, sound, frequency, and the contribution that music therapy research can make to a new understanding of arousal and anxious states. Otherwise, the alternative is to run the risk of maintaining the status quo with the central tenets of the arousal theory only, and this will limit knowledge and understanding. As Porges offers in one of his earlier articles introducing the polyvagal approach:

> The flexibility and variability of autonomic nervous system function is totally dependent upon the structure of the nervous system. By mapping the phylogenetic development of the structures regulating autonomic function, it is possible to observe the dependence of autonomic reactivity on the evolution of the underlying structure of the nervous system, and consequently the dependence of social behavior on autonomic reactivity. (2001, p.126)

It is essential to consider the evolutionary approach with regard to shifts in the brainstem and cranial nerve morphology, and "functions from a digestive and cardiopulmonary system to a system that integrates the regulation of facial muscles, cardiac output and the vocal apparatus for affective communication" (Porges, 2001, p.127). What Porges explains in these shifts aligns completely with the major operations within music psychotherapy clinical improvisation and its primary mode of affective communication being instrumental and vocal music-making.

The HPA axis

From the physiological perspective, stress activates several systems in both parallel functions in a chain reaction. When an initial shock or surprise feeling occurs, or stage one in the GAS, the brain responds by activating the hypothalamus–pituitary–adrenal (HPA) axis, which, in turn, releases hormones. The specific hormones of concern here (because they impact when we harness the physics and components of music to de-stress) are adrenaline and noradrenaline. These hormones are responsible for physiological arousal, and are activated by increased activity in the sympathetic nervous system. The heart begins pumping more blood and cardiac output; alongside this process, the hypothalamus sends messages to the adrenal glands to tell it to release the primary stress hormone, cortisol. Cortisol plays a vital role in setting the body up for managing a stressful occurrence. First, it increases glucose levels or sugars in the blood, which helps the brain use more glucose. From this process, the body can repair tissue and slow any non-essential functions that will impede the preparation for survival, also known as a fight=or=flight state of readiness. This system happens on micro and macro levels on any given day. As Aldwin (2007) describes, it changes the quality of an experience in the person–environment transaction (de Witte, Spruit *et al.*, 2020). Incidents occur ranging from a feeling of nervousness about taking a test, going for a job interview, needing to confront a friend or family member about an issue, to performing or speaking in public or going on a first date. These are part of the ebb and flow of daily life for people who do not have fear that is related to any of these situations. Other physiological parts of our body can be activated to de-stress.

Breath and stress

Using breathwork, such as belly breathing, activates the vagus nerve and increases oxygen flow throughout the body. The action tells your brain to tell the nervous system to activate neuron circuitry. There are 350 neurons in the brain that connect breathing to arousal. Scientists of breathwork, such as Yackle and colleagues, have found a brain region called the pre-Botzinger complex (Yackle *et al.*, 2017). In their 2017 study on mice, released in the medical journal *Science,* Yackle and colleagues found a subset of neurons in the system (located in the pons section of the brainstem), which transmit signals in the pons area to modify feelings of alertness, attention, and stress. Furthermore, these neurons showed activation of two proteins, cadherin-9 (CDH9) and developing brain homeobox (DBX1). These proteins are controlled by two genes, Cdh9 and Dbx1. The team effectively muted these two genes in genetically engineered mice, which allowed them to delete the 350 neurons associated with breath, stress, and arousal. They found that after doing so, the mice were in calm states for more extended periods. As the authors suggest, for panic—and I would also suggest for phobic conditions where breathing can lead to hyperventilation—this is a potential direction for further research and development in the medical field.

But what if we also take it further in the realm of the physics of music and music therapy? What if the clinical applications of voice and breathwork in music therapy can also target this neuron system? After all, stress is a physiological, emotional, and person–environment transaction. The same can be said for the role and function of music in contexts of therapist–client encounter. The field has already produced excellent research on the impact of music therapy and neuroplasticity in rehabilitation settings, but it lacks the translation of this knowledge into music psychotherapy and mental health contexts.

The critical difference in characteristics of stress and anxiety, however, is between the fear responses, as in the fight/flight physiological sympathetic nervous system responses, and the anxious, worry, and perception-based responses that create state anxiety that doesn't involve a panic or phobia response. They are concerning either the autonomic structures in the brain and body reactions or arousal structures. According to Lucas and colleagues, a key feature of threat is that" it mobilizes neural networks that are quick to respond—a fast circuit—which bypass brain structures involved in conscious models of behavior change such as Social Cognitive Theory until such times that threat has passed or is neutralized" (Lucas *et al.*, 2018, p.11). For example, when the body-brain-mind is in a fearful state, the sympathetic nervous system and the HPA axis prepares for mobilization and movement. The movement can be either direct action or avoidance and possible freezing behaviors. When the HPA axis is constantly overloaded or there is a chronic activation of the HPA axis, the consequences can lead to system-wide dysregulation (Lucas *et al.*, 2018). Similar effects can also occur with avoidance of threats and can lead to "a chronic unconscious presence that disrupts adaptive neural circuitry adversely, affecting both physical and psychological health" (Lucas *et al.*, 2018, p.11). Immobilization is also possibly triggered "by [the] activation of vagal motor fibers originating in the dorsal motor nucleus of the vagus. Fatigue and depression are often symptoms of an immobilization response to trauma" (p.11), when it feels as if there is no escape, no end in sight, and no possible way out of a perpetual, chronic situation.

A clear understanding of these two significant areas helps us to think about anxious responses to stimuli and anxious behaviors due to those stimuli, on a continuum of intensity. Another critical operational consideration is of when and where anxious responses are within a normal and functional realm, and when they go beyond that helpful purpose, impede human lives, and become pathological. Stress and anxiety come in different intensity levels as human lives are shaped alongside experiences and encounters that activate fight/flight and fear responses. These functions and sequences are anxiety "responses'" as they are part of a functional and operational system designed to support human sustenance, not impede it. As complex as it is, when the neurological functioning that informs the psychological functioning is understood, I believe that we can get closer to a multi-dimensional way of thinking and treating anxiety through music as a critical mechanism in therapy contexts—and in music therapy specifically. As neuroscience informs our understanding of anxiety, we learn more about the pathways between anxiety and neurology, psychology, biology, and physiology, across the domains of the body.

Expressions of anxiety

Anxiety and stress are closely related and can "look" similar in behavior and emotional manifestations. When the body expresses anxiety, it works from all cylinders: from the brain systems out through to the external stimuli and back to the brain again. For more in-depth information, see Lisa Feldman Barrett's book *How Emotions Are Made: The Secret Life of the Brain.*

Your body, brain, and mind on anxiety– going beyond the amygdala

As Siegel (2020, p.7) writes: "Human connections shape neural connections, and each contributes to the mind. Relationships and neural linkages together shape the mind."

In recent years, there has been a rich conversation on developing theories, evidence, and treatment approaches for anxiety and stress. One of these areas is Stephen Porges's work on polyvagal therapy, and another is the work on mind consciousness, collective trauma, embodiment, and neurological connections by Daniel Siegel.

A neurological perspective

There is a hierarchy of structures and sequences that make up the human brain's defense system related to fear and anxiety (Gray & McNaughton, 2007). This system helps us to understand the intricacies between corresponding fear responses to danger (the fight/flight mechanism) and anxiety responses to threat (the more complicated response system). Several significant areas of the brain are a part of the whole defensive system for both response sequences. In the case of fear, considered *defensive avoidance* (when there is little to no time to respond to an impending dangerous situation), the anterior cingulate responsible for discriminate avoidance interacts with the amygdala, which generates active avoidance. The medial hypothalamus is responsible for a directed escape from danger, while the periaqueductal grey is responsible for the undirected escape. On the other set of structures (and not mutually exclusive from one another) is the *defense approach.* This defense approach is part of the behavioral inhibition system, a sequence involving the posterior cingulate responsible for discriminated avoidance. It is part of the continuum of the cingulate response across both structures. The septohippocampal system, responsible for passive avoidance, is on a continuum of sequence with the amygdala. The stimulus for danger, such as sound, can interact and activate both chains of sequential events due to the geniculate, activating the auditory cortex, and threads into either the defensive avoidance sequence or the defensive approach sequence. Understanding the basics of the structures and sequences of the defense system helps us to know when these internal processes manifest in behaviors. A psychological assessment and treatment plan for each client can be fitted to suit the specific kind of defensive response. A music therapy assessment, for example, relates directly to sound-shaped interventions, which could be triggering auditory stimulations rather than helpful and well-thought-out music therapy interventions. Another way to understand this is to think about it from the lens of processing levels, the behavioral response, and accompanying neural substrate function. A critical operational function to consider is if a life-threatening situation from which there is little to no escape occurs or if there is a need to survive at the cost of extreme stress that causes a spike in arousal and physiological reactions.

Reactions also need to be considered in the psychological trauma responses that include both the physical, psychological, and physiological chain reactions of a threat to the body and danger to self in any single moment of extreme stress. That is where connections between gene expression, epigenetic processes, and maladaptive patterns in human responses to stress and the interpersonal causes of anxiety require our deepest attention (Banjamin, 2018, p.177).

The brain and panic responses

A way to understand the functioning and developmental trajectory of anxiety in the brain is to think about how it supports our functioning either from the "bottom up" or the "top down."

When we consider the bottom-up route, we are exploring older parts of the brain that support survival: fight, flight, and freeze responses in that area function through the periaqueductal grey. Regarded as the lowest level of the defense system, it responds to the environment, which links to defense signs. The response of undirected escape appears here, such as an animal, which is very close to a predator in need of an immediate exit from the dangerous situation. There is a body of research that shows the periaqueductal grey as a "major component of the fight/flight system before control is passed to nuclei concerned only with individual components of defense reaction, and that, by itself, it does not control particularly sophisticated defense responses" (Gray & McNaughton, 2007, p.99). Gray and McNaughton progress to discuss it as being considered the main area to generate panic in human beings.

Escape themes: The medial hypothalamus

The medial hypothalamus is connected to the periaqueductal grey and shares similar functions, generating panic responses. There are critical differences in function: a) there is no immediate jumping in the level of response and more intermittent levels of response that shape more distance in the defense sequence; b) escape is also blocked, which, interestingly, is a reciprocal sequence between these two areas; c) aggression is decreased in this part and increased in the periaqueductal system. This activation may spread to higher levels in the defensive system, stimulating and activating a panic response.

The amygdala function

Until recently, the amygdala was considered the neural house for fear responses. It remains understood that several significant structures within the amygdala send and receive information (the lateral nucleus, basal nucleus, corticomedial complex). This is information that is specifically related to potential threats. When the amygdala gets information that danger is impending, it sends out a series of outputs to eight structures that activate a sequence of events to create a sign of fear. Authors who study the emotional brain responses and the function of the amygdala, such as LeDoux (1996) and Feldman Barrett (2017), provide arguments for other co-occurring neural activity beyond the amygdala. On the topic of stereotyped fear response findings, Feldman Barrett explains:

> Yes, the amygdala was showing an increase in activity, but only in certain situations, like when the eyes of a face were staring directly at the viewer. If the eyes were gazing off to the side, the neurons in the amygdala barely changed their firing rates. Also, if test subjects viewed the same stereotyped fear pose over and over again, their amygdala activation rapidly tapered off. If the amygdala truly housed the circuit for fear, then this habituation should not occur. (2017, p.20)

Research also sheds light on the nature of anxiety and its complicated but not sole relationship to the amygdala's function. Nevertheless, the system is complex but helps us to understand specific behavioral responses and neurological mechanisms behind it to inform music therapy interventions for anxious people—particularly in light of newer information on relationships between and impact of anxiolytic drugs, nerve cell transmission, and music as a model for managing levels of serotonin and noradrenaline.

Fear themes: Startle response

One of the considered expressions of fear and a typical theme of generalized anxiety disorder (GAD), startle response and its sequences that occur in the amygdala's central nucleus has a pretty significant body of research behind it in all areas of concern. Startle response is also known as potentiated startle response. According to Davis and colleagues (1993), it is an *anticipated or expected* shock where physical changes occur in the body. These include raised heart rate, respiration, scanning for danger and vigilance, freezing, salivation, and ulceration, which are associated with themes and features in GAD (Davis *et al.*, 1993). A most critical point is the fear-potentiated startle, as it is blocked by the majority of anxiolytic drugs (ethanol, barbiturates, benzodiazepines, buspirone, propranolol). But Davis and colleagues also explain the beginnings of links between neuroplasticity and fear conditioning, which are crucial in considering the music psychotherapy treatment of startle response.

Startle response is of particular interest in music psychotherapy because of the growing understanding of the response's auditory circuits and neurophysiology of music. According to Ray and colleagues (2009), "the startle reflex is a set of skeletomuscular contractions viewed as a behavioral interrupt that prepares the organism for action. It is elicited by an intense stimulus of sudden onset and generally measured by its eyeblink component in humans" (p.147). In their research, Ray and colleagues highlighted an important finding, revealing that, with non-anxious participants, "both anticipation of aversive situations (e.g., anticipation of shock) and processing negatively valenced information (e.g., viewing slides, imagining fearful situations) augment the startle reflex. Positive states related to picture viewing diminish the reflex" (2009, p.148). More recent findings have also shown the impact of induced positive affect and impact on startle response (Ruiz-Salas & De la Casa, 2021).

A *startle reflex modulation* shows a pattern of how impactful these findings were on links to negative and positive experiences/surroundings (person–environment transactions). The reflex's modulation can be increased or decreased based on how negative or positive the individual's experiences and surroundings are, and the co-occurring emotional responses in the brain. There are other contexts in physiology and psychopathology where startle response patterns show up. The key feature of concern for music psychotherapy purposes is the reflex behavior and fear-potentiated startle response behaviors and affect modulation in the emotional responses. The physiological response can symbolically be applied musically and creatively in structured, storytelling methods. Concurrently, the physiology of music—frequency speed, tempo, rhythmic structures—is also activated in interventions in the musical alliance and change process. If all of this information is transferred over into considering how to apply: 1) the imagination and 2) music-specific interventions within music therapy treatment design, physiological symptoms, and state-related stress in music psychotherapy, integrated interventions that apply a skeleto*musical* and interpersonal perspective could also modulate autonomic responses to support more sustained outcomes. Moreover, the possible prevention and maintenance of the *anticipatory signs* and *characteristics* of the startle response and arousal/action cycles associated with stress in anxious people is a much-needed specific direction to take our research and treatment.

PART III

CLINICAL-CULTURAL DIMENSIONS OF MUSIC, MUSIC THERAPY, AND ANXIETY

CHAPTER 9

Music, Stress, and Anxiety

The meaning of music in our lives

The way I think about music and my musical experiences integrates into how I conceptualize music therapy. My worldview on music is that it is a form of organizing experience to understand, live, and connect that begins before birth occurs. Ruud (2010) describes this as the "relational turn" (p.21) and a "communicative musicality" where "there are reasons to believe that sounds constitute an important presupposition when the infant experiences both an inner and an outer world" (p.23). He progresses to discuss this concerning identity development, where "there is a link, then, between biologically programmed behavior and the music cultural expression" (2010, p.25). Humans, therefore, shape musical experiences by organizing frequencies and sounds in their inner and outer environments, which enables opportunities for connections on multiple levels of human experience. This idea blends neuroscience, psychology, and creativity together to explain that humans are relational beings and use explicit (conscious, left side of the brain) and implicit (non-conscious, sensory, right side of the brain) ways of knowing. Humans require a connection in their relationships to people, places, and things, in order to evolve and feel fulfillment. As Oliker (2013) describes:

> Implicit knowing is non-symbolic, non-verbal and non-conscious, involving parts of the brain that do not require conscious processing during encoding or retrieval. In general, implicit knowledge involves circuits in the brain that are tied to experiences involving behaviors, emotions and images. Unlike explicit knowledge, implicit knowledge or knowing is present at birth.

Ruptures in these necessary connections occur locally and globally, through systemic structures that shape socialized patterns of undermining behaviors towards others in various cultural and community contexts. There are intrinsic connections between music and health in music therapy's cultural contexts. It is vital to explore, discover, and connect theory to practice from this lens. Kenny (2006) describes her understanding of this through her model of the field of play.

Music, physics, and physiology

My research and interest in music, physics, and music therapy began during my music technology course at Goldsmiths College in London. I remember learning how to use the mid-1990s Power Macintosh computers in the studio and was fascinated by how to shape sound into compositions that went beyond acoustic work and mirrored human physiological representations of energy and experience. During my music therapy graduate training at New York University (NYU), I attended a class that was, again, transformative. My teacher, Frank Bosco, who remains a dear mentor and friend, laid out a system and framework called *elemental music alignment*, which incorporated laws of physics, sound, and energy bodywork in music therapy theory and practice. At the same time, I was interning in the trauma training unit at Bronx State Hospital. Under the expertise and supervision of Gillian Stephens Langdon and Kristina Muenzenmaier, I began to find connections between music, psychology, and trauma. The deep-rooted physiological, psychological, creative relationships between music, physics, and unconscious traumatic cellular memory within therapeutic relationships fascinated me. The stress and fear cycle was present in every single person with whom I worked. I found a passion for continuing to explore frequency, resonance, and relationships in the shared musical space of improvisation and between music, music therapy, and chronic stress and anxiety, which would eventually become my life's work and dissertation research in 2012. If all things are energy, then I thought considering individual and collective relationships as they are impacted by stress is imperative in understanding the meaning, role, and function of music in all its contexts.

According to Schneck and Berger (2006) and Schneck (2015), there is a *music effect* whereby the whole human system is impacted, from laws of physics through to physiological, psychological, and neurological impacts. They describe a framework which is organized into six areas. They ascertain how there is a symbiotic relationship between the body and music and that conversation may occur between *potential* energy and *kinetic* energy, which are cyclic, and they comment that "manifestations of energy are [therefore] vibrational" (Schneck and Berger, 2006, p.41). With this in mind, music is, therefore, energy, and energy must vibrate through various materials and intervals. This underlines that all things are energy, and reminds us of the deep connection and transformative, medicinal, and wellness power that music has on humans.

There are infinite manifestations of energy, such as nuclear, cosmic, infrared, thermodynamic. Sonic energy is where music comes from, and sound is a sub-form of such energy, heard through auditory senses and felt through the tactile senses. Energy can have a flow, create a sense of status quo, or be disturbed and cause an imbalance in perception of the world around us. When people are stuck in the fear response loop and experience chronic stress, the whole human system's status quo shifts. The body is in a constant high gear of functioning, the fight-or-flight state. Ultimately, this high gear is an unsustainable state to be in, as seen by the impacts and manifestations of stress and anxiety on human life detailed in the previous chapters. It is energy-zapping! Light energy, sound energy, chemical energy, mechanical or thermodynamic energy, and gravitational or inertial energy and proprioceptive receptors (sense of "self"—the non-visual perception of internal bodily conditions and limb orientations in space) can impact our various physiological senses of sight, hearing, tasting, and touch. They affect both the physical sense responses and the internal sense of "self, such as limb orientations in space and internal bodily conditions" (Schneck & Berger, 2006, p.42).

Music and anxiety

Schneck and Berger (2006, p.114) write that:

> The person caught in a fear spiral may not be aware of the state of physio-logical stress and anxiety that his or her system is enduring. In fact, fight-or-flight behavior might be so deeply instilled that it feels like a familiar and perhaps even "comfortable" way for that "me" to be. After all, how would the brain know that the information it is processing, or cannot process, is not the norm?"

Anxiety has many shapes, forms, structures, and soothing symptoms, and is only one part of a complicated whole. There are other voices of anxiety that require a platform for expression. There are ample examples of imprinted quotes about music's power over the collective psyche that may not be interpreted as originally intended, losing the quality's essence. It is essential to understand the current thinking on what activated systems are in the human response to music from a scientific perspective. The following section addresses important findings on this subject.

The interplay of music, brain, and anxiety

Vuust and Kringelbach (2010) discussed the most recent studies available connecting music and the brain. They included theories about the variety of emotional responses to and expectations people have of certain qualities of music. Qualities mentioned were rhythm, tempo, and stem cell events that connect music to physical and emotional arousal. According to Vuust and Kringelbach, music is possibly an integral part of human evolution and survival. They discuss how the human brain's frontal lobe area has adapted to music to function beyond cognitive activity (as previously understood) and now acts as an auditory mirror of our experienced emotional state.

Two concepts that may inform a developing theory on the treatment of anxiety with music are musical expectation and musical prediction. Both highlight the constant flux of auditory structures during the music experience and that the brain response is dependent on the structure of the music (Vuust & Kringelbach, 2010). The information gathered by Vuust and Kringelbach (2010) provides some basic knowledge that can be used to assess the neuroscience literature of today. They proposed certain qualities of physical and emotional arousal and flux of simultaneous auditory mirrors in the brain when making music with another person. Such attributes may add to the level of intimacy that occurs and may also be responsible for activating the imagination.

Other researchers have found connections between music, imagination, and perception. For example, Kandel and colleagues (2010) explored the relationship between body orientation and imagination. They investigated certain activations in the brain (posterior parietal cortex) that showed that individuals possibly use the imagination to orient their bodies to an actual figure. This information suggests that brain structures use those pathways for both imagined and real-world experiences (p.394). In their book, Schroeder and Matheson (2006) also provided a theoretical context for the ideas and theories of how the imagination's architecture is designed and operationalized. Also, in their investigation on hearing in the mind's ear and musical auditions, Zatorre and colleagues (1996) found that when vocalist participants listened to a song they were preparing for an audition, similar regions of the auditory cortex area of the brain were activated as those when they were imagining practicing the same song (p.29). This evidence points directly towards the imagination as a multisensory mechanism. It also supports the idea of harnessing imagination as a psychodynamic tool in therapy to call on an experience (past, present, or future), with the therapist as a co-creating witness. These are attributes of the uniqueness of the creation of intimacy that are of interest in decreasing anxiety through music. One prominent theme, and one on which Zatorre and colleagues

(1996) also commented, is the predominance in the field of neuroscience research on music listening in contrast to any body of literature on the effects of music-making.

Music and wellness
Music: Nature's adaptogen

If superfoods can be associated with adaptogens, then music is the non-dietary version, but just as good and medicinal for our bodies. Music in healthful contexts is non-toxic; it has a non-specific response in the body, shows resistance to stress response and stressors in the body, and has a normalizing influence on the body. Sims (2021) describes adaptogen function as "irrespective of the direction of change from physiological norms caused by the stressor": "In other words, an adaptogen is a substance, typically a plant extract, that can help the body adapt to stress and promote and/or restore normal physiological functioning" (2021, p.32).

Remember the stress response system's anxious predictions/bias-behavioral response-physiological response and the general adaptation syndrome of alarm to resist–adapt–exhaustion from Chapter 8? Sims explains that "Adaptogens help us stay in the resistance phase longer, via a stimulating effect that holds off exhaustion. Instead of crashing in the midst of a stressful moment, task, or event, or attain equilibrium and soldier on" (p.32). The impacts on fatigue, inflammation, and cortisol are combated with music interventions.

Researchers in musicology and music therapy have long been interested in the relationship between the brain and music, and many theories, ideas, and experiments have resulted from this interest. There are established and approved approaches for working with anxiety in both fields, the most common being *clinical neuromusicology* and *neurologic music therapy*. One music therapist who has written about music listening, neuroscience, and relaxation is Robert E. Krout (2007). His writing represented a change of tide in the perception of using music therapeutically as a wellness tool. From Krout's perspective, the combination of processing music and relaxation in the brain has such a malleable effect that people can use it for various purposes, including coping with anxiety. With this in mind, it is necessary to reflect on the concepts mentioned above in working with typically functioning adults who are experiencing anxiety and who do not want to take medication or use cognitive-behavioral methods to treat their anxiety.

Function and quality of music
Music expectation: Response to music

According to Vuust and Kringelbach (2010), there is an operational mechanism in the brain that they have conceptualized as music expectation. These theorists believe that the brain's function predicts what is coming next in the music (e.g. whether music violates, delays, or confirms expectations). Such expectations are dependent on an individual's perceptions of what breaks, delays, or establishes an expectation. The concept is based on the listener's experience of an induced emotional state via the music. But the implications for using this knowledge in clinical improvisation or music-making and anxiety theory seem promising. For instance, for formulating interventions that aim to regulate affect through steering the client into a state of heartbeat regulation. Vuurst and Kringelbach (2010) mention that the sensation of predictability was apparent when the structure of the listened music was repetitive with holding cadences, thus creating a sense of confirmation of expectation (p.258). The concept and function of music expectation pose the idea of applying it to treat anxiety in music therapy. If operationalized in practice, other significant and difficult-to-treat symptoms could be positively affected, such as inability to relax, fear of the worst happening, and nervousness. The flexible quality of music allows the music therapist to apply and translate the three-dimensional response system (violate, delay, or confirm an expectation) into a clinical intervention.

Concetta Tomaino is a seminal author in music therapy and neuroscience, and an early advancer and trailblazer in music therapy and neuro-rehabilitation. She spent her early career with neurologist Oliver Sacks working on projects involving people suffering from brain trauma, Parkinson's disease, Alzheimer's disease, stroke, or uncommon neurological diseases such as encephalitis lethargica. Sacks (1973) wrote a book called *Awakenings* that addresses these issues. The literature shows that Tomaino has continued to advance this work through her scholarly collaborations with other researchers (Potok, 2002). These experiments shed light on how music bridges short-circuit areas of the brain and can be a powerful source in bringing isolated people back into the community.

Music and community

Music is a global resource that people use in their communities to create sustainability in the village, town, or city where they live. There has been a surge in music and the arts as health tools in recent years. For example, the compendium released by the United Nations, *Music as a Global Resource* (Heinemann & Hesser, 2011), contained reports of several different studies and projects that used music in education, as art, and as therapy. Those studies and projects collected revealed positive outcomes in quality-of-life issues in various communities worldwide. The current conversation is occurring in the United Nations and World Health Organization, as evidenced by the emergence of global group projects and compendiums like the groundbreaking scoping review from the WHO (Fancourt & Saoirse, 2019). The sentiment of social agency and music in the community is also apparent within the formal study of musicology. Traditionally, musicology has been the study of how music is constructed and represented. However, emerging theories show a paradigm shift from the traditionally based structural analysis of music constructs to an action-oriented direction of individual and collective social agency (DeNora, 2004; Ruud, 2010).

Music and interventions

Music and intervention are among the more contemporary conversations that are happening across disciplines of study that use music for health. The rise of interest in music as a health tool has also increased experimental research, approaches, anecdotal stories, and accounts from cases in the community on this topic. It is no surprise, though, when attention is paid to the fact that music has been around us since we evolved into mammals. That makes it one of the biggest evolutionary phenomena in human functioning, alongside the human body itself. Music fulfills homeostasis. How and why we use it as the intervention is vital to understand because music has *POWER* when integrated into our social network system, as Porges (2017) reminds us. Given the movement of arts in health, interests in neuroscience, nursing, medical, physical fields, therapeutic musicians, and music therapy's work. It seems that any way we turn these days, research or work is happening around music as a health intervention. Music is a health tool and a universal global source to which human beings are programmed to align and attune. This is because of the physiological, psychological, aesthetic, and core intrapersonal and interpersonal musical processes that drive humans to a sense of transformation, of a movement from one state or emotional landscape to another.

For example, let's remind ourselves of how guided imagery and music as an intervention help decrease sleep disturbance from the study by Beck and colleagues (2015). In music as intervention, Du Rousseau and colleagues found in their controlled pre-post experiment with frontline law enforcement workers a significant improvement in the quality of sleep, mood, and everyday functioning (see table 1, p.392 original study). They used what they named "brain music (BM), and music-based neurofeedback therapy." So, while it is not music therapy, these findings provide further support for listening-based interventions as a means of decreasing sleep disturbances and increasing quality of sleep in work-related contexts.

In a recent meta-analysis, de Witte and colleagues (2020) uncovered the broad scope of settings used to explore these benefits of music, in particular related to stress and anxiety. They found two impactful areas (psychology and physiology) where the studies showed that music reduced stress. In a groundbreaking systematic literature review and meta-analysis of music interventions and stress, de Witte and colleagues found incredibly exciting results in physiological and psychological domains. A big finding was on the effect on various physiological states: heart rate, blood pressure, and stress-related hormones (2020, p.303). An interesting characteristic of this finding was a trend in larger effects on physiological stress-related outcomes than those found in studies conducted in Western countries (p.304). On psychological stress outcomes, they found that music interventions reduced stress-related symptoms of state anxiety, nervousness, restlessness, and feelings of worry. Finally, they found a trend with music interventions and tempo (60–80bpm) showing a clear difference from treatment as usual. De Witte and colleagues offer ideas about the potential benefits of listening to intentionally curated preferred music to reduce physiological and psychological stress.

Finally, they discovered a trend with music interventions and tempo (60–80bpm) showing a clear difference from treatment as usual. The authors offer ideas about the potential benefits of listening to intentionally curated preferred music to reduce physiological and psychological stress. In terms of stress reduction, group settings where music was used in interventions showed better results than non-music interventions, and greater results from single session, first session to proceeding second and third sessions. They concluded that:

> Overall, we found significant small-to-medium effect of music interventions on physiological stress-related outcomes (d =.380) and medium effect of music interventions on psychological stress-related outcomes (d = .545), indicating that music intervention groups benefited more than the comparison groups. We conclude that music interventions are effective in reducing physiological and psychological stress-related symptoms in different settings (mental healthcare, polyclinic medical settings, during medical surgery and in daily life situations. (de Witte, 2020, p.306)

Music, physiology, and stress

When the homeostatic mechanisms can no longer maintain equilibrium and stable cyclical frequency output, they become overloaded. The central nervous system begins to receive signals encoded with stressors and disrupts all significant central nervous system and limbic systems. The signs indicate a threat situation and begin to pump more chemicals around the body, particularly adrenaline, and move the system into the fight/flight mode for survival. With chronic stress and anxiety, the system becomes conditioned, and with that persistent conditioning occurring, the system operates at that as its new normal, or "programmed learning" (Schneck & Berger, 2006, p.105). The ripple effect can put people at risk for some other serious health concerns that compound the situation, such as an inability to focus or concentrate on simple, yet necessary, life tasks.

Foundational knowledge on stress responses and how music functions in the response system to interrupt the physical stressors is an essential part of the practice and research of music therapy and anxiety. It informs every aspect of treatment planning and is at the core of the work to provide symptom alleviation in severe cases of acute stress and exhaustion.

Coping with stress musically

There is a musical, physiological, emotional, psychological response system within a single musical experience. The upcoming chapters describe methods and techniques of applying ways to manage and cope with stress. Generally speaking, identifying the stress first, and whether it is physiological dominated or cognitive-behavioral, psychological dominated, helps to identify routes and structures of either listening to music, producing and playing live music, or listening and playing concurrently to combat the various aspects of stress. Setting up routines and patterns in daily life that allow for music to be a central de-stressing tool integrates the power of prediction and expectation. Integrating the research to work with slower, steady tempos, breath, and imagination activation is also a core factor to assist with stress and to calm and relieve the body–mind–brain connections.

CHAPTER 10

Conceptualizing Musical Environments as an Anti-Stress, Sustainable Movement: *Music, Health, and Performed States*

A golden age of understanding the actual health benefits of music is emerging. Fields such as psychomusicology and ecomusicology generate new information that can harness the greater good for health and well-being. Music therapy has had a growing movement of community music therapy (CoMT), which is an alternative music therapy practice guided by ecological perspectives. It is a way of thinking about music and wellness on local and global levels, which helps in understanding and thinking about music as and in life. Major tenets that resonate with me are the elements of concern in CoMT, which are music and health in interactive, performed states within and around the systems people exist in. Pavlicevic and Ansdell's (2004), Rolvsjord's (2010), and Ruud's (2008) thinking about music in situated psychosocial and socio-political contexts has influenced the way I think about the nature and purpose of music for health and mental health continuums. I think in a dimensional way about the local and global contexts where psychodynamic, informed, community-based philosophy intersects and interconnects in my research and practice.

In his similar approach to thinking about CoMT, Wood (2016) offers a matrix for CoMT and provides an outline of key features in its formulation. He discusses the various tenets within the matrix, including the *range of musical impact.* He explains this in the context of the people, places, and spaces that we work in and with that "such a lot happens when we make music in that sort-of-private, sort-of-public situation, where bodies physical, professional, and politic combine. In CoMT, we attune to that broad range of possibilities" (p.29). It is at this point where psychosocial and sustainable philosophies between fields of study in music intersect. It offers a way to bridge an idea of sustainable musical environments that inform each other. Ansdell and DeNora (2016) approach the helpfulness of music in our everyday lives by offering a way of understanding the multiplicity and holistic functions and social responsibilities of music in certain contexts. Musical worlds, musical experience, musical personhood, musical relationship, musical communities, musical transcendence, and musical flourishing are all aspects of how music is in our lives as a function and purpose. With this interdisciplinary lens, the music therapy field is well positioned to use this information to combine our expanding knowledge of why change occurs in the therapeutic contexts and advance how and why we shape interventions and integrate them in our practice, research, and teaching. Landscape and the sounds that occur in them are no different. These related music fields are interested in the environmental influence of the soundscapes that we dwell in and create to respond to the spaces in which we spend our lives—mainly as a means to minimize sound stressors in our environments. Music therapists and musicians are impacted in aesthetic, cultural, and clinical ways. These impacts bring us closer to the immediate importance of considering how we interact with our art and the world, and the effects (negative and positive) on our mental health, wellness, work health, and global health ecosystems.

Music, environment, and health

Anyone participating in musical practices is part of the preservation of the cultural expressions of World Heritage concerns. As Ansdell and DeNora (2016, p.295) beautifully put it, "We love music because we need music."

The intersections between musical cultures and our environment

Au (2016) reminds us about the arts and cultural preservation by highlighting the importance of support from organizations such as UNESCO: "The importance of cultural preservation for all humanity is recognized by UNESCO and international conventions established to protect World Heritage sites and intangible cultural expressions like traditional knowledge, skills, music and dance" (Au, 2016, p.26).

Anyone participating in musical practices is part of the preservation of the cultural expressions of World Heritage concerns. Yet, at the same time, we are also participating in the globalized music industry in ways that intersect with the current climate crisis. In my opinion, all musicians in all sectors of the music industries, including music therapy, need to be concerned with action-based practices that move towards the "greening" of musical cultures, production, and musical expression. Our musical values must reflect our environmental values, which need to impact global sustainable values and actions. With this in mind, we cannot ignore how this intersection impacts our lives in the various ways of how we learn, how we communicate, and how we expand and evolve. Furthermore, for music therapists and musicians in the healing practices, it is a multi-pronged area of teaching, research, and practice that poses both concern and hope for advancement via sustainable practices in clinical, collective, and cultural, public, and organizational ways.

Within the fields of ecomusicology, ethnomusicology, musicology, sociology, education and leadership, and organizational behavior, topics that address environmental activism appear in music culture sustainability (DIY artists, heritage ensembles, sustainable music-making using technology, indigenism), industrial ecology (instrument crafts, tracing the instrument back to the tree, and "more-than-musical" themes, renewable energy), public health (literacy, bullying, school environments), and organizational behavior (arts and learning as sustainable ways of knowing higher education environments, sustainable teaching, and performance or "pianism" (James, 2012). These all address one primary concern—how do we continue to express and share music as a resource, while at the same time preserving heritage, resourcing our communities, and nourishing, not destroying, our relationship to the whole, the environment, and, as Gibson (2019, p.185) describes, our non-human others.

Music cultures and sustainable values

The ethnomusicologist Jeff Todd Titon has influenced my learning and thinking about music in contexts. I came across his field research in my ethnomusicology training at Goldsmiths College. He explains that music cultures need to be considered ecosystems and that applied fieldwork must be reciprocal and relational (Titon, 1984). These pillars of the scholarship stay with me today, in my own music cultures that I share in the field of music therapy and my other musical contexts. I seek and aspire to create all of my musical contexts as relational, reciprocal, and sustainable ecosystems that reflect the individual and the collective diversity in each class, group, ensemble, composition. I see this emulated in a variety of community-based musical scenes. All of the music worlds appear to have these core relational aspects to them.

DIY artists (those individuals and bands who have an ethic and philosophy to do everything—write, compose, manage, and perform) are a musical community population. They are naturally inclined to think about sustainable practice because being a DIY musician is an ecological existence and balance between very different-looking tasks and functions. The DIY musicology model offered by Oliver (2010) speaks to the links between those balances and understanding local music scenes and sub-sectors of music industries as an ethic and a way of self-sufficiency. It relates to themes found in his study concerning perspectives of artistic processes, managerial processes, and information systems, and offers a foundation for the DIY artist or band to be self-sufficient through these critical areas.

Heritage instruments and sustainable practices require consideration of the variety of skills needed and the critical characteristics for a well-thought-out design that emulates the traditional feel and sound and cultural representation. Inkeri Ruokonen and colleagues address this in studying the five-string Kantele, a Finnish national heritage instrument (2014). They found several key characteristics—creative, ecological, economic, aesthetic, and socio-environmental—from their interviews with music education students who had their sixth-form students make and play them. It is a repertoire that shapes heritage discourse, meaning that maintaining an extensive repertoire ensures cultural representation and heritage management sustainability. In his work published in the *Malaysian Journal of Music*, Associate Professor of Ethnomusicology at Universiti Putra Malaysia, Made Mantle Hood shows this in the ethnographic exploration of two significant gamelan orchestras located in Bali, Indonesia (Hood, 2014). Hood also lifts out the reciprocal elements of heritage related to community partnership, hierarchies, religious ritual, and service to the community aesthetically and economically—not just from top-down systems, but from stewards of the tradition that provide sustainability peripherally. These are aspects of any informed CSR program (discussed in Chapter 4).

Immersive online learning in musical spaces has been investigated more in the past ten years and more than ever in the current Covid-19 pandemic fall-out. Brunt and Johnson (2013) offer ideas on sustainable active music-making cultures through web-based interactive music. While they were ahead of their time on many levels, since then, a rising amount of knowledge and research is emerging due to the digital requirements in a pandemic.

More recently, and most imperatively, in her review article in 2020, Klisala Harrison (2020) discusses Indigenous music sustainability during climate change. Harrison critically analyzes the concept, shedding light on Indigenous peoples as being among the most affected by climate change due to a host of historical and current ramifications, from colonization, forced geographical relocation, and other threats such as loss of natural substances to create instruments for the sustenance of musical cultures. I might add that the impact of sickness induced by infection—the most recent one being Covid-19—adds insult to injury.

Industrial ecology

The sale of instruments in North America alone is a 1.5 billion-dollar industry (Au, 2006). Certain environmental activist groups such as Greenpeace have been attempting to educate the public on this since 2006. The Greening North America project aimed to promote "good wood" musical instruments that have been certified by the Forest Stewardship Council. This is wood that has been sustainably sourced and limits the logging of particular tree wood typically used for its quality, such as in guitar soundboards. One of those trees in the North West that researchers and scientists are concerned about is the Sitka spruce. Chris Gibson addressed this state of the "Anthropocene" in his research that traced guitars back to the tree. He describes musical instruments as "gateway objects that invite contemplation of material and corporate relations" (Gibson, 2019, p.183). He says that "such relationships bind together musicians and non-human others" (p.183). I agree and draw from Kenny's (2006) ecological theory in music therapy to align with this philosophy.

Gibson's research on tracing guitars back to the tree lifted out themes of co-generation between human and non-human others. He named them "more-than-musical." These more-than-musical themes were the "Enchanted Wood," where materiality and the agentic capacities of non-human others co-exist; "Corporeality," where body, affect, and emotion impact the qualities of sound in the body-space relationship, and the ability to affect and be affected as it links physiology to the environment; and "Volatility," representing the dimension of unpredictability and upheaval and of the reconfiguring of the relationships between species extinction, musicians, and musical instrument makers in these current times of resource scarcity and regulation. These more-than-musical themes had an impact on me on a multisensory level. They felt in some ways magical, otherwise frightening, like children's tales with metaphors of danger and peril, as well as hope, agency, and regeneration. The links between the third theme particularly moved me as representative symbols of therapeutic processes and the evolving prevalence of the concept/experience of eco-anxiety. The concept of time, materiality, and temporal layers in the musical and planetary dimensions were discussed. A recent study from Philipp Kohl (2020) on how music offers alternative ecologies of relating in deep time and in musical time provides food for thought on the meaning of reciprocity and relational access between human and non-human existences in cultural, environmental spaces.

Au points this out in an interview with Yuen Shi-Chun, a civil engineer, artisan, musician, and environmentalist who introduced the concept of "eco-diversity" to the Chinese manufacturing of traditional orchestral instruments. One of his actions was to replace reptile skin with a recyclable polyethylene terephthalate (PET) latex membrane. The benefits of this alone produce a more resonant and robust vibration and frequency of the instruments, which is better for concert halls and larger spaces. Aesthetically and artistically, the orchestra can express differently, and the audience can receive and experience a better quality musical experience, improving all kinds of emotional, physical responses. Furthermore, as Au also states, "with over 500 000 traditional stringed instruments now fabricated in China every year, production required four meters of skin for roughly every 12 instruments made—the equivalent of killing 60,000 endangered pythons" (Au, 2006, p.29).

From acoustic musical instrument concerns to electronic musical instrument innovation

The research in eco-industry and music is shining a spotlight on powering instruments, bands, and performances. This research is informing all performing arts, from live shows to DJ equipment and cloud-based musical engineering. The choices to curate relevant and creative interventions are broadening quickly.

SOLA: Sustainable Orchestras of Laptops and Analog is a project developed by Perry Cook, Scott Smallwood, and Dan Trueman at Princeton University's SoundLab (Cook & Smallwood, 2010). The project consisted of a group of meta-instruments, laptops, interface equipment, and a hemispherical speaker designed to be powered by solar power. It highlighted the use of solar batteries as a form of powering computers and amplifiers. Projects like these represent the kind of research that will inform a green trajectory for the mainstream public. Think of concerts that use renewable power, like solar power, and the cultural access to provide for remote locations and off-the-grid areas—the show will go on.

Sound environments

The idea of sound environments comes from two angles. On the one hand, there is the environment that we cannot control—our natural environment, the one we live in. New York Jersey City was a loud and urban sound environment; Cornwall was the complete opposite. On the other hand, there is the sound environment we can control, from macro to micro sounds. Think of the pace and tempo of work spaces, the way people speak to and with each other. All are made up of sound. How are the sound bites in your environment? Loud and intrusive or completely the opposite? Consciously producing sound throughout our spaces and structures is important. The organization, quality, and the ways that we do it, all impact the stress response system. When communities are better equipped to sculpt a healthy sound environment, there is an improvement in the quality of interactions, ideas, and relationships.

Public health

The growing appreciation for the presence, meaning, role, and function of the arts and the sustaining impact on public health has become more apparent in the public and collective psyche. The global pandemic's aesthetic and identity impact has brought humans from the balcony to apps like Soundtrap, Zoom, Houseparty, and socio-artistic responses and movements such as quarantine karaoke closer to their needs for health and vitality through the arts. In a recent interview with Al Jazeera early in April 2020 about the pandemic and music, I talked about reciprocity and reflexivity (Zarate, 2020). When people can sing and play, they produce a health relational mechanism, and shape music cultures. When people do not have a culture of convening and arts as a way of knowing, it leaves a health void. The environment loses essence, and then we begin to lose our essence and need to find other ways to be creative. From positively impacting bullying with groups of 11–14-year-olds singing traditional, familiar songs in Spain (Epelde-Larrañaga *et al.*, 2020), to addressing the intersections between street musicians, outdoor acoustics, and movement flows of public spaces (Clua *et al.*, 2020), more studies are examining our relationship to the music on mass, collective levels, as I believe we have a need to respond and heal and reclaim our musical world and our music cultures.

Organizational behavior, music and creativity: Active factors

In her 2016 article in the *American Review of Public Administration*, Alisa Moldavanova writes:

> Instead of seeking results, sustainable thinking asks, "What is important for my organization, and what kind of legacy would it leave for the future? What are its core values, and what would it take to preserve them?" In other words, strategic and sustainable thinking are different, albeit connected, ideas. Indeed, sustainability often builds on strategic thinking. (p.536)

Moldavanova critiques institutional survival as insufficient and offers an intergenerational concept on organizational sustainability that bolsters those mentioned above in a two-level approach. She is an advocate for considering culture as the fourth pillar of sustainability to unify various systems with culture and organizational economics. In her research on a collection of museums, music, and performing arts centers and spaces, she found two major themes emerging: narratives of institutional resilience and institutional distinctiveness. Elements that highlighted an institution's resilience were structural adaptability, such as institutional change, hybrids, and social and community relevance, such as public–private partnerships. Distinctiveness emerged as capitalizing on the uniqueness, such as staying true to the core mission, occupying a unique institutional niche, shifting towards a semi-instrumental role, and the distinct value of the space's value (museum, music, and performance spaces). Higher education can serve as a buffer for external arts organizations, which provides a baseline for funding and access to quality human resources, built-in audiences, technology, and funding (Moldavanova, 2016, p.532). Other essential areas contributing to sustainability practices and ethics were public outreach that provided and supported social and community relevance, including addressing access and commitment to social equity (Moldavanova, 2016), p.534). The most important finding was that arts and learning and sustainable ways of knowing emerged via the vital role the results showed in the space's actual function. Moldavanova describes the importance of looking towards the future with a lens for different learning models that are centralized in the personal multisensory experience of these spaces and writes:

> unlike traditional learning, which relies on cognitive experience, logic, and rationality, the learning model offered by museums which are grounded in emotional perception, experimentation, interaction, and the personal experience of creativity. The ability of the arts to evoke creativity, to teach people to look at their lives and societies critically, and to re-examine social stereotypes is particularly valuable for thinking about the future. (2016, p.536)

Emotional perception, experimentation, interaction, and the personal experience of creativity—isn't this what we are concerned with in music therapy and the creative arts therapies? What if the model of intergenerational sustainable processes and practices offered here could be applied within and beyond other public and private sectors, which included in-house music therapy and creative arts therapy for mental health and well-being? What if we were to develop leadership programs and tracks for our emerging therapists and leaders for our field's evolution and sustainable practices?

These reasons alone promote the necessity for a sustainable, conscious, action-based philosophy in arts and health, musical cultures, music therapy, and the wider creative arts therapies community. Furthermore, practical, intergenerational sustainability has to be equitable for the generations ahead. There is an imperative need for organizational research. For these reasons, mental health, arts research, and practice come together to support the global demand for mental health resources in our environments where we work and learn. These are critical, translatable assets of a sustainable model that includes artistic ways of knowing and legacy evolution in and out of the field of music therapy and musical cultures. The possible combinations for community, social wellness and productivity are boundless!

CHAPTER 11

Music Therapy Research and Practice: *Anxiety in Context*

The current landscape

There has been a growing interest in music therapy's effects and impact on anxiety over the past 10–15 years, with significant advances in music therapy and medicine, particularly with regard to pain relief with children and adults in oncology, cardiovascular, pre-operative and post-operative pain and stress management, in prison and disenfranchised community populations, and even in dentistry. Although not specifically identifying areas discussed in detail so far, there is a broad interest in the field that does cover some areas of physiology and environment in therapeutic change.

Music therapy and stress

While stress and anxiety are deeply related, the field is combining the two. I offer a suggestion here to organize our strategy on music therapy and stress research. We conceptualize the whole topic, from stress to a diagnosed anxiety disorder, along a continuum of treatment and approaches. According to Martin and colleagues (2018):

> [the] consequences of stress are constant agitation, exhaustion, burnout, helplessness, fear, and eventually a weak immune system or even organ damage. The inability to cope with stress is a risk factor for various epidemiologically significant illnesses: cardiovascular, muscular or skeletal diseases, depression or anxiety disorders. (p.1)

As mentioned in Chapter 1, stress is cited as a sign to take action, mainly when chronic and acute signs of stress are reported. Within the body of empirical research, there are clusters and areas of interest in music therapy and stress. You can find them in work-related stress, burnout, and job satisfaction (Beck *et al.*, 2015; Brooks *et al.*, 2010), performance-related stress

121

with musicians (Brodsky & Sloboda, 1997; Kim, 2008), women's reproductive health and pregnancy (Chang *et al.*, 2008), parent stress (Jacobsen *et al.*, 2014), elderly in residential home care (Mohammadi *et al.*, 2011), medical staff (doctors, nurses, health and social care workers), relaxation and re-entrainment of the circadian system (Rider *et al.*, 1985), self-esteem with children and adolescents, and academic learning stress (Sharma & Jagdev, 2012; Smith & Joyce, 2004).

In their randomized controlled trial, on 20 Danish workers with stress-related incapacity to work, Beck, Hansen, and Gold (2015) used therapeutic guided imagery and music (GIM). They conducted six two-hour sessions over nine weeks. Workers showed significant improvements in well-being, sleep disturbance, and physical distress. They also reported that early intervention led to a faster re-entry to work. Clinically speaking, they saw significant positive effects on stress, mood, sleep disorder, depression, anxiety, and physical symptoms of distress (see table 2, p.339, in the original study).

Some newer studies have shown results that indicate a lasting effect for one or two more weeks post-treatment and then a relapse back to stress and worry behaviors. Interestingly, we also see differences between receptive/passive and expressive/active music therapy approaches and the intake, "in treatment and post-session results" (Gutierrez & Camarena, 2015). Although representing only a tiny body of knowledge at this point, it is nevertheless an exciting movement in what I consider the right direction for music therapy and anxiety research and treatment—particularly given that new emerging research on change mechanisms in creative arts therapies and music therapy can integrate into future studies and practice (de Witte *et al.*, 2021). Studies show longer-lasting impacts on anxiety from more than one single session to manage stress, even further down the clinical research path. From my research, I've seen more connections between the clinical and the collective, the neuropsychology and the creative psychology of the impact of what we do and how we work in music therapy. There certainly seem to be pockets of interest and work clusters that speak to the psychological, physiological, and cost-effective impact of music therapy on stress and anxiety. In medical settings, the instant relief of pain and distraction from pre- or post-operative stress related to those contexts and improvisational-based music therapy are crucial.

Based on this current and emerging body of knowledge, there seems to be a need to organize the interest in music therapy stress and anxiety research into a strategy or plan that can be integrated into our educational and clinical practices. Figure 11.1 offers a way to approach the different treatment needs and outcomes required for areas of concern with stress and areas of concern with anxiety. It shows a visual representation of considering these concerns as a continuum of treatment. In this way, it can help towards clarifying what is actually being identified in terms of intensity of the experience, and what interventions will be needed to support the individual being treated.

Stress . . . . Anxiety

Topics and experiments	Topics/experiments
Instant, no follow-up	Action-oriented approach
Single session	Dialogical processes
Immediate symptom relief	Integrational processes
Distraction	
Receptive-based approach	

Figure 11.1: Continuum of care in music therapy and anxiety research

Core components: Music therapy can help with stress and anxiety
Tempo and steady beat
In improvisation, the use of a steady beat and specific tempo impact anxious states. For example, in 2011, Gadberry (2011) experimented with manipulated tempo and steady beat. Her study tested two groups; one group received the steady bass bar beat in interventions, and the other did not. Her findings showed that playing in this way, using the steady beat, reduced anxiety. De Witte and colleagues (de Witte, Lindelauf, *et al.*, 2020; de Witte, Spruit *et al.*, 2020) also had significant results involving tempo and predictable, steady beats.

Voice, breath, music therapy, and stress
A body of literature has been progressively building since the mid-1990s involving clinical case studies and theory (Bunt, 1994; Newham, 1998). More recently, there has been an emergence of specific improvisation techniques, methodology, and theoretical development that supports de-stress breath and vocal interventions. This has also been seen in the recent literature from Austin (2008), Magee and Davidson (2004), and Warnock (2011) as well as Baker and Uhlig (2011).

Music therapy and performance anxiety
On reviewing the music therapy literature, I found there to be a keen interest in performance anxiety from musical and occupational perspectives. There is, however, a noticeable gap in the peer-reviewed literature between clinical

psychology research and clinical music therapy research. Only one article from psychology bridged the two and used music therapy research within the reference material (Osborne & Kenny, 2008). The significant studies in clinical music therapy research are in the *Journal of Music Therapy* and lean towards behavioral psychology in design and approach to address cognitive responses. For example, Orman (2004) experimented with virtual reality and graded exposure to elicit physiological and psychological changes in performing musicians. Kim (2008) explored how improvisation-assisted desensitization and music-assisted progressive muscle relaxation and imagery aid in musical elements and their effects on anxiety (Silverman, 2010). Elliot and colleagues (2011) explored characteristics of relaxing music as a means of controlling anxiety levels. They stated, "Music for anxiety research has generally adopted one of two approaches, a participant-centered approach in which the participant selects the music or the experimenter-centered approach in which music is selected by the experimenter" (Elliot *et al.*, 2011, p.267). The authors pointed out that this has driven a bias and has not focused on musical elements or constructs that make music "relaxing." Medium complexity in the music was a pertinent element in their results. Their findings suggest that relatively constant music with few dramatic changes in volume, melody, and key, but with some structural changes, is effective. This research type was helpful to think about from a music psychotherapy perspective, because individual sessions require more direct interventions to address various anxiety symptoms. This shed light on the effectiveness of using relaxing music to relieve symptoms, and also provided information as to what kind of musical elements cause irritating arousal. Furthermore, this knowledge included information about which psychodynamic interventions are appropriate to give voice to the feelings underneath the anxious energy. Another study, by DeLoach (2003), on genre, song choice, and anxiety levels contributed to the body of literature.

Kirchner and colleagues (2008) investigated performance experiences from the perspective of a sense of relaxation or a sense of flow. They used a survey design to gain more knowledge about individuals' experiences while performing. Levels of the following were reported:

- Relaxed/feelgood/enjoyment
- Emotional expression
- Loss of awareness of time/pain/sound
- Reaching goals/getting the right feel effortlessly
- Being absorbed/immersed/focused
- Transcension/dissociation
- Not having to think.

One author who has contributed a significant body of knowledge to performance wellness is Louise Montello (2002, 2005, 2010). Based on her research with musicians who experience performance anxiety, Montello has applied findings to create an integrative music therapy model known as performance wellness. The theory and methodology of essential musical intelligence (EMI) (the innate ability to use music as a self-reflecting, transformational tool) are applied within this model. In her study, Montello (2010) provided a newer concept that further shaped her approach to performance-related disorders. She merged psychological and psychosocial constructs of the polarizing effects of a narcissistic injury in personality structure and performance-related pressures to create what is called "the polarizing perfectionist" (2010, p.112). The performance wellness model aimed to transform the musical themes' polarizing elements through various improvisational techniques, such as musical self-statements and group music improvisation.

Music listening as a music therapy method: Receptive music therapy

Authors Grocke and Wigram (2007) define receptive music therapy as encompassing "techniques in which the client is a recipient of the music experience, as distinct from being an active music maker" (p.15). The authors recognize the Bonny method of guided imagery and music (BMGIM) as the most internationally known receptive music therapy model.

A small body of literature has emerged since 2007 addressing the impact of music listening on anxiety. One study experimented with music listening and neurophysiological responses to music (Krout, 2007). Another experiment examining the effect of a short, one-session live music therapy session on anxiety in the workplace produced significant results (Smith, 2008). Also, Kim (2008) explored the effect of live music-making on performance anxiety in musicians. All three authors suggested using music therapy intervention to teach people how to cope with real-world situations. None of the studies addressed preventive tools for anxious individuals living in the community attending therapy in private practice.

The overall evidence gained from these searches showed that the field of creative arts therapies has predominant modalities in the body of literature. The modalities are music therapy and art therapy. The available music therapy and art therapy literature offers such a wide breadth and variety of research on anxiety that it is difficult to clarify which studies address specific anxiety symptoms and which part of the studies' interventions affects the clients' stress. There is ambiguity about what anxiety is, where it comes from, and how to treat it in the creative arts therapies literature and, more significantly, in the music therapy literature. Certain studies reflect a movement towards defining anxiety from the perspective of stress in the workplace (Smith, 2008), but based on the literature, the field is far from presenting a comprehensive knowledge of the treatment of anxiety based on empirical evidence. Although relatively new to the scholarly dialogue, there is a discussion about the relationship between neuroscience, music, and stress that may support music therapy's theoretical development in this area.

Music therapy, therapeutic relationship, and anxiety

Scheiby (2005) illustrated the therapeutic music relationship's uniqueness as a more "mutual relationship than the typical relationship in verbal psychotherapy. Because the music therapist also plays music in work [and] for transformation to take place, the music therapist and the client must go on a musical journey together" (p.10). Baker and Wigram (2005) stated that "The process of creating, notating, and recording lyrics and music by the client or clients and therapist within a therapeutic relationship [is used] to address psychosocial, emotional, cognitive, and communication needs of the client" (p.67). From a multicultural perspective, Shapiro (2005) stated that "Appreciating, learning about participating in another person's musical culture, and encouraging them to share it with others can be influential in forming therapeutic relationships, especially with people who cannot speak the dominant language" (p.29). Oldfield (2006) also emphasized the intrinsic interactive qualities within the therapeutic alliance in music therapy.

Music therapy and academic anxiety

Studies are emerging in the field that addresses academic anxiety in students across the learning spectrum. From a global perspective, in Indonesia, for example, one study carried out by Situmorang and colleagues (2018) found academic anxiety manifesting in students through thoughts and feelings of sadness. This was as a result of worry associated with the *process of preparing* for final papers, such as theses. The authors identify four important indicators of anxiety that are vital for music therapists to understand further: patterns of anxiety-engendering mental activity, misdirected attention, physical distress, and also use of appropriate behaviors to cope and manage with academic anxiety (Situmorang et al., 2018).

In their comparative study on the effectiveness of group counseling, receptive/passive music therapy and expressive/active music therapy, and CBT on millennials' academic anxiety, Situmorang and colleagues (2018) found that receptive music therapy was more effective from pre-test to post-test, compared with active music therapy, which was more effective between post-test and the two-week follow-up. Their findings suggest two things: first, music therapy methods were successful in decreasing anxiety in group student contexts; second, they reveal an essential component of music therapy research and practice regarding the possible relationships between the intersections of physiology, group work, and receptive-based music therapy for relaxation and calming, alongside the potential connections and intersections between physiology, stress, worry, creativity, psychology, and music in clinical contexts. They discuss this as working due to techniques specific for passive music therapy (e.g. listening to music and guided imagery) and active music therapy (e.g. composing, improvising, and re-creating music), with the trained music therapist helping the students to realize the negative thoughts that cause the academic anxiety indicator, such as the thesis project, to evaluate them, explore alternatives, and problem-solve around them with coping skills and insights, in creative and non-traditional ways. The findings indicate a continuum of treatment that speaks specifically to the use of receptive/passive music therapy as working with certain aspects of academic anxiety, such as the physiological and biological arousals linked to fear. Expressive/active music therapy works towards the physiological and psychological change, and the therapeutic relationship steers the clinical discourse of decreasing symptoms and improving the situations that cause them. Situmorang and colleagues write that:

> the use of music in counseling can increase the production of all four positive hormones present in the human body, namely endorphins, dopamine, serotonin, and oxytocin. The functions of these four positive hormones can make the body more relaxed, reduce anxiety or stress, increase happiness, improve intelligence, and increase self-esteem. (2018, p.52)

The academic community saw the havoc wreaked across the world in 2019–2021 on teaching and learning due to the global pandemic. There is an immediate and necessary need to build on this body of work and respond to and address this issue globally. As a higher education professor, I understand the stressors from both the teaching and programming levels and the learning challenges for students which the Covid-19 pandemic caused. It illuminated the significant systemic societal dysfunctions of racism, economic and health poverty, access to employment, healthcare, and healthy food. Alleviating and supporting communities through our research and practice will help families, students, and teachers in individual, community, and collective ways to recover and cope with the colossal stress of academic anxiety. This is a vital role and function that music therapy is well positioned to take on.

Music therapy, healthcare worker and first responder stress and anxiety
Music therapy as a flexible continuum of treatment for crisis response

Music therapy has a critical part to play in current times in harnessing receptive and active-based approaches to deal with healthcare and first responder stress. Providing weekly support, self-help style groups with self-selected and pre-selected music that aids with physiological impacts and psychological processing are also part of the therapeutic program approach. Shaping an environment held in these ways by music therapists for individuals and groups and the larger institutional community has the potential for the greater good across all hospitals to support the healing needed after any crisis. Most importantly, there is an immediate need in the medical and frontline community services. Anecdotal reports are coming out daily of even seasoned physicians showing signs of acute stress, such as inability to stay asleep and remember facts. As Abdulah and Musa (2020) illustrated in their cross-sectional survey of frontline healthcare workers on the impact of treating Covid-19 patients, with regard to insomnia and stress, 93 percent of the 268 physicians surveyed reported stress, and 68.3 percent of them reported sleeplessness. Furthermore, the sample's mean age was 35.06 in an age range of 30–70-year-olds, and a meaningful experience level was 10.13 years. Considering that frontline healthcare workers represent a large percentage of the workforce population, these individuals' mental and physical health is of utmost concern for care. The authors also found that women respondents were more sleepless and stressed than their male counterparts. There was also a significant positive correlation between the number of days the physicians had dealt with Covid-19 patients and sleeplessness.

This is where studies like that of Beck and colleagues (2015) are crucial reminders of the importance of the clinical and therapeutic use of music for sleep disturbance and work-related stress. A hybrid continuum of care approach is needed in any work with Covid-related music therapy. From the compounding issues of acute and chronic stress responses and exhaustion through to the lasting and lingering issues from long Covid, the ability of music interventions in music therapy to harness the physiological, psychological, and aesthetic aspects must certainly be utilized to support such an immense need for recovery.

CHAPTER 12

Critical Improvisation: *A Transformative Framework in Music Psychotherapy*

Clinical improvisation: Flexibility for individual change

Improvisation isn't a mere approach, method, or technique in music therapy. It is a practice and a transformative interpersonal philosophy of life. Applying and integrating improvisation to the things in our day generates inspiration, creativity, and flexibility, builds relationships and connection, shapes attitudes, and changes minds and even policies for more significant social, community, and cultural transformation. Improvisation restores, renews, and heals connections. The dialogical processes and characteristics in improvisation are among the most powerful tools for change because of two essential functions; the nature of music is an antigen, and the nature of improvisation is transformative. There is a shared responsibility within those functions for the care of the therapeutic relationship. I use the acronym ART as a way of thinking about it:

A critical approach to clinical improvisation through:

Aesthetics
Relationships
To be: Identity.

Artistic expression and musicality are central to the approach's transformative power, similar to those in other improvisation-focused music therapy models such as creative music therapy (Nordoff & Robbins, 2007) and artistic music therapy (Albornoz, 2016). In its essence, it is a music-centered music therapy model.

I centralize music's role as the primary mode and function of change, and therefore also in how and why I apply music-centered practices to interventions. Aigen (2104) says that "Because the music-centered position seeks to explain the efficacy of music therapy within specific musical structures and processes, it allows greater specificity in musical interventions" (p.20). The critical improvisation framework creates a structure to address symptoms of anxiety and its various dimensions from a specific musical lens. It also offers a model called critical social aesthetics and a method called clinical listening-cultural listening. The method's core skills are rooted in the highly relational and action-oriented clinical improvisation environment. Each skill reaches and connects dimensions of anxiety in clients in a process-driven way, and the music therapist can use a range of techniques and apply them to each skill. It is also inclusive of the realm of sense and perception of beauty, play, and enjoyment, and approaches the theme of aesthetics from a holistic and socially responsive lens. To be socially responsive means to have a practice of responsiveness in theory and in practice. The framework is also a challenge to more traditional ways of sensing and perceiving aesthetics and improvisation in music therapy. I include a lens of social transformation within a social justice framework. Adams and colleagues (2016) identify social justice as "both a goal and a process" (p.3). It's actually a *practice of personhood and becoming*. They describe social justice in the following way:

> The goal of social justice is full and equitable participation of people from social identity groups in a society that is mutually shaped to meet their needs. The process for attaining the goal of social justice should also be democratic and participatory, respectful of human diversity and group differences, and inclusive and affirming of human agency and capacity for working collaboratively with others to create change. (Adams *et al.*, 2016, p.3)

The authors highlight the principle of "power with others" as opposed to "power over others" from Kreisberg's paradigm developed in 1992 as a means of attaining social justice goals (Adams *et al.*, 2016). In Chapter 3, I described the idea of *productive power* as a collaborative and coalition-based principle in a social justice and music therapy frame.

Figure 12.1 shows how these ideas have come together. The theoretical model flows from the top, theoretical approach through to the method and skills, and finally into the applied techniques.

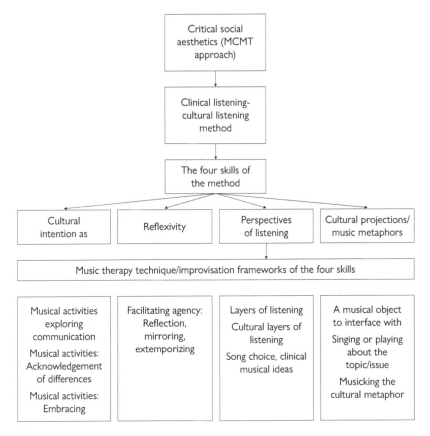

Figure 12.1: A music-centered music therapy (MCMT) model using a critically informed approach to clinical improvisation

Critical social aesthetics: A transformative approach to clinical improvisation

Paul Stapleton (2013) discusses the concept of "improvisational responsibil-ity" from a critical perspective (p.170). It is a concept that suggests shared, social learning and a journey of becoming. He also discusses the social power of improvisation and that "improvisation is not an expression of a diachronic personal narrative [of just the client's story], but rather one of the conditions in which a self comes into being" (p.170). The therapeutic relationship in clinical improvisation brings therapists and clients together in a unique, highly relational, and creative context. That creative space shapes musical products or objects, representing both the client's and therapist's learned social behaviors about the world and each other. When I work with the specific anxiety symptoms—let's say, excessive worry—the musical object can now represent excessive worry and all its collective, social contexts and their clinical implications. The musical object distributes through creativity and relationship to therapist and client as they are each perceived. They get to know and understand each other as the process evolves.

Elliot and colleagues (2002) describe the need for the creation of new terminologies and considerations of how art forms are sensed and perceived when they explain that "these challenges for the social sciences and humanities involve nothing short of the adoption of entirely new principles for evaluating cultural productions with the fullest possible understanding of the social, political, and economic conditions in which they are produced" (p.7). They go on to discuss the potential impact of such new terminologies when considering "explanations for how and why elements of creative production affect us as they do" (p.7). Creative productions derived from core relational music therapy processes expand on these fundamental challenges to our theory and practice in mental health and apply to real-time improvisation techniques. In their article on critical perspectives, Sajnani and colleagues (2017) discuss the need for responsiveness and responsibility in how we care for people, health, and art in the multiplicity of the clinical artistic process.

Clinical listening: A critical improvisation skill

Clinical listening has been defined as a multisensory way of learning about the world of the client. Several authors discuss the various modes and multisensory listening experience in the finer details of music therapy practice, including Abrams (2011), Aigen (2007), Ansdell (1995, 2014), Forinash (2000), Forinash and Gonzalez (1989), Kossak (2015), and Viega (2014). According to Lee (2016), "detailed musical inquiry must invite more refined listening" (p.21). His framework supports the idea that simultaneous factors occur within the improvisation-aesthetic experience. These concurrent factors must include the therapist's intrapersonal, interpersonal, intersubjective, and culturally socialized responses. While some models and approaches in music therapy have discussed multisensory perspectives, there remains a lack of consideration of aesthetics as transformative cultural competency in the act of clinical listening. Essentially, this is a gap that I am attempting to bridge with the framework.

Forinash and Gonzelez (1989) adapted phenomenological analysis approaches from Ferrara (1984) and advanced listening levels in music therapy called open listening, listening for syntax, listening for semantic, and listening for ontology. This process helps analyze and evaluate the therapeutic process and progress in improvisation. I also approach it as a practice of listening in the therapeutic process. The intentional space occurs from start to finish, and listening must occur at all times, through music, speaking, and silence. I value clinical listening as an identified competency that requires integration with other skills, such as empathy, presence, artistry, humility, relational being, and so on. Clinical listening-cultural listening began as a way of listening clinically, integrating the principles of clinical listening (Forinash & Gonzalez, 1989; Lee, 2003, 2016), music aesthetics (Scruton, 1999), and critical social theory (Calhoun, 1995; de Freitas, 2008). The combination of these theories reflects the possibilities and importance of the multisensory, social, ecological environment of Kenny's (2006) theory of the field of play within clinical improvisation. Within an aesthetics framework, it is crucial to acknowledge because how we "sense" and how we "perceive" music is fundamental to an aesthetics link and informs how we *sense and listen* and how we *perceive and listen* to each person's story in improvisation moments. In the case of anxiety, how the symptom is sensed and how the symptom is perceived by our clients and by ourselves in the act of listening and improvising is essential to attend to. In her relational music therapy approach, Trondalen (2016) defines how these shared life worlds are expressed through the concept of musical intersubjectivity. Grounding music as an art form, she explains it as a field of belonging and acting in multiple *lived* ways:

> It concerns creating mental contact. It is about meeting with the other's mind, a joint and shared experience within a relationship that is established through music and interactive in nature. Such a mental contact is non-verbal (implicit) and happens within a procedural framework. Musical intersubjectivity links to participation in a moving-along process, from meaningful concrete interplay (for example, improvisation with limited elements) to the ability to create meaning for oneself and others through words (for example, songwriting). This developmental process includes a kind of flow, an implicit and procedural knowing, where experience, body, and affects are essential. (Trondalen, 2016, p.121)

The method of clinical listening-cultural listening (CL-CL)

A core component of critical social aesthetics is clinical listening, called clinical listening-cultural listening (CL-CL), which I consider a multidimensional, social-cultural experience undertaken by the therapist to understand the therapeutic process. There are four skills used in CL-CL: 1) intention, 2) reflexivity, 3) perspectives of listening, and 4) social/cultural projections. The method is inspired by music therapy and expressive therapy authors who are interested in aesthetic values and analysis of listening. For example,

Lee's music analysis lens for working with clinical listening (2003, 2016), the phenomenological methods of listening and improvisation analysis (Abrams, 2011; Aigen, 2007; Ansdell, 1995, 2014; Forinash, 2000; Forinash & Gonzalez, 1989; Kossak, 2015; Viega, 2014). Ansdell's (1991) model of mapping the territory had a significant influence on how I approach listening in real time, and in analysis and assessment of recordings of sessions (see Chapter 14 for details on the evaluation procedure). From these authors, I gained an overall appreciation of the holistic approach to listening that considers the multiple layers of existence through the reciprocal processes of active music-making. CL-CL is how I currently think about listening, integrating the four core skills into a skillset that provides a way for music therapists to sense and perceive music socially and culturally in improvisation.

Let's look at the four skills of CL-CL in a bit more detail.

Intention refers to an attitude of cultural responsiveness and empathic acknowledgment of difference in the clinical music encounter. Intention is defined as understanding the presence of stigma in social structures and an intention to transform these structures to mitigate mental health oppression.

Reflexivity hones the capacity to recognize oneself as an agent who can identify, question, and change one's place in the social structure of the improvisation encounter and therapy process. Reflexivity refers to people's capacity (in the current context, therapists) to recognize themselves as agents who can identify socialization norms and reflect, question, and change their place in a specific social structure (de Freitas, 2008). Wood (2016) discusses the multiplicity of reflexivity as complex and states that it "occurs within multiple timeframes, involving multiple levels of information, including material circumstances, prevailing ethos, individual and communal timing, music therapy purpose, and political impact" (p.80).

Perspectives of listening highlights ways of listening to the improvisation environment from multiple perspectives (self, other, client, worldview, environment, transient, social, and cultural).

Finally, the skill of *social/cultural projections* leans on aesthetic principles and constructs influenced by Scruton's theory of music metaphor and image schemata (1999). Working with social/cultural projections in improvisation is the skill of entering into the therapy encounter with the person or people's perception of themselves (both client and therapist) as social/cultural beings. They are represented in a musical theme within the music improvisation environment. During this encounter, cultural metaphors, objects, and musical images are then produced out of the creative, active improvisation music (sounds, motifs, themes, patterns, etc.), causing the social/cultural projections to take shape into an idea or topic. Those projections of, let's say, the anxiety symptom or a related subject are transferred into the music in the improvisation environment, shifting from the original intention to insight about the music's social/cultural representation of the symptom. The most prevailing ailment concerning that symptom will emerge and concretize into the story, people, places, and things that are behind the symptom. It applies in two ways: free-floating, non-referential improvisation, which allows for the most prominent topic surrounding the symptom to emerge, and referential improvisation, which directly and explicitly works with a symptom itself. From there, the various physical, social, and cultural impacts of the symptom concurrently emerge. For example, if I want to use the method to assess cultural dimensions of nervousness in the music, I will choose to use non-referential improvisation. If I am working on specific cultural humility topics as a process for a group or individual to gain insights into the presence and meaning of stigma and anxiety related to one's relationships and socio-cultural location, I will choose referential improvisation.

CL-CL is the method that determines how I approach improvisation as a participant clinician, how I listen, and how I work with my cultural and social projections. I consider this a vital competency in the overall clinical process, which helps me design, generate, analyze, and present clinical data from the improvised work as authentically as possible. CL-CL is designed to be flexible so that it affects the individual (therapist and client) in how they feel and perceive artistic information in clinical contexts.

Figure 12.2: The architecture of the clinical listening-cultural listening method and its interaction between the theory of critical social aesthetics (CSA) and the four skills of the method

CHAPTER 13

Psychodynamic Assessment and Evaluation of Anxiety

The treatment continuum and assessment

The therapeutic process in music therapy involves various functions and purposes that support a solid clinical treatment program from start to finish. Those are a sound referral system, clear and relevant assessment systems, time for case conceptualization, applied treatment planning and interventions, the evaluation and development of scope of practice, and the termination process. Lindahl Jacobson and colleagues (2019) explain that assessment involves a series and collection of tools and strategies, including "reviewing pertinent records, documents, and clinical artifacts; employing effective interviewing skills and methods; carrying out appropriate observational strategies; and selecting, administering, and interpreting findings from clinically relevant tests and measures" (p.19). It is an ongoing, flexible system that is not linear and requires revisits to case conceptualization, re-evaluation of psychological progress, and analysis and interventions that lead to the eventual termination of treatment as clinical goals and objectives are met.

As Barbara Wheeler states, "assessment may take on many forms" (2013, p.344). These forms range from systematic procedures that accumulate scores to compare across one session with different activities or sessions (also see Wigram's evidence-based procedure with improvisations in the event-based assessment developed from Bruscia's Individual Assessment Profile), and more ongoing observations. A good music therapy assessment reflects a clear understanding of its purpose and a systematic way of gathering and accumulating information that determines strengths and needs (Hanser, 1999, p.76). Bruscia (1987) offers categories that cover: diagnostic, prescriptive, interpretive, descriptive, and evaluative purposes of assessment in music therapy. Wigram (1999) also follows a similar framework but has developed slightly different descriptions for certain categories, such as general assessment within the prescriptive category. A good referral system will align these components, supporting the initial case conceptualization with unique information and skills required to begin music therapy treatment.

136

The uniqueness of music psychotherapy assessment of anxiety

Client behavior and responses are unique in music therapy contexts, particularly regarding the combination of the physiology of music and the stress response system and action-oriented music psychotherapy approach. Different representations of people happen when they are music therapy clients. These representations offer unique aspects and co-occurring indicators of symptom relief, symptom story, and symptom cause that may get lost with current, traditional cognitive, linguistic-based assessments. Wheeler (2013) points out that "while existing assessments for learning and psychological development, for example, can be helpful, it is only through music therapy assessment that we can know the strengths and needs of the music therapy client" (p.348). While there is room to grow, I see the uniqueness as a strength to continue evolving and integrating into our growing body of assessment tools in psychodynamic music therapy. These tools represent the music psychotherapy client's change process in music psychotherapy terms. For example, using specific tools to assess in music-centered areas for interpersonal and intrapersonal growth processes, representing and reflecting the music therapy client's cultural identity, community roles and functions, creativity, and aesthetics in our assessment practices are vital for strengthening our models. All these areas are, of course, centered within the most important aspect of the psychodynamic music assessment, which is the role and function of the therapeutic alliance.

For example, using musical data to reflect potential diagnostic timeliness of musical data, musical and non-musical transference and countertransference, or projected *musical objects* helps to glean insight into past attachment trauma in a specific moment and at the *point of interest* (see the Critical Improvisation Anxiety Symptom Assessment model).

Cultural, creative, and critical considerations as de-stigmatizing actions

There is always a pertinent need for music therapy-specific assessment to include the creative, cultural, and transformational community concerns of consumers, patients, and clients. For instance, in the case of panic-related disorders and symptom presentations, tinnitus, neck soreness, headache, uncontrollable screaming, or crying may be culture-specific and need to be discounted from assessment findings and inclusion (American Psychiatric Association, 2013, p.208). These cultural components or domains of evaluation are even more critical when working in mental health situations, particularly regarding stress and anxiety. Remember that, as discussed in

Chapter 3, after all, there are cultures of exploitation in the community (work, social, etc.) that imply what Andrea Tone calls *the emblem of struggle as a badge of success* (2009), which is a problem that remains largely unseen, unnamed, and, therefore, untreated.

A continuum of assessment: Clinical, cultural, critical, and creative contexts

In a presentation for the European Creative Arts Therapies Educators Conference in 2019, my colleagues from expressive therapies and I described how we understood the therapeutic process as a five-point continuum of assessment where formal Big-A and informal little-a occur. We placed these within clinical, cultural, critical, and creative contexts and questioned certain power areas in assessment processes. For example, where are the dynamics of power in any assessment? What is its context? Who gets assessed? How do we facilitate and teach a co-created assessment process? The formal evaluations involve absolutes—powers to determine a course of treatment in collaboration with interdisciplinary teams; the multiplicity of music and the other art forms in creative arts therapies; understanding clients' needs; role, function, perceptions, representations that appear inside the musical space and outside, within the therapeutic relationship, which shapes clinical discourses. The informal assessments are in the continuous observations, in-session dialogical processes, and real-time assessments of needs and capacities. They require a relational attitude and way of facilitation, an improvisation-based practice that incorporates creativity, relational-cultural identity, and, most importantly, acknowledgment of the value and importance of the music therapy therapeutic relationship as a mechanism of growth and change.

Assessments in music psychotherapy, mental health, and anxiety

Music therapy assessments in mental health have evolved through psychiatry, and mainly from work in inpatient settings.

A brief history of the emergent psychiatric-focused assessments

Psychodynamic music therapy approaches and perspectives of assessment are historically grounded in psychiatric music therapy. The 1980s was a period where new policies were introduced to aim towards more holistic and representative assessments for patients. The prominent title of "activity therapist" was what most music therapists were given. I also worked under that title as a new hire in child and adolescent inpatient psychiatry. The

138

legacy of that marker in policy continues in current-day practice. Thankfully, the emergence of licenses in music therapy and creative arts therapies is helping to change that misrepresentation. Policy-makers in the mental health field are being educated on the music therapist's function and skills, which benefit the individual and the collective.

A turning point in our assessment and psychiatric music therapy history was the formulation of music/activity therapy intake assessments for psychiatric patients. The assessments included competency, treatment evaluations, and effects scales. The Psychiatric Music Therapy Questionnaire (PMTQ) (Cassity & Cassity, 1991), for example, developed the findings from surveying clinical training directors, and created an accompanying comprehensive manual, the *Multimodal Psychiatric Music Therapy for Adults, Adolescents, and Children: A Clinical Manual*, based on Lazarus's multimodal therapy model (1975, 1989). The combination of test, interview, and questionnaire takes a total of 30 minutes, making it an efficient all-around assessment for psychiatric work. Meanwhile, in New York, in the clinic and private practice settings, Florence Tyson's work highlighted the more psychodynamic and mental health focus and practice which led to the use of the identity of *psychiatric music therapist*. Some may argue that alongside the early work of Brusica, Isenberg, and Hesser, it was the beginning of what we now have as the *music psychotherapist* identity and music psychotherapy practice.

Improvisation and assessments

There are excellent assessments in music therapy, and I cannot cover all of them here. If there is interest in learning more about them, I suggest a closer look at the Wheeler (2013) reference and the Lindhal Jacobsen *et al.* (2019) reference—both have been cited by me here because I find them extremely useful. Among the current 18 or so empirical assessment tools that exist, the ones that have influenced my assessment of anxiety and attachment trauma are rooted in observation, analysis, and interpretation of the musical and non-musical data. The primary psychological theories that inform my assessment of anxiety are the social architecture of anxiety theory and attachment theory, discussed in Chapters 3 and 4.

The major methods that I incorporate are influenced by models grounded in creativity, action-oriented improvisation, and here-and-now-based approaches. Assessments that inform the Critical Improvisation Anxiety Symptom Assessment music therapy (CI-ASA MT) are Juliette Alvin's (1977) free improvisation method and phases of assessment, Bruscia's assessment model of domains in the Individual Assessment Profile (IAP) (1987), and Wigram's (2004) event-based analysis of improvisations using the IAP. They all capture the element of flexibility-based, artistic, qualitative work, alongside systematic documentation of motifs and themes that arise in the series of improvisations that I conduct on anxiety symptoms in the assessment phase. They are also flexible enough for me to use with any age group. I also include other age-related and population-related tools based on the individual referral, which offer aligned criteria to assess and have cultural considerations, such as the Individualized Music Therapy Assessment Profile (IMTAP). In cases where I need to create add-on methods of evaluation for certain unique characteristics and qualities that arise, I go to various other assessments and analysis tools that are available. The International Music Therapy Assessment Consortium (IMTAC)[1] is one source, alongside the literature mentioned above, and Wosch and Wigram's (2007) comprehensive book on microanalysis in music therapy.

Standards for Assessment in Music Therapy Practice

The American Music Therapy Association (AMTA) sets the clinical practice standards and assessment for mental health, covered in Section 2, which are described below:

2.0 Standard II—Assessment

A client will be assessed by a Music Therapist for music therapy services.

2.1 The music therapy assessment will include the general categories of psychological, cognitive, communicative, social, and physiological functioning focused on the client's needs and strengths. The assessment will also determine the client's responses to music, music skills and musical preferences.

2.2 The music therapy assessment will explore the client's culture. This can include but is not limited to race, ethnicity, language, religion/spirituality, socioeconomic status, family experiences, sexual orientation, gender identity or expression, and social organizations.

2.3 All music therapy assessment methods will be appropriate for the client's chronological age, diagnoses, functioning level, and culture(s). The methods may include, but need not be limited to, observation during music or other situations, interview, verbal and nonverbal interventions, and testing. Information may also be obtained from different disciplines or sources such as the past and present medical and social history in accordance with HIPAA permission regulation.

---

1   www.musictherapy.aau.dk/imtac

2.4 All interpretations of test results will be based on appropriate norms or criterion referenced data.

2.5 The music therapy assessment procedures and results will become a part of the client's file.

2.6 The final decision to accept a client for music therapy services, either direct or consultative, will be made by a Music Therapist and, when applicable, will be in conjunction with the interdisciplinary team. Screening may be used as part of this process.

2.7 The results, conclusions, and implications of the music therapy assessment will become the basis for the client's music therapy program and will be communicated to others involved with the provision of services to the client. When appropriate, the results will be communicated to the client.

2.8 When the assessment indicates the client's need for other services, the Music Therapist will make an appropriate referral.

2.9 The music therapy assessment will include current diagnosis and history will be performed in a manner congruent with the client's level of functioning to address the following areas: 2.9.1 Motor functioning; 2.9.2 Sensory processing, planning, and task execution; 2.9.3 Substance use or abuse; 2.9.4 Reality orientation; 2.9.5 Emotional status; 2.9.6 Vocational status; 2.9.7 Educational background; 2.9.8 Client's use of music; 2.9.9 Developmental level; 2.9.10 Coping skills; 2.9.11 Infection control precautions. (American Music Therapy Association, 2015)

Section 3 covers treatment planning, and Section 4 is implementation, reflecting the premises discussed above.

Issues for anxiety

Several significant factors need to be considered for a person who is struggling with anxiety:

- The specific symptoms experienced, particularly if it is an inability to relax, a sense of perpetuated unease, nervousness, fear of the worst, or being judged, or extreme worry about something, or a co-occurring general nebulous feeling that something terrible is going to happen.
- The prevalence of those symptoms.

- The general context of the anxiety in the person's life: fear-prevalent or panic-prevalent.
- Themes of loss: loss of function, agency, self-worth, self-esteem, career trajectory, education trajectory, and/or function in social circles.
- Themes of isolation.
- Themes of anger.
- Themes of feeling "stuck," hopeless/helpless.
- Themes of guilt.
- Themes of a limited to no affect (in disorganized attachment in children particularly).

Once the *themes* of anxiety are identified during intake and assessment, the *routes* and *road map* can be developed further by identifying *patterns* related to these themes. The patterns can then be placed into a continuum of stress responses to the *context* of the stressors—the people, places, and spaces where the anxiety appears. This is an essential step in the formulation of a music therapy treatment plan. Based on music therapy research on stress-related outcomes and anxiety-related outcomes (described in Chapter 9), choosing receptive-focused or expressive-focused interventions in the critical improvisation framework will dictate the treatment's impact and quality. No matter which is the prevailing stress response, it is all stored in the body and its memory. With that in mind, a cautious and careful approach is vital when using any musical intervention—remember that, for any age group, anxiety is just the surface of the underlying root causes such as attachment trauma.

A continuum of treatment for anxiety and music therapy

The continuum of anxiety is the process that occurs through a panic-related attack or an ongoing stressful, debilitating, real-world fear. When a client participates in music therapy, the encounter will bring up the whole parts of the continuum—from the early attachment disruption through to more conscious and accessible reflections of day-to-day occurrences. Both systematic assessments and behavioral analysis are crucial in the continuum of assessment. A helpful and identifiable hermeneutic-informed music psychotherapy assessment offered by Lowey (2000) explains 13 qualitative areas of inquiry. Several of those areas include assessment of the musical, verbal, non-verbal reflection of awareness of self, assessment of others and of *the moment*, the *thematic expressions* that occur, *listening*, and the qualities, expressions of the music, and the felt sense of the *collaboration/relationship* (Lowey, 2000, p.45). Other resources are also offered for improvisational assessment and analysis (Bruscia, 1987; Wigram, 2004; Wosch and Wigram, 2007).

Due to the powerful multisensory environment in the music therapy encounter, there are ethical and clinical responsibilities that need consideration. It is the music therapist's responsibility to know and understand this process as part of the continuum. Music can be used to support holding various dimensions and contexts of the anxiety simultaneously, or movement through each or one single phase as an intervention, through to directly working and dialoguing with a symptom. These are just a sample of the ways music can be used to work with the complexity of anxiety and the specific symptoms. Overall, however, any method we choose allows for the body–mind connection vital for establishing a recovery process. Many of my clients have described the felt sense of anxiety as *being in the cells*, which is true (see Chapter 8), and music also operates "in the cells" (see Chapter 9). The body–mind connection can be activated and worked within powerful, yet gentle and creative, ways that are unique to music therapy. Setting out *routes* helps us to consider clients' current functioning in their anxiety continuum. The routes include client patterns of onset, activation, resistance, and recovery, the cultural, economic, and other dimensions of the context of the stress or anxiety. The therapist's relationship to these factors and dimensions, and possible relational dynamics that may ensue form the groundwork to a treatment plan with music therapy.

Routes for coping with stress

Routes to designing treatment informed by observations and client reports of symptom presentation and patterns that are fear-prevalent or panic-prevalent.

Table 13.1: Routes for designing treatment

Route	Stress response continuum	Improvisation method
Route 1	Psychological—physiological—psychological	Expressive prevalent
Route 2	Physiological—psychological—physiological/psychological. Onset: fear and panic occur rapidly together, as in phobic responses.	Receptive prevalent

Table 13.1 shows a focus on the top four symptom categories that I work with across age groups. Referrals need to fit these top categories for the most productive and effective outcomes. They have shown to have the most impact in decreased intensity in reporting over time. This information has come from my lab, clinical anecdotal work and experience, and from other music therapy studies that have focused on improvisational-based,

interactive music therapy technique and change factor research in creative arts therapies (Ahonen-Eerikäinen *et al.*, 2007; Baker & Uhlig, 2011; de Witte *et al.*, under review; Martin *et al.*, 2018; Popa, 2015). Table 13.2 below describes these areas of clinical concern based on the domains in the *DSM-V*. It offers a guide to designing a focused treatment plan with the main areas of stress and anxiety-related disorders that music therapy can help with.

Table 13.2: General guidelines and taxonomy for working with anxiety in music therapy

	Generalized anxiety	Social anxiety (social phobia)	Panic-related anxiety
Major symptoms and features	Fear of the worst (in a real-world context); unable to relax; nervousness (jump from multiple symptoms throughout the day, and often present as overwhelmed).	Fear of social situations and possible scrutiny by others or being negatively evaluated; children express by crying, tantrums, freezing, or not speaking; adults by avoidance of intimate settings—present as submissive or controlling. In older adults, exhaustion from medical symptoms causes social avoidance.	Fear and persistent worry of losing control, fear of dying, e.g. fear of heart attack. Recurrent unexpected panic attacks. Quick surge of intense fear— coming from a calm state or anxious state. Nervousness. Physiological responses: palpitations, sweating, trembling, shortness of breath sensations, nausea or abdominal stress, chills/heat sensations.
Primary CAT/MT approach	Interactive, dialogical, improvisational: trauma-informed, attachment-based. Or receptive/ combination with active-based approach.	Interactive, dialogical, improvisational: trauma-informed, attachment-based.	Receptive, listening-based: trauma-informed, attachment-based.

CAT/MT change factors for intervention guide	Shared musical experience; physical act of making music; musical synchronicity; musical attunement; safe and structuring nature of music; increased flow.	Shared musical experience; musical synchronicity; safe and structuring nature of music; increased flow.	Shared musical experience; safe and structuring nature of music.
Methods to consider	Clinical listening-cultural listening; process-driven, group-improvised songwriting.	Clinical listening-cultural listening; process-driven, individual improvised instrumental music as primary method.	Clinical listening-cultural listening; listening and playing simultaneously.
Technique to consider	Facilitate musical cues for affect regulation, induced memory recall in improvised songs.	Facilitate musical cues for affect regulation, induced memory recall in improvised songs.	Specific 40–60bpm tempo/pulse of the song being listened to. Tone and alternating, predictable rhythms
Research/ studies	(Baker *et al.*, 2015; de Witte *et al.*, under review; Landis-Shack *et al.*, 2017; Passaili, 2012; Robb, 2000)	(Landis-Shack *et al.*, 2017; Potvin, *et al.*, 2018; Robb, 2000)	(Ansdell *et al.*, 2010; Baker *et al.*, 2015; de Witte, Lindelauf *et al.*, 2020; de Witte, Spruit *et al.*, 2020)

The Critical Improvisation Anxiety Symptom Assessment (CI-ASA) assessment procedure

Assessing and evaluating the symptoms

Assessment of the level of intensity and frequency of symptoms, and where they are activated or show up in a client's life, is critical in the design of the treatment plan. It allows for the cross-section of parts of a client's functioning (clinical, social, creative, etc.) to identify a specific context to the symptom(s). Once that appears, the story behind the symptom can then unfold and have dedicated focus.

It also covers the possibility for more symptoms to be identified and named by the client, such as panic-related symptoms or other symptoms where improvisational-based work may not be the best choice. Receptive approaches and listening-based techniques have a shown impact on panic-related, physiological symptoms such as dizziness. The assessment procedure allows for categories of "other" and "music that helps calm, soothe, relax," which provides an opportunity to indicate potential receptive, listening-based interventions. Inclusion of the particular sounds of anxiety as treatment begins is also necessary to document and monitor the treatment discourse.

Observations as evaluation

Observations are an important part of assessing and evaluating treatment progress. Several angles occur within the clinical listening-cultural listening method. Doing self-observation, client observation, and art observation (music) concurrently offers key clues and clinical data as to what might be happening for the client, and for the therapist.

Social-emotional learning self-report tools

Social-emotional models of assessment fit well for affect regulation issues, and offer some essential tools and ideas to support the child music therapy client with stress and anxiety. Not all models are made equal, and a reminder for cultural, ethnic, and racial experiences in social settings of the child to be included. whenever considering these models and frameworks. Ultimately the goal is to infuse the practice of self-care within the whole approach. Dena Simmons is a scholar whose work on Social Emotional Learning and equity should be every reader's go – to point on this topic. Another excellent resource is the girls leadership group, https://girlsleadership.org/author/catherine-macdonald-burns on check ins.

In some cases, there are colorful and age-appropriate cards and worksheets that have a positive strengths-based and coping philosophy. They can range from feeling states, visual representations of the individual-collective community models of practice, to emotional zones that range from cool zone to red zone with their associated feelings and their manifested behaviors. All target the objectives of insight into self-awareness, self-management, social awareness, relationship skills, and responsible decision-making that shows understanding of actions and consequences. Skills for self-soothing, self-care, and relationship building are ultimate goals in anxiety work with children and adolescents. When preferred music is blended into this kind of approach, a space is intentionally provided to validate and honor the individual's experience. Intentional empathic listening, and empathic dialogue need to occur by the therapist in relationship to the child or youth's response to whatever complex social experience has occurred and the music that allows for those real and healing conversations to occur.

	Feelings/states	Creativity-based music coping skills
Green zone	I am feeling… Happy, focused, present, and ready for my day. Yes/No	1. Happy playlist (receptive). 2. Active-based music therapy on identified song from playlist.
Blue zone	I am feeling… Sad, down, ill/sick, nervous, bored, stressed out, tired. Yes/No	1. Resource playlist; people, places, things. 2. Active-based music therapy on identified song from playlist.
Orange zone	I am feeling… Worried, fidgety, silly, excited, a bit unfocused, not fully in control. Yes/No	1. Organizing playlist. 2. Active-based music therapy on identified song from playlist. Sing/play at the same time.
Red zone	I am feeling… Angry, frustrated, out of control, want to yell, harm. Yes/No	1. Cool-down playlist. 2. Vocalize—sing to 10 (active).

*Figure 13.1: Example of a check-in card based on
social-emotional concerns with affect regulation*

Suggested questions to stimulate the process:

Pre-music:

> Q1. Can you circle which zone you are feeling?
> Q2. What instrument would you like to play that sounds like that feeling?
> Q3. Is there a song that you want to sing (either about the feeling, to the feeling)? Ask questions that enhance, heal, help, and/or resource.

Post-music:

> Q4. Did today's music help with your feeling zones?
> Q5. Was today's music-making helpful? What was your favorite instrument/song/music activity for that?
> Q6: What is your feeling zone now (after music)?

Sample intake questions that integrate questions to integrate into other social-emotional self-report tools of private practice, school, clinic, and other community-based settings. The following statements can be aligned to the associated emotional zones from the chart above.

The Revised Children's Manifest Anxiety Scale (RCMAS) ("What I think and feel")

Read each question carefully. Put a circle around the word YES if you think it is true about you. Put a circle around the word NO if you think it is not true about you.

1	I have trouble making up my mind	Yes / No
2	I get nervous when things do not go the right way for me	Yes / No
3	Others seem to do things easier than I can	Yes / No
4	I like everyone I know	Yes / No
5	Often I have trouble getting my breath	Yes / No
6	I worry a lot of the time	Yes / No
7	I am afraid of a lot of things	Yes / No
8	I am always kind	Yes / No
9	I get mad easily	Yes / No
10	I worry about what my parents will say to me.	Yes / No

Brief, general information on the revised scale factors
Anxiety Scale Factors: Confirmed by Reynolds and Paget (1981):

Physiological Factor: 1, 5, 9

Worry/Oversensitivity factor: 2, 6, 7, 10

Concentration anxiety factor: 3

Lie scale factors:

Lie 1: 4, 8

Lie 2:

Table 13.2: Adult Client Self-Report Worksheet. Intake Indicators, and Ongoing Treatment and Evaluation of Treatment Indicators—Part I

Anxiety symptom	Rating 0–5 (pre-musical) 0–1: low 2–3: medium 4–5: high	Rating 0–5 (post-session) 0–1: low 2–3: medium 4–5: high	Manifestation of symptoms in everyday life/behaviors (behavioral assessment)	Contexts for the anxiety (affective assessment)
Unable to relax				
Fear of the worst				
Nervousness				
Heart pounding/racing				
Other 1)				
Other 2)				
Other 3)				

Symptom prevalence and characteristics can be evaluated with several valuable tools:

- The Revised Children's Manifest Anxiety Scale (Reynolds & Richmond, 1978)
- Beck Anxiety Inventory (Beck & Steer, 1993).
- State-Trait Anxiety Inventory (Spielberger *et al.*, 1983).

 Table 13.4: Client Self-Report Worksheet. Intake Indicators, and Ongoing Treatment and Evaluation of Treatment Indicators—Part II

Anxiety symptom	Music listening/ playing that helps to calm, soothe, relax (affective)	Music that is unhelpful to me. Music to avoid. (behavioral)	Musical sounds and themes of symptoms
Unable to relax			
Fear of the worst			
Nervousness			
Heart pounding/ racing			
Other 1)			
Other 2)			
Other 3)			

CHAPTER 14

A Music-Centered Psychodynamic Evaluation Method

Music psychotherapy assessment and evaluation tool

The evaluation tool that I use integrates the clinical improvisation approach and clinical listening method. It works to provide a mapping process of phenomenologically informed clinical musical data that decreases the presence, frequency, and intensity of symptoms of stress and anxiety. It allows for the client's story to be acknowledged and tracked. The method helps to lift out and document accumulated moments representing the interpersonal roots of any attachment trauma behind the symptom. Once the patterns are established, the mapping process allows for ongoing evaluation of progress that moves towards some form of psychological resolve and physical relief.

I map what happens in a session in five stages, which cover the visible and invisible territories or boundaries that are moved through. The order in which I use the maps is not parallel to that of a session. Instead, I order them in terms of my observable process. I came up with the idea 20 years ago and have been developing it along the way. It underwent a national pilot study with colleagues within the American Music Therapy Association in 2014. The study's findings have been invaluable in continuing to develop the idea and method. One of the major learnings has been about how the maps and their procedures complement and align with the stages of psychotherapy (supportive, re-educative, re-constructive). For example, the physical territory map is a good introductory-level way of analyzing what is happening in the music and the musical-relational interactions, and practicing listening skills for the role and function of the therapist, client, and music. The other stages of the mapping process move deeper into understanding what else is going on in the therapy process. My students and colleagues at Lesley University in Cambridge, Massachusetts, continue to provide invaluable feedback about it. It captures the physical and invisible interplay of the deep roots of severe anxiety dynamics, the accompanying sematic memory held in the body, and the meaning of transitions in the therapist–client music therapy relationship. It is a synthesis of the psychophysiological impact of music in the therapy context, and the ways early attachment trauma *play out* in, through, and out of the body in its cultural contexts.

Map 1: The physical territory

This map represents the physical territory, the present, obvious here-and-now—what can be seen by the conscious eye. This is the most obvious to me when I begin a session and is why I mark it first. Observations such as what instruments are chosen, how they are played, and when they are played are the crucial factors here. The map is divided into 14 segments. Each segment is assigned its musical element. For example, form, idiom, instruments played, vocal, meter, rhythm, and so on are marked. The session's music-making timeline is marked from the center of the circle to the outside line, representing zero minutes at the center and the final minute of the improvisation on the outside line. Guidelines for the session's duration are marked along the timeline. This information comes from listening to audio and, where possible, video recordings using the clinical listening method and procedure. The map is then separated into the various transitions that happen in the session. I observe this by noting any transitions a client may move through from one event to another. Each transition is represented by a circle, which is always drawn in blue ink for consistency. I call these *transition circles*, and they vary from client to client, and session to session. To adhere to the uniqueness of each client's transitions, I use fill-in lines to represent the most abrupt transition from one event to another, with a dashed line with much space in between to mean the most fluid transition. Of course, by marking the extremes, I give myself room for any occurring transitions that are less extreme. I code these with less space in between dashes, or longer dashes, and so on. Once the transition circles are marked, bands are formed where I can write in all the specifics relating to the transition.

The following hypothetical examples will highlight this method. A client moves from the *welcome song* into another song without closure, so I will mark this with a dashed circle near the center of the physical territory map. If a client abruptly switches from singing hello to playing an instrument or beginning to talk, this is marked with a filled line, indicating a structured, rigid musical transition. Doing this provides me with an opportunity to see how a client copes with transitions, either induced by me or by them. It also provides visual information to accompany my logs of the number of transitions a client makes in a session. This, in turn, leads me to find a client's musical and verbal patterns where I can then have a sense of working towards goals explicitly dealing with the musical and physical events. This map is taken and adapted from Ansdell (1991). It is a zoom-out of the whole physical session.

Two forms of evaluation occur in the analysis process. First, while in session, I carry out here-and-now observations and make a note to self to document a particular moment and point of interest. Second, I remember those moments, and pay attention to new awareness and insights when I listen back to the recording. It is an inductive process of analysis and evaluation.

Figure 14.1 exemplifies a 30-minute session with two points of interest observed. The first, at the ten-minute point, and the second at the 15-minute point. The first point of interest shows the event as very abrupt, with a filled-in line. The musical environment changed obviously, and the client ceased to sing and instead played the conga drum in a faster, staccato 4/4 rhythm. The transitional circle is marked accordingly. The second point of interest was completely different. It shows a fluid transition from singing "Twinkle Twinkle Little Star" to another song, "Mary had a Little Lamb." Everything—quality, tone, tempo, form, and so on—stayed the same in the musical environment, indicating this fluid movement from one event to another. Therefore, the transition circle is marked with a dashed line.

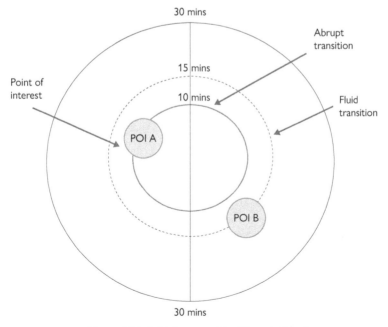

Figure 14.1: Initial map to identify point(s) of interest(s), showing two points of interest

Table 14.1: Template for analysis of the physical
territory of the music in the point of interest

Physical territory items	Timeline and description 0 min
Tempo	
Rhythm	
Meter	
Melody	
Vocal	
Continuity	
Phrasing	
Form	
Physical	
Idiom	
Facility	
Force	
Articulation	
Instrument	

Map 2: The focused, specific event of the session

This map is like a zoom-in of a specific event and point of interest in a
session. I place emphasis on what I feel are the most relevant experiences for
either the client or me, or both of us, by circling the individual events. Such
events and/or experiences will involve any physical movements of playing
an instrument that I observe, any transferences and countertransferences,
or projections—basically, absolutely any experience, visible or invisible, that
seems to cause an effect to the flow of the therapy. Each event/experience is
focused on individually, using the format of this second map. To continue
using Figure 14.1 as an example, one significant event that happened was
when the client switched from singing a song to playing the conga drum in a

faster, staccato 4/4 rhythm. This is classed as a significant event—movement from one phase to another—and will be circled in blue ink.

By circling all of the most important events in each weekly session, I get a picture of where a client is in terms of their process regarding transitions. Moreover, I have found that the events that I circle are generally related to a musical interaction that occurred, which triggered a response either from me in the form of musical and non-musical countertransference, or a physical response from the client, resulting in them transitioning from one musical event to another. Information is then gained regarding what instrument or song triggered the movement, and when it happened (see Figure 14.2).

- Event occurred in the tenth minute of the session.
- Abrupt physical movement from singing to playing the drum quite forcefully.
- It felt as if the song had triggered a reaction, which the client seemed to be conscious of.
- The client seemed to be physically looking down at the drum with no apparent awareness of me in the music with her.
- I felt shocked, and scared, like a four-year-old, as well as isolated. The client felt to me as if she was an adult ignoring a child, about 18–20 years old.
- I played the piano with her throughout the movement from singing to playing. Moving with the mood change as well. Key change from major to minor, clustered chords with drum.

Figure 14.2—Map 2: the significant moments and points of interest

I can see when in the session the event happened, as well as noting observations of the client's affect, whether she seemed to be conscious of a memory, or not. My own reactions can be observed and noted. In this case, there were reactions of shock and feelings of being scared and isolated. The instruments and music I played can also be observed and noted here. This is where I also go through the CL-CL method's procedure, checking in on my cultural intentions in the music, my agency and client's agency, perspective of listening, and any musical, cultural objects that may have occurred.

This is where my interest in what happens with both the visible and invisible dynamics of the music therapy session is developed further. Map 2 provides a gateway into the invisible realms of the therapeutic relationship, which ultimately allows me to explore how music can be a trigger to take a client into their experiences of consciousness, as well as how I experience this. Thus the process evolves into a musical dance of the therapeutic dynamics, yielding exact, visible information of what instrument and/or song caused the transition, how the instrument and/or song was played and/or sung, how I was feeling within this transition with reference to musical and non-musical countertransferences, and when in the session it happened. This information ultimately shows me where a client's (and my) boundaries are regarding physical, observable realms, as well as what the invisible boundaries are doing, via projections, countertransferences, experiences of consciousness, through memories being triggered, and so on. In terms of a boundary perspective, the physical boundaries are just the beginning of the musical interaction.

Maps 3, 4, and 5: The invisible territories
The following maps (3, 4, and 5) are all drawn in the same format. They are designed to be placed in sequential order over a reduced version of map 2. This modified version of map 2 then becomes the center for the third, fourth, and fifth maps.

From this center, the maps have four bands moving outwards. These bands represent a movement away from the center, which is the conscious, physical experience, through to the outer layer, which represents a more expanded experience, either a growing older in age or a movement into unconscious realms. Within these bands are areas that are also experienced and moved into and out of, so they are permeable, and are used as a reference point for a certain age or level of consciousness. All arrows marked in these three maps move in the same direction, implying that there is an invisible flow of experiences around the present, physical session, which is the center circle. These maps ultimately represent the important fact that music psychotherapy can provide an arena for both present and past experiences to happen at the same time, while moving slightly closer to the specific questions of how, when, and why music can do this in the therapy setting.

It is of importance that the reader simply acknowledges each map in its own right at the moment, as part of the whole working process. Each map can only function as a part of the whole model, which comes together with the addition of the fifth map.

The hypothetical example from Figures 14.1 and 14.2 is continued in the following examples of the rest of the mapping process.

Map 3: Transferences and countertransferences (musical and non-musical)

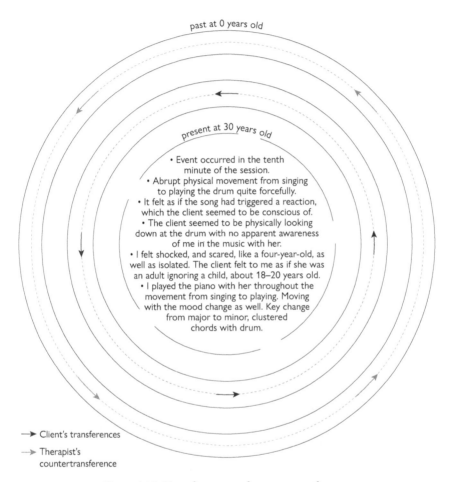

Figure 14.3: Transferences and countertransferences in the specific event of the session

Here I look at any transferences and countertransferences that occurred in the specified event. I place this map in third position simply because it is what I pick up on after my initial physical observations. It represents the invisible forces that occur in the music therapy session. I will explain each band and its purpose by describing it from the outer band line through to the most inner. The fourth, outer band line represents a client's life from when it began; it is labelled 0 years. It also represents the furthest past of a client's life, in terms of transference and countertransference information.

The third band line from the center circle line signifies a client's childhood years. The second from the center circle line signifies a client's adolescent years. The first band line from the center circle line signifies the adult years, right up to the center circle line, which is classed as where the client is in their physical, present age. The example I use below shows that the client is 30 years of age at present. The band lines are guidelines to enable me to mark ages that I feel from transference and countertransference of the specific event in question, which is marked in the center (Figure 14.3), that fit in between two bands. I mark a client's transferences with green ink, and my countertransference with orange ink.

Map 4: Boundary benchmarks—when past attachment ruptures occurred

Once I have an idea of where the transferences and countertransferences are moving, in terms of age and past experiences, I then take a look at the developmental boundary benchmarks and write in where any known attachment trauma and developmental ruptures happened. The marked boundary benchmarks usually coincide with the transferences and counter-transferences. This map is adapted from Black and Enns' (1997) model of developmental transitions, and the developmental benchmarks explained in Chapters 16 and 17. The outermost band line from the center signifies the *pre-childhood* boundary benchmark. The third represents a client's *childhood* boundary benchmark, the second from the center circle line represents the *adolescent re-enactment* boundary benchmark, and the first band line from the center circle line exemplifies a client's *adult re-enactment* boundary benchmark. I mark in brown ink where the trauma happened in a client's life, if they were neglected, had a parent who was dismissing or ignoring emotional needs, or were abused, and/or if they were the neglectful object or abuser. I also note whether the attachment neglect or abuse was physical or sexual, which can cause different attachment styles and stress responses that shape the dynamics of the therapy relationship.

For the sake of this example, I am suggesting that my hypothetical client was sexually abused by her stepbrother at the age of four. The stepbrother was 20 when he violated her developmental attachment boundaries. As you can see, the information from the boundary benchmark map and the trans-ference/countertransference map coincide. Even if this does not happen in other cases, it is still relevant and important information for the therapist to obtain. It may provide the therapist with insight into events that might not even be documented in a client's records. This leads on to the fifth and final map of the process, the adapted version of Wilber's (1977, 2001) spectrum of consciousness.

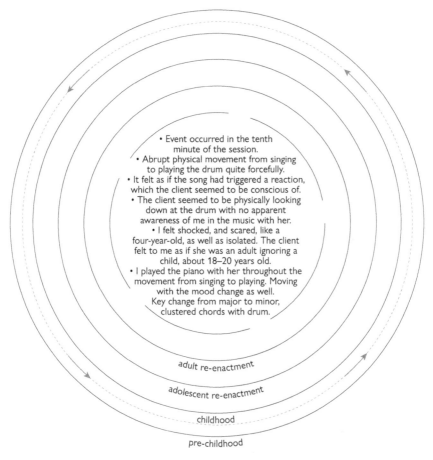

Figure 14.4: Developmental boundary benchmarks.
When the attachment trauma happened

Map 5: Spectrum of consciousness

The last phase is taking a look at the spectrum of consciousness to see where, in terms of awareness, the client may have been for this event. The outer band line represents *unity consciousness* followed by the third band line, which represents the *centaur level*. In between these two lines is where the *transpersonal bands* reside and move. The second from the center circle line signifies the *ego level*, which is followed by the fourth band line, the closest to the physical center circle, which represents the *persona level* of consciousness. This is the area of consciousness within which most humans function, in terms of projecting unwanted personal material onto others.

This final map is like the icing on the cake. It captures the culmination of all the information from the preceding maps because it actually gives me a reference point to work with regarding where a client may have been in terms of consciousness of the event. It is extremely relevant for my work with survivors of sexual and physical abuse who have complex and severe social, fearful-avoidant anxiety disorders, because it enables me to have a handle on the process of therapy when working from a trauma model such as Herman's (1992) stages of recovery. If a pre-composed song arises, I can take this method and find out whether a client is ready, in terms of recovery, to address the issues the song represents for that person. It provides me with information about what musical activity/event was happening at the time the transferences and countertransferences were occurring, which leads to whether they were linked to any abuse that happened from the boundary benchmarks. It also provides me with important information concerning the way in which the musical event may or may not have aided a client with coping with her psychosis because I can document, in terms of consciousness, where a client moved via the music. This map is adapted from Wilber (1977, 2001) (see Figure 14.5). You will see in Figure 14.5 that I have marked the client's conscious experience in both the persona level and the centaur level. This is because the information gathered up to now from the other maps shows that the client is projecting, and hence functioning, on the persona level.

However, the physical reaction, as embodied by the abrupt transition in the music, highlighted the fact that something, in terms of memory per-haps (going by the transferences and countertransferences), was triggered. I therefore mark the client's conscious experience in the centaur level as well, since this band represents an integration of body and mind experi-ences. The somatic experience of sexual abuse is important to note here. A memory could trigger the physical reaction in the music. This memory could be a sensation without words, yet the instruments provide the voice. The amalgamation of all the maps together provides important information regarding the exact moment when the specific transferences and counter-transferences occurred, along with the music which triggered them—and, more importantly, where, in terms of experiencing consciousness, the client was operating.

160

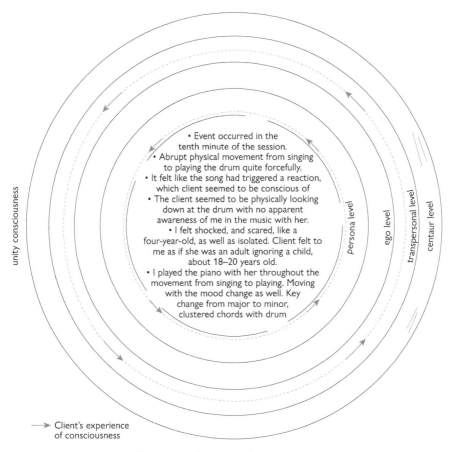

Figure 14.5: Spectrum of consciousness

Transitions as change factors and critical response actions
Documenting progress with the music maps

The mapping process begins with the transitions, which I view as symbols of psychological change processes happening in the therapeutic music alliance. The analysis of these points of interest is crucial to gain more insight into what is happening in the therapeutic process and the relationship. It is a way of unpacking psychological phenomena. Transitions represent the manifestations of psychological processes at work in the therapist–client relationship and the musical play space.

The child was singing and playing merrily. A sense of attachment was occurring within the therapeutic relationship. Suddenly, he stopped and began to ask questions about his favorite food and how much time remained of the session…

CHAPTER 15

The Sounds of Anxiety and Their Meaning: *Musical Expressions, Representations, and Themes*

When...
...the door knocks...
...the monitor beeps...
...the footsteps get closer...
...there is a loud surprise sound...

These are all statements and memories that I hear when I work across age groups. Important anniversary days for birthdays, holidays, and so on are accompanied by the sounds of abuse and trauma, particularly with the young people who are 16 onwards and have lived in social care and been through countless admissions to inpatient psychiatry or are in the system of outpatient therapy. These are the young people and adults I try to reach most because they are the ones who are in many ways the least protected people in our current societies. They are our future, and yet, at the same time, the system does not protect or regulate them at the same level as when they were children. The experiences of disrupted attachment and trauma stay with them in their memories and, unfortunately, play out in the dysfunctional systems within which these vulnerable children, teenagers, and young adults are at risk of being absorbed. There is a need to support these youth with current treatments. It requires an individually-focused balance of symptom management and behavior modification that includes trauma-informed therapeutic approaches of creative arts therapies. As Cruz and Feder (2013) explain, '...just alleviating or even getting rid of the symptoms, through medication of behavior modification, for example, may not get to the root of the problem' (p.32).

The auditory system is the first to be developed and typically the last to decompensate in the human body. It links, as explained in Chapters 8, 9, and 10, the whole body–mind–spirit. This is why the sounds of anxiety are trauma memories of various gradients. Like a virus dose, we don't know how intense or prevalent or even lasting it will be, but the trauma infection is a reality with which our vulnerable youth live. In clinical improvisation, these life story themes come through the music and are implicitly expressed or felt and explicitly heard and expressed. Both contribute towards the self-expression of specific themes of the active sources and inactive (memory) sources of anxiety. My research experiments explore these themes, and, so far, have found that certain musical qualities represent particular and specific symptoms (active, present, and past (inactive) present) that are representations of stress and anxiety, particularly social anxiety and generalized anxiety disorders. Critical improvisation, and its dynamic, systematic frame, targets the nebulousness of the feelings and states that the anxious symptoms bring on. It also enables me to work with a symptom directly, which releases the interpersonal and intrapsychic story behind the symptom. The transformative work can then begin to alleviate and even eliminate symptoms that have evolved into an anxiety disorder over time. The primary symptoms that I address with my clients and my research range from mild to severe and typically involve an experience of nervousness, an inability to relax, a fear of the worst, and the heart pounding or racing.

This chapter discusses what these symptoms sound like, based on my research and experience in clinical improvisation contexts. It offers insights into the musical, physiological characteristics of stress and anxiety that may not be fully detected when treated as a comorbid disorder of depression. Let's tie in the stress response system, environment, and how our bodies respond (see Chapters 9 and 10). For example, it is essential to gain clinical information when making connections between the explicit and implicit qualities of sounds. Let's take the fragile-like sounding musical qualities (explicit) and silence qualities (implicit) of nervousness to talk in public and fear of being ridiculed, and think about them occurring with potentially extremely high arousal levels (silence, implicit). The high arousal may be happening in the background with a high frequency and rapid tempo. It may not get noticed or picked up on as quickly in non-musical interventions. What is not explicitly expressed verbally may be highly active symbolically but may not get a chance to *speak* of what is going on in the individual's *sound environment*. The story is only half told. Understanding these essential clinical components of the disorder is imperative for successfully implementing critical improvisation methods and treatment techniques.

The two domains of treating anxious sounds in improvisation

The intervention design of treating anxiety's musical qualities has two domains—either expressive, active-based improvisation or the soothing calming, containing domain that focuses on receptive-based interventions. The reasons are tied to the various domains of the body's physiological stress responses and arousal, the type of anxiety disorder—fear or panic-related—the client's music and sound preferences, and the adaptogen influence of music qualities and components. As explained earlier, each dimension needs attention when choosing techniques for intervention design for the CL-CL method. Think about how to tie it all together within the structure and framework of CL-CL. It is all about considering the characteristics and qualities of the symptoms and domain choice to establish the sound patterns—in this case, the musical expressions and sequences and musical objects produced in the improvisation dialogue.

When dialogue is necessary, or when containment and holding are needed, the expressive and the soothing techniques to use are detailed in Tables 15.1 and 15.2.

Table 15.1: The expressive domain
Technique: active-based, projective

Symptom	Technique	Reasons for selection
Inability to relax	Dialoguing	
	Thematic development Identifying "antsy" Matching, mirroring, Dialogue-based instrumental Dialogue-based vocal Consistently grounding	This was also connected to nervous energy but not identified by the patient.
Numbness—in fingers		
Constant worries Psychosomatic	Grounding—as a warm-up Extemporizing Amplifying	
Fear of losing control in environment Heart racing, shock sensation/startle response	Dialoguing with "antsy"	

Fear of the worst happening	Matching, mirroring, reflecting Extemporizing Reflecting Dialoging Extreme fear of worst: grounding, reflecting	
Performance anxiety	Projection/symbolism	

The below examples contextualize certain combinations of sounds, symptoms, and applications to use in either domain:

He couldn't relax and experienced constant heart pounding. He also had rare but unpredictable panic-related responses with breathing when stressed. Tempo manipulation, dialoguing with the sensations both instrumentally and vocally (with tempo and velocity manipulations), would be the initial clinical response.

She couldn't relax and had constant worries about being fired and maintaining employment. Grounding, extemporizing, and amplifying techniques would be the clinical response to express and empower, to a) name and express the worry, and b) build confidence.

Their identified symptom was nervousness, which was activated in moments of conflict in the workplace. Fears of authority and "speaking up" created heightened arousal and stress responses, which prevented her from sharing her ideas. Grounding techniques, such as repetitive octaves and manipulation of the slower tempo would be the clinical response. Matching and mirroring vocally in soft, predictable tones would also be an excellent way to address childhood attachment trauma alongside exploring the nervousness related to other relationships.

Table 15.2: The soothing and calming domain
Technique: accompanying/receptive-based

Symptom	Technique	Reasons for selection
Nervousness	Vocal grounding Grounding	
Difficulty breathing	Vocal grounding Grounding	

cont.

Symptom	Technique	Reasons for selection
Fear of the worst happening	Fears of fitting in Multiple fearful behaviors: agoraphobia Extreme fear of worst: grounding, reflecting	
Fears of fitting in Multiple fearful behaviors: agoraphobia	Dropped out of college because of it Grounding, soft, proximal distance, but able to handle intimacy in the music Played guitar a little bit He was empowered when he played the guitar Could not go beyond a whisper Reflecting	

The below examples contextualize certain combinations of sounds, symptoms, applications to use in either domain:

> *She was 19 and so scared to leave the house that she needed a close and trusted caregiver in the family to accompany her at all times.* Stress responses were constantly firing at all cylinders. Many young people in our communities live in terror of the outside world due to their anxiety and agoraphobia. There is a great need for a community-based Anxiety-Informed Recovery Approach in Music Therapy (AIRA-MT) that breaks down the traditional four-wall clinic and a green light to telehealth music therapy methods to reach this specific population.

So, in effect, we must address the psychophysiology of music to think about anxious symptoms musically. Overall, some general characteristics can be associated with each symptom. Still, there will always be layers and nuances that also require consideration when working with any individual or group. The characteristics of the sounds of anxiety are offered as a guide to understanding your anxious states and contexts and others' consciousness of taking care of clinical, sustainable, and cultural contexts. It is a tall order to be so attentive to oneself and others, but in my opinion, it is a necessary one.

Let's begin with addressing each of the symptoms.

The sounds of nervousness

It helps to close your eyes for a moment to imagine and connect with this state. What are the key characteristics and chain events in the body that lead to feeling nervous? When I ask my students this question, the range will be broad, from heart racing, sweaty palms, to dizziness. It is always within the physiological chain reactions. There is always a story attached to it revealed in the musical experiential on the specific contexts and their sounds of nervousness.

At this point, your body is releasing hormones to handle the surge of reaction that is about to happen. Adrenaline is being pumped all over your body to activate the sympathetic nervous system, which suppresses the parasympathetic nervous system, which in turn moves the adrenaline responsible for creating sweat, increased pulse, and even increased blood pressure. Musically, the sounds will be characterized by rhythm and tempo because they will represent an increased heart rate, increased pulse, and increased flow of activity in the nervous systems. Pitch will be on the higher end, and the melody will be unstructured and have a frenetic and kinesthetic quality to it. Vocal characteristics will also reflect these qualities. Something will be there to show there is a sense of nervousness. A person's voice may present and sound calm, but the rhythm or the tempo or pitch may show signs of the presence of nervousness.

The sounds of "I can't relax"

The core characteristic of this symptom presents more explicitly than its counterpart of nervousness. It will typically accompany its close buddy, fear of the worst, with its feature of endless worry. When this is expressed and presented musically, it will be characterized by its melody. Melody is a sequence of connected tones. When someone cannot relax, the melody does not seem to have a predictable flow or line. From the physiological perspective, the brain is working hard to try to predict. In states of stress, the prediction function cannot secure a satisfactory ending, so the cycle of neurological-physiological events continues. When we put tones and sequences to that state, the music also doesn't show any form of predictability and this is a vital characteristic of this symptom. When we consider untuned instruments, the "state of the sequence" played will sound disconnected, non-directional, and unpredictable.

The sounds of "what if…" The fear of the worst

This is a little harder to detect because of its cognitive and psychological characteristics and requires more musical and song-based storytelling and autobiographical content in improvisation work. The important thing to remember is the context of the sense of fear and endless worry. Getting to the context is key because the sounds come as a dialogue with that context. It can be difficult to have someone stay with it and not use the physiological responses to music to calm themselves and alleviate symptoms. This symptom's key characteristic is the unanswered question of "what if…" What if the house burns down while I'm outside? What if I get run over by a bus? What if my parent doesn't come back home? The "what if…" is presented musically as an unanswered question that is expressed through several components. First, when there are tuned and harmonic instruments involved, the harmony is lower in its tones, and the tempo is not as fast as it is in nervousness. The tempo could present as calm, but remember, the arousal level in this symptom is exceptionally high due to the panic connected to fear. This is one of the more complex qualities to pick out in the music. Fear is presented musically with a sense of vastness—so harmonies that cluster together, an ambiguous landscape with silences in it, will most likely be expressed. The therapist's sense of the music is essential to pick up on because of the arousal present. It is important to assess physiological responses when playing with this symptom. Getting the bio-feedback on that and playing out the symptom will provide more information for the arousal level. Without intervention, straight-up playing would not pick up on it, and it would remain a latent manifestation of the fear.

Increased heartbeat

Think of times when a situation caused you to have an increased heart rate, but you needed to be completely confident. Performance anxiety is an excellent example of this. From sports, performing arts, to presenting to colleagues, we endure this level of latent-based symptomology of stress and anxiety. When it is played out, it can sound unforgettably powerful.

Cultural context is essential always to remember because where I might have ears trained to think of increased musical pulse for this symptom, it may not be that for someone from another culture or country to me. This situation happened to me in an international teaching context, and it was compelling. I was working with small groups of music therapists in the class, and each small group had chosen one of the significant symptoms being discussed here and explored what that sounded like for them. The group that chose this symptom did not increase the tempo but increased the dynamic and slowed the tempo. It was captivating for me to listen to. It was played on a bass tone bar, ominous, low sounding, with a heartbeat pattern. The intensity reflecting an interpersonal story behind the symptom revealed a sense of fear and unpredictability. The intensity of the sound's quality, loud dynamic, predictability of expression of the human heartbeat, and concentration of the whole group listening in silence showed that while we can predict certain musical sounds and musical presentations of these symptoms, the cultural considerations of each context are crucial. In this case, it was a non-Western context.

The sounds and their contexts

To get to each symptom's unique sound, the context for all symptoms is critical and will lead to the story behind the sound or improvised song.

The intensity of the symptom is crucial to identify. Frequency and repeated patterns are also critical to understanding whether this is a stressful moment in someone's life or whether the stress has developed into an anxiety disorder. Musical improvisation can represent multiple symptoms at the same time. This is a blessing and a curse because we want to be specific, but we also want to acknowledge the context causing the symptom(s). The reality is that no symptom occurs on its own because of the cycle of anxiety, such as anxiety attacks and stress-provoking situations. But, because of the intensity of these cycles, understanding the symptoms is vital to understanding the whole context better and alleviating each symptom that occurs in any given situation.

I remember teaching a graduate course of theories of music therapy for the first time as a junior professor. My heart was pounding (adrenaline), I feared what the students would think of me (what if I don't remember my facts and research in my lectures?). I didn't sleep well the night before because I felt nervous about the upcoming event (more adrenaline and performance stress/anxiety). Of course, it was fine, and I left feeling relieved and excited to be doing the work. But the three-stage stress response system is a vivid experience which, for some, can be terrifying and even deadly.

The sounds and their musical motifs

A musical motif is a pattern that occurs and reoccurs in a composed piece of music. When improvising, we create motifs that emerge and are used and clinically developed. They might inspire the development of a composed piece, or they might fill the purpose in the here-and-now for the improvisers and never be created again. When anxiety motifs occur in the music, they

169

infuse characteristics of their sounds and move the improvisation development into the musical story of the stress or anxiousness. Combining the context (historical, current, cultural, social) of the symptom and the sounds shapes a situation where individuals can symbolically tell their story through the musical medium. It is essentially creating a narrative, an autobiography of their anxiety that has shape, sound, action from intrapersonal processes outwards to interpersonal processes, and engages in a creative act that simultaneously impacts a sense of aesthetic, action-based, physiological, and physical actions all at once. Depending on the treatment program, these motifs will reoccur, and this is the next window into the inner world of the individual's response to the symptoms and the story. Motifs will differ, but the fear of the worst may bring someone back to the roots of a particular symptom, to childhood years, and a close caregiver's actions and behaviors impacting development.

It could be a situational context where the motif represents a literal person in the individual's life responsible for either causing or perpetuating an anxiety-provoking dynamic.

An individual's anxiety story's musical motifs are another critical component of working within the sounds framework. It has helped me fine-tune interventions that can go more deeply and broadly into the unconscious motivations and responses, or blocks that never got a chance to be worked through and interrupted in developing years for adults. For children, naming and characterizing the motifs in play contexts is incredibly helpful in working through the anxiety symbolically and playfully. I can choose certain instruments within the musical dialogues that align with the characters of the motifs.

The cycles of anxiety and their sounds

The cycles of anxiety include the onset of the situation and its relative symptom(s), active physical and psychological reaction, and the sense of loss and bewilderment and relief at the event ending. When people work with their anxiety symptoms and their stories, the cycles' activation is symbolically, creatively, and physically re-experienced. This is why it is critical to know what the symptoms sound like in improvisation and their accompanying motifs.

The complex psychological and biological events that occur at the onset of anxiety lead to the intensified physiological responses of the anxiety attack's activation, or stressful moment, and end with a completely depleted adrenal system and psychologically drained individual. In musical contexts, when a cycle is being worked on, it is critical to take one section of the whole cycle on at one time. Spending time with each section of the cycle allows sensitization and familiarity to happen, again symbolically, and through the specific sounds that come through—without it leading to the complete and actual onset or activation of an anxiety attack.

A single dialogue-based approach, or, as Oldfield (2012) describes, a *musical conversation*, particularly with children, can also address a cycle in a single improvisation when used with the symptom. Whether it is a person, place, or thing, there will be a cycle of emergence, anger and frustration, and resolution, or development towards resolution. The motifs will reflect this process, and new motifs will enter into the music that are part of the processing of the material.

Overall, the use of the sounds and motifs within the cycle of anxiety can be constructive when working on a specific person, place, or thing in an individual's life connected firmly to the symptoms and their consequences.

Elements of an Anxiety-Informed Recovery Approach in Music Psychotherapy (AIRA-MPT)

- Establish structure, predictability, and safety. Don't break this—it's fundamental for the rest.
- Establish the therapeutic relationship and build trust. Use your strengths for this, and your clinical knowledge; it goes a long way in professional development and relationship-building with clients.
- Identify inner and outer resources—strengths and grounding forces in the individual's life such as people, places, and things.
- Validate feelings of worry and fear.
- Identify and explore boundaries.
- Identify the stressors and their contexts and scenarios.
- Identify and explore the stress and anxiety symptoms and behaviors (fight, flight, fear responses) related to stressors: behavioral, social, emotional.
- Identify and explore coping strategies: behavioral, social, emotional. Undo harmful connections to fight, flight, fear responses.
- Identify creativity and improvisational strengths: "Thinking on your feet!" The four Rs: re-establish, redo, renew, repair connections to people, places, and things.
- Build (re-build) self-esteem, empowerment, and interconnectedness (intrapersonal and interpersonal processes) with self, friends, family, and community.

Conceptualization and overview of treatment

Conceptualizing a therapy program for any client involves asking who, what, where, when, and how you will work with a client or group. Consider the clinical framework (critical improvisation in this case). Include and address musical, personal, identity, and culture issues and your musical and individual responses to the client's situation, including possible biases, empathies, and over-identifications.

Overview of treatment

Assessment

Administer the Critical Improvisation Anxiety Symptom Assessment (CI-ASA) at intake, and ongoing (the Big-A and the little-a process explained in Chapter 13). Music-centered music therapy requires an assessment framework and tools that underscore and amplify the meaning of the client's musical symbols, responses, and behaviors. I typically go to the Improvisational Assessment Profile, and the Event-Based Assessments, and the pre-post symptom and music preferences information.

Preparation

Preparing for sessions is often more energy-zapping than actually being in the therapeutic encounter, particularly if you need extra supervision, guidance, or consultancy from colleagues on a case. Be sure to spend time thinking about each session's details from start to finish and plan with attention to detail. The details need to include the whole session from start to finish—the non-musical events and procedures alongside the musical events and procedures.

Observation

Operationalizing the critical improvisation framework is crucial at this point in treatment in music therapy because of the need to be working on multiple levels all at once. Apply the CL-CL method by following the four skills within an observation context—self-observation, client observation, and the art observation (music). Focus on your cultural intention to be present, your reflexive processes, ways of listening, and the cultural objects that occur in the physical and the transference/countertransference environment. Notice essential transitions in the improvisation, and make a mental note to yourself about analysis and evaluation time. All offer key clues and clinical data about what might be happening for the client, especially if the client cannot be vocal or express in traditional and dominant ways of interacting.

Procedures
Apply to methods:

- Initial engagement with the symptom.
- Freeing and feeling. Source of breath, vibrations.
- Immersion with the symptom: "the invitation to stay fully with the phenomenon."
- Incubation (time away from the symptom).
- Illumination (new perspectives).
- Explication (understanding and meaning-making).
- Creative synthesis—it all comes together to form a cohesive whole.
- Improvised songs of process.
- Improvisational music (Wigram).
- In the here-and-now.
- Adapting to the moment.

Methods
The method I use is CL-CL method with the critical improvisational framework (see Chapter 12).

Techniques

- Musical predictability—steady beat—reflects the neurological processes of familiarity.
- Musical contact comfort—and active seeking of musical behaviour.
- Soundscapes—the musical coping space.
- Resourcing—identify inner and outer resources such as strengths and grounding forces of people, places, things.
- Felt security and proximity.
- Musical attunement.
- Songs of the sounds:
  - product driven
  - process driven.

Analysis
In some settings where I have worked, it has not been possible to record details due to case confidentiality. In those instances, an immediate detailed analysis is needed after the session. This is needed to shape the clinical discourse and create a clinical road map that integrates the art (symbolic) and the reality into a description of the work that can translate into written and verbal language for the interdisciplinary teams typically involved. Table

15.3 is a helpful resource to document clear, concise, and detailed analysis notes of a session.

Table 15.3: Documentation template chart for conceptualizing treatment in AIRA-MPT

Point of treatment	Musical	Non-musical
Assessment		
Preparation		
Observation		
Procedures		
Methods		
Process and post-session analysis		
Anxiety technique		

CHAPTER 16

The Sounds of Anxiety:
Methods for Working with Children and Adolescents

Working with anxious children and teenagers in improvised music is incredibly useful and productive because therapists can incorporate elements of play and music skills into techniques and methods to process feelings. In this chapter, there is a guide to treating anxious young people with best practices to consider, followed by a step-by-step example of how to do the method. The therapeutic musical encounter addresses several significant areas that are often not explicitly presented in the child or youth, such as intense states of heightened arousal that may appear selectively mute, flat, or disinterested. Robarts (2003) writes about this in her own work by sharing, "whether in a rush of joy or anger, in the turmoil of anxiety or the tranquility of music and reflection, when a song grows from spontaneously expressed feelings it is in a sense both a container and transformer of feelings, whereby new meanings may be forged (p.159). Levine (1996) has explained such phenomena with the theory of the survival cycle. He states that the cycle is incomplete, since the person did not have a chance to take the fight/flight option. Instead, they were left in the state of shock. He comments that, "these 'frozen' kids, while appearing calm (if not unresponsive), are still internally prepared for the extremes of activation necessary to initiate the flight or fight procedures they never had a chance to execute" (p.5). If left incomplete, and unprocessed, the feelings will be stored physiologically in the body, since they have no way of being released. They will then cause psychosomatic complaints. Attachment and complex theory, social contexts, and the application of the sounds of anxiety model in the critical improvisation framework all come together here, particularly in children with consistent high states of arousal. In school-age children and youth, these experiences may be compounded by other sustained academic anxiety stressors—which

175

have significant prevalence in our academic and community cultures. A high prevalence of anxiety exists with most children and youth that I have worked with who have been in some form of social care. The late teenage years are particularly impacted. Health anxiety, eco-anxiety, academic anxiety, and social anxiety are significant concerns for today's children and youth. The organizing factor of structure in the music acts, as Robarts describes, the *container,* and the expression of the sounds of anxiety in the improvised music acts as the co-occurring *transformer of the feelings* and their contexts the child associates with the anxiety. The path towards meaning-making of those combined experiences is then set in place for musical explorations of the people, places, and things that support and cause anxiety.

Anxiety activators and the onset

There is always difficulty discerning the activating moment or point of onset of worry because the symptoms and their contexts have been emerging and sustained for significant periods before signs of distress. They could be related to other neurological challenges, physical disorders, or ailments and diseases that co-occur with anxiety in children. Often, the symbolic play of the *sounds of anxiety* and the psychodynamic projection methods that uncover the feelings and experiences attached to the *anxiety story* are the two pillars for a case and intervention conceptualization. The child or teenager's attachment style and socio-cultural contexts are critical signs to observe for responses to potential relational and systemic stressors.

Recognizing anxious feelings

It is crucial to help families and children recognize anxious feelings and their dimensions and contexts. These feelings stem from bullying and cyber-bullying behaviors from social media, isolation, loss, disinterest from an unforeseen circumstance out of their control (natural disasters, war, mass shootings, or a pandemic) (see Sutton, 2002), through to family distress and lack of understanding of the impact on the children. In cases where there is an evident and severe sustained stress causing the anxiety, such as a specific person or group associated with stalking or bullying tactics, the music therapist must work within an interdisciplinary community-based team to alleviate symptoms as quickly as possible. The multi-pronged approach is critical to provide support and safety for the child or youth. The music therapist can provide a crucial role in helping to cope with the stress, empowering selfhood, and strengthening identity, particularly with teenagers who may go to music for healthy and unhealthy coping reasons (see McFerran, 2010 for more information). It is most important to work on symptom alleviation through creative and symbolic expression.

For the music therapist, a specific, focused, and knowledgeable approach to the treatment of anxiety is optimal, allowing for educating children and their families about what it *looks* and *sounds* like in their everyday lives and on ways of coping and communicating the associated emotions.

Goals for learning healthy, non-anxious attachments across development
Infants and toddlers

- Sense of safety and emotional regulation from "object constancy" and "attunement" from a caregiver.
- Mirroring of expressions with familiar people.
- Creativity and imagination in play.
- Following rules and routines, to help build independence skills.

Latency, elementary children

- Identifying and building strengths and areas of creativity.
- Connection to feelings, emotions, actions, and consequence sequences.
- Learning how to problem-solve and make decisions.
- Learning how to be in a peer group, make friends and build empathy.

Adolescents

- Friendship building and peer support—the focal point of identity building.
- Building skills and talents.
- Learning how to establish, set, and achieve goals.
- Creative problem solving to attain aspirations and goals: behavioral, social, and emotional.
- Developing self-awareness—advancing understanding of actions and consequences: behavioral, social, and emotional.

Examples of methods
Remember to infuse the AIRA-MPT in your methods and intervention designs!

There are essential steps and components to consider when working with this population in both group and individual contexts. I use the following procedure within the critical improvisation framework.

Treatment procedure

1. At intake, be sure to use the Anxiety-Informed Recovery Approach in Music Psychotherapy (AIRA-MT) but apply age-appropriate language to set goals and objectives. Include an IAP that fits the child.
2. Consider the child's cultural and social contexts and the various dimensions of anxiety that intersect with their daily experiences (e.g. ask questions about their sound environments: are they chaotic, loud, quiet, silent, etc.?).
3. Understand the various characteristics that may need to be worked with, such as music to calm down and transform intense, stressful states, music to tell the story of the symptom (e.g. control and boundary issues).
4. Include the projective technique of creating a character for the primary symptom. (This becomes invaluable for improvisation and for processing the encounter through play.)
5. Allow the child to describe the character through storytelling (either verbally or creatively using puppets, instruments).
6. Move the story into musical contexts.
7. Identify creativity and improvisational strengths: "Thinking on your feet!" The three Rs: re-establish, redo, renew, repair connections to people, places, things.
8. Integrate music and physiology into a methodology for interventions, such as tempo. Apply methods, clinical listening-cultural listening at all phases.
9. Structure the room so that there is space to interact and, at the same time, a sense of intimacy and holding with a set amount of instruments to work with for that day, but not so overwhelming that making choices will seem impossible.

For your professional development:

Conceptualization and overview of treatment

With whom am I working? Set intention for being culturally responsive and aware.

Individual methods example

Assessment

Part I of The Critical Improvisation Anxiety Symptom Assessment (CI-ASA) indicates the early teenager has a high rating for fear of the worst happening at pre-session. Manifesting behaviors of the fear show up in tearful breakdowns and avoidant emotional expressions of the symptom, causing delays in leaving home in the physical transition between home to school. The affective assessment reveals a strong sense of constant worry and fear that something terrible is going to happen to them, with no specific person, place, or thing when asked. Part II shows a high preference for (age-appropriate) music listening to preferred music to cope. The client identifies music that helps as songs by Cardi B. The client also identifies music that is not helpful, which is trap music. At this point of assessment, the symptom has a nebulous and all-consuming presence in the client's life but does have a clear behavioral and affective context. Coping skills for the problem show signs of a fearful-avoidant response to stress with some indication of a panic response. There are clear musical indicators to use as interventions.

Preparation

Apply receptive dimension and coping response route first: music listening to preferred music choices. Provide predictability of routine and musical and non-musical interventions with physical, emotional, and psychological transitions. Consider accompanying and improvised singing using preferred songs as the initial framework. Acoustic and electronic tools required: digital player and access to the preferred song choices for music listening.

Observation

They respond positively to the coping with stress music listening intervention. Ask questions that support identity empowerment and skills with feedback on lyric understanding and conceptualization. Concurrently, the somatic environment feels very high energy; the vocal presentation is rapid, high up in the larynx, and there is little eye contact. There is a sense of secondary symptom presence of nervousness.

Procedures

GOALS

Identify the feelings associated with the inability to relax and worry; build creative coping and resourcefulness skills when the symptom is activated; increase self-awareness of actions and consequences with school tardiness (behavioral manifestations); identify and problem-solve the issues with the transition between home and school (affective/emotional manifestations);

explore social/collective connections to the symptoms (social/systemic manifestations); decrease frequency and intensity of the inability to relax and worry, and undo harmful links to the stress response attachment cycle.

OBJECTIVES
Apply a planned and guided mindful music breathing exercise to name a place to cope and calm; use song and metaphor: music listening exercises with preferred music choices, and which the therapist has chosen, to express action and consequence, behaviorally and musically (symbolically); use rupture and repair, structure and predictability in music, accompanied by live music-making and drawing.

Methods
CL-CL.
There is room to be creative with the techniques, as long as the clinical rationale remains grounded in identifying the symptoms and their contexts. I provide a few examples here, and focus in on one called the sound-wave technique: "Cope and Calm" Mindful music applications using Soundscapes, "the sound-wave" (drawing and music). People, Places, Things.

Technique
Apply the sound-wave technique:
Phase 1: The client draws a figure of eight on a piece of paper, using oil pastels or something similar that is smooth and flows. The therapist also draws and matches the tempo, rhythm, and breathing, and finally uses sound concurrently with the client. The therapist invites the client to imagine the oil pastel is a boat on a wave that isn't going too fast or slow or too high or too calm, providing a baseline to return as needed. Invite the client to align breathing to the movement and move into sounds of "inhaling" and "exhaling." The intervention includes consistency, predictability, and mind-body-creative connection.

Phase 2: Progress from the drawing-sound-movement to listening to a background (live or pre-recorded) with the loop-like, cyclical qualities of the figure-of-eight images. Continue to shape the coping musical space.

Clinical and cultural intention: Attune to the presentation of the client and how the symptom is being expressed in the here-and-now. Observe and scan for speech and body tempo, for stress response activation and response to the therapist. Identify and observe the cultural musical and non-musical expressions individually and in the therapeutic alliance. Focus on breathing patterns and align accordingly to match.

Reflexivity: Moves between matching and reflecting the musical and breathing qualities of the drawing exercise. Maintain presence but pay attention to remain out of the way of the client's sense of agency in moving to their tempo and rhythm. Hold and contain.

Listening: Listen for the multisensory inputs and contexts of the act of drawing-moving-breathing-vocalizing in an ongoing cycle with you as co-creator, witness, and observer. Listen and observe for transitions in movement, breath, and vocal, and where there are more intense or shallow inhales or exhales.

CULTURAL PROJECTIONS IN THE MUSICAL OBJECT:
HARNESS MUSICAL COUNTERTRANSFERENCE AS AN
EFFECTIVE TOOL TO GIVE YOU INFORMATION
Observe and assess the musical object's emergence from the co-created container of breath–movement–drawing actions. The loop-like quality of the shape and the sounds acts as a metaphor for the expressions and the repetition of the behaviors linked to transitioning for school. The act of moving "up" and "down" and "around" can also operate as a symbolic means of self-regulation. By doing so, it generates insight into the onset and resistance cycles of stress and activators. Observe any connections to the larger picture of social and collective contexts using musical countertransference. Embodying the movement and drawing via the wave imagery and musical components and client expressions of the wave creates a coping skill to use when there is no material to use but the relational and experiential memory of predictability, expectation, and the creative act of mindfully calming.

Group work methods example
Conceptualization and overview
Creative problem-solving, identity-building, goals, managing conflict, actions, and self-awareness are all developmental skills addressed in structured music therapy group work. For community-based approaches, often an open mic arena, structured band work, and performances are formats for group music therapy to address low self-esteem and isolative behaviors associated with social and generalized anxiety, particularly in the teenage years. In more extreme cases, smaller groups of three or four young people will be needed.

Use a clinical framework for working with identity, culture, and personal responses to the client's situation, including possible biases, empathy, and over-identifications.

What interventions and treatment plans will fit these areas?

Assessment
Individual assessment occurs pre-group. In-group assessment occurs for the here-and-now presence of anxiousness and stress responses.

Preparation
Obtain an overview of presenting individual symptoms and stressors. Formulate a plan that addresses the predominant presenting overall symptom with intervention choices. Characteristics in the techniques require structure and simplicity, predictability of placement and use of core instruments, and structural musical outlines of sessions, such as the hello/welcome songs, main musical events, and goodbye/closing songs and music. Use musical, creative, and non-musical projective techniques. Use various finger puppets and props for characters as needed to launch the storytelling.

The group of three latency-aged children was in the middle of a 12-week treatment program due to exposure to violence in the home. Startle responses alongside fearful-ambivalent patterns and nervousness were high for all three children.

Observation
In an instance of musical transference (Scheiby, 1998), during improvisation on nervousness, after vocal holding on "ahs," one client makes an abrupt transition (of psychological and creative inspiration) and begins to sing the theme tune "My Heart Will Go On" from the movie *Titanic*. At this moment (point of interest), roll with the process, accompany, and assess. The other two members join in, and all three sing with conviction and expression. The musical environment is filled with intense emotion. The quality of the music and affect of clients singing it is aligned with the song topic of individual and collective hope, death, and loss. The group members seem to need the catharsis and connecting to layers of the story of the *Titanic*.

At this moment, the clients are connected to the song and to nervousness. There are a couple of ways to move the process along. Either with a bridge section to sing a phrase of affirmation and link it back to nervousness, or hold and contain to allow for the meaning-making, which the client may be nervous about to continue to evolve, as it is still in a pre-verbal, unconscious, or subconscious level. By doing so, the clients spend time singing and playing with this song. The song then becomes the core structure and symbol of nervousness for the next four sessions. The group process with the clients is strengthened through using the song as the symbol for the symptom. The clients build confidence and skills through unison singing and solo singing, and the members complement each other and build trust. The members appear to experience joyful moments of singing together, and at the same time are able to work through their nervousness. To continue to drive the process, other interventions follow, such as introducing other sounds and characters in the scenario that each member chooses. The clients use these characters in musical storytelling and improvised song techniques as a means of exploring the sounds of nervousness and their musical themes. The clients begin to unpack the stories behind the nervousness, as the expanded and manipulated versions of the initial song unfold in the improvisations.

Procedures
GOALS
Increase confidence and skills building; identify and explore feelings of nervousness; identify coping with stressful situations and safety-seeking behaviors.

OBJECTIVES
Use unison singing and solo singing to increase *comfort contact, proximity seeking,* confidence, and skills.

Apply structured and predictable music routines (e.g. the same, simple, yet highly flexible and adaptable hello song).

Methods
CL-CL.
Vocal psychotherapy, vocal holding.

Technique
Vocal psychotherapy, vocal holding: Unison, harmony, melodic singing. Accompany with two-chord, oscillating, predictive pattern.

Themes/sounds identified: "My Heart Will Go On."

> *Intention:* Attend to the cultural contexts of the client group. Provide subjective empathy skills for staying present with potentially harmful and unhealthy learned coping mechanisms.
> *Reflexivity:* Nervousness is the predominant symptom. Provide a non-musical intervention for a discussion if they are able or stay in

the music if it feels as if the children want to play it out and shape a musical story about nervousness or a song on their mind.

Listening: Listen to the multiple sensory inputs and contexts. Listen for the story to emerge in the improvisation's melody and musical direction.

Cultural projections and music metaphors: Musical transference as a mechanism for the emergence of the music metaphor.

Regarding the member who initiated the *Titanic* song, cognitively, the act of singing the song helps her memorize the words and how they connect her to the lyrics and their meaning. Psychologically, the song feels as if she is using it as a letter of sorts to connect with someone or something (people, place, or thing). Emotionally, she appears to be transported to wherever the creative space leads her, and she seems to be responding to the pain of the loss—the individual and collective loss.

Analysis

Point of interest: when the client's affect and emotion fitted the words to the song, a sense of intense feeling and presence was felt. There was musical transference of the song "My Heart Will Go On." It seemed to come out of nowhere in the moment but had a symbolic meaning of death, loss, hope, and resilience. The nervousness she described was connected to the song, but it was not yet conscious in that session. The client took the therapist and group members into the story of her nervousness about losing her mother to opioid addiction and the feeling of being in a family and system that presented as the symbol of a sinking ship, where there was no point of return.

The nervousness that she was experiencing knew what was going to happen on an intrapsychic level. The other group members affirmed her in the shared singing as a coping mechanism to deal with the stress, to not feel alone in her experience, and to be able to process the unconscious level of worry in a structured and predictable creative environment. The improvisational skills required were to pick up on the musical surprise and roll with the client's process using accompanying and mirroring clinical musicianship skills.

Without the analysis of looking specifically at the transition as a point of interest, the therapist and team may have missed the symbolic relevance of the song as a musical transference of a clinically relevant musical object.

Transitions in community contexts

Transitions occur in everyday life outside the therapy session, or just before, or just after a session has occurred. These can be extremely stressful for children and youth, especially those who reside in congregate settings. Using action-oriented and pre-recorded intentional music and/or visual and music activities and artifacts that assist in lowering the panic and stress before or after events is important as a music therapy intervention.

The Bunnies Project

My first experiment with testing anxiety and transitions in a community setting was in 2005 in my work at the child and adolescent inpatient unit at Bronx Lebanon Hospital Center, New York. The team observed high levels of anxiety and stress before, during, and after visiting hours. It was a busy time on the unit, with all congregate spaces needed. The room that was potentially good to use would need either recorded music or a video-musical piece that was created intentionally to have a rhythm, tempo, visually calming objects, and so on. I collaborated with a non-profit company that curated artwork for community spaces that needed it. It found a perfect fit for our needs—an artist willing to provide a video for visiting hours. Between the creative arts therapies team, we configured a set of recommendations to infuse into the video that slowed tempo, maintained a predictable experience, and was child-friendly and appealing. The result was a video of two bunnies interacting and just "being" in their space and in their world. There was no music, which made it feel more natural to have the outside come inside visually and via movement. Decreases in acting-out or anxious behaviors were observed by the interdisciplinary team. Since that moment, my work has connected transitions inside and outside the therapy room. More recently, community transitions have also gained some attention in the field's research from the positive findings of the Bibb and colleagues' (2016) study on the impact of music therapy group work on circuit-breaking the anxiety around mealtime in a supported post-mealtime intervention.

I hope that more research can be done with this idea in other community-based settings, because it works!

CHAPTER 17

The Sounds of Anxiety: *Methods for Working with Adults*

Across cultures, races, and ethnicities, the significant themes in adulthood are setting meaningful and realistic goals, managing developmental gains and losses, managing motivations, and developing emotional stability. When anxiety impedes the normal developmental tasks of any stage or boundary of adulthood, it can mean losing the autonomy to flourish and work, or the necessary means to simply survive. The inner critic voices that Benjamin (2018) calls the *family in the head* disrupt and dismantle function, which needs to be reclaimed, restored, and eventually recovered.

Goals for adulthood attachment development
Early adulthood

- Independence and autonomy.
- Identity expansion and establishing preferences and philosophies.
- Gaining more emotional stability.
- Setting meaningful life goals.

Middle age

- Generativity—expansion of identity and influence.
- Managing developmental gains and losses.

Late middle age

- Changes in parent–child roles.

Late adulthood

- Adapting to changes in physical and social identity.
- Dealing with losses.

Examples of methods
Remember to infuse the AIRA-MT in your methods and intervention designs!

Treatment procedure

1. At intake, be sure to use the Anxiety-Informed Recovery Approach in Music Psychotherapy (AIRA-MPT), make any adjustments for age and capacity to set goals and objectives. Include an IAP that fits the adult.
2. Consider the cultural and social contexts and history of the adult and the various dimensions of anxiety that intersect with their current daily experiences.
3. Understand the various characteristics that may need work, such as music to calm down and transform intense, stressful states or music to tell the story of the symptom.
4. Include the projective techniques that create an opportunity to talk or play about the presenting symptom, talk *to* the presenting symptom, or, more advanced, *become* the presenting symptom.
5. Allow for the adult to engage in the creative process by drawing on identified creative and improvisation strengths in everyday life.
6. Move the story into musical contexts.
7. Integrate music and physiology into the methodology for interventions, such as specific tempo at 60–90bpm, or the frequency, tempo, and pitch of your vocal sounds and speaking voice. Apply clinical listening-cultural listening at all phases.
8. Structure the room to allow space for interaction, and at the same time, a sense of intimacy and holding with a set number of instruments to work with for that day, but not so overwhelming that making choices will seem impossible and cause potential chaos (not a good idea for an anxious person).

For your professional development:

Conceptualization and overview of treatment

Who am I working with? Set intentions for being culturally responsive and aware.

Individual methods example

Assessment

The client identifies a "collection of symptoms" of constant worries about employment, heart-pounding, and a fear of losing control. He experiences it as what he calls "itchy." His IAP reflects musical domains of incredibly soft vocals, barely audible at times, expressive and inconsistent rhythmic patterns, and an emotional and expressive quality to playing a melody on the piano while being accompanied. His preferred music is electronic dance music (EDM), rap, and hip hop, also identifies as his resource music. His least helpful music—music that he places as increased "itchy" emotional and behavioral responses that reflect his perception of angry and rageful, and musically—is anything that has a chaotic rhythmic structure with elevated volume.

Preparation

Apply the expressive dimension and coping route.

Music qualities need to include grounding techniques with repetition and predictability so his brain–body–mind can know what to expect. On the piano—accompanied at first—stay out of the way, close enough but not too close. Provide choices to play at the piano or on an instrument of choice—acoustic, something like a tone bar at first (simple frequency distribution and resonant). Octaves in the left hand of the piano on a two or three-chord progression with open chords, moderate volume. In the studio, create a holding accompaniment that includes these features in a "chill" version of EDM to set up for breathwork and potential for an improvised song procedure.

Observation

He seems to respond positively to initial improvisation on the bass tone bar with piano accompaniment using the grounding techniques. He stays in the musical frame provided, which gives room for the jerky, inconsistent rhythms of "itchy" to be expressed. He responds in the musical relationship to interventions when using mirroring to move into dialoguing with "itchy."

Procedures

GOALS

Validate the feelings of worry; identify coping strategies; identify creativity resources and strengths; re-establish connection to resources (safe haven); improve self-confidence; strengthen interconnectedness.

OBJECTIVES

Use grounding to secure the predictable environment; use matching and mirroring to validate the sounds of "itchy"; provide elements of "space" in the music for "itchy" to have a voice and "come out."

Methods

CL-CL.

Technique

Clinical and cultural intention: Stay attuned to musical nuances and respond with simple mirroring techniques in the melody at first: I see you, I hear you, I'm with you.

Reflexivity: Harness reflection techniques in the overall structure of the improvisation. Be aware of the role of agency. Facilitate the musical discourse that reflects his emotionality in the music note so that if you need to lead, it is in service of allowing "itchy" to be acknowledged and expressed. Be aware of countertransference and stay curious.

Listening: Listen in the multiple sensory inputs and contexts. Listen for the story to emerge in the improvisation's melody and musical direction—where does the rhythm go and end up? Where do the dynamics go? These are essential observational and assessment clues to the story.

CULTURAL PROJECTIONS IN THE MUSICAL OBJECT: HARNESS MUSICAL COUNTERTRANSFERENCE AS AN EFFECTIVE TOOL TO GIVE YOU INFORMATION

Observe and assess the kind of *musical object* shaped and created in the improvisation. What are the cultural representations for the co-constructed music? How is identity being represented? His musical melody of itchy has echo-like qualities to that of a typical EDM chill track. What else is behind that? My music preferences for electronic music as a grounding intervention also shape an aesthetic appreciation in the cultural-social musical space. The therapeutic relationship is being established and developed. The music's role provided the experience of metaphors and representation of the feeling that his expression of the emotion cannot identify beyond "itchy." Processing at the end of the improvisation together in music terms can occur, and from the perspective of the musical experience of playing *about* "itchy" together.

For you personally:

The Musical Attachment Journal

Think about the styles and kinds of music that you go to for a sense of agency and purpose. Write seven down and organize them into a soundtrack. Pick one every day to listen to (and play). Use the CL-CL method to engage with each piece of music or song, and explore the three resources (people, places, things) to which you attach your music when actively engaging in the method. Write what comes up during (if listening) and after listening or playing. Reflect on what the process reveals and highlight significant themes of insight.

Continue every week with the songs that resonate and new ones that come up.

Group work methods example: The Worry Cloud

Assessment

The young women's empowerment group reaches the cohesion phase in the group process and they are ready to develop more dialogue with the themes of fear and continuous worries, which they all identify as sharing in their various contexts. All report high levels of fear of the worst in the AIRA-MT as the symptom associated with the worry.

Preparation

Group members are familiar with each other at this point and able to engage in a meaningful way. A procedure that ends up with a musical product that is representative of the shared experience of worry and at the same time continues to build trust and empowerment is an apt intervention for this group at this phase. Songwriting is the example used. Select and gather relevant tools to be used. Set up a circle of chairs for all group members, and set up instruments in the middle or side of the room, and any tech and electronic tools to use.

Do five minutes of grounding breathing techniques before the group to clearly set your intention (I'm with you, I see you, I hear you), and focus on the four areas of the CL-CL method before the group begins.

Observation

Observation is the ongoing form of in-session assessment and evaluation. Use music physiology to guide and inform initial scans of the members as they enter. Look and listen for pace, tempo, pitch, speed, and overall quality of member voices. One girl has to repeat herself several times because her voice production and quality are barely audible and soft, and have an invisible-like effect. Or, her affect looks calm and restful, and when she speaks to another member, her voice sounds shaky, with up and down tones with a speedy tempo. Clinically, it sounds as if she is in a fearful-ambivalent state and possibly moving towards a sense of feeling stuck or being in relentless cycles of the stress response hyper-activated.

Procedures

GOALS

Decrease the frequency and intensity of stress responses that lead to continuous worries and fears of the worst happening.

OBJECTIVES

- Use improvisation methods and projective techniques to gain insight into trigger points of stress responses.
- Identify coping strategies, musical and non-musical, and decrease the intensity of moments of the stress response.
- Use the group process and the group music process as a vehicle for gaining further insight into the attachment stories behind the worry.

Group songwriting exercise to work on objective 3

Stages/phases of songwriting

The songwriting procedures are influenced by Baker and Wigram (2005) and Baker & Tamplin (2006, p.200) and integrated into the AITA-MPT.

Stage 1: Decide on the most acute symptom to play about, sing, and explore musically (endless, ongoing worries).

Stage 2: Identify the thoughts and emotions associated with the symptom. Generate group process via creativity process to get to the emotions that represent the stories.

191

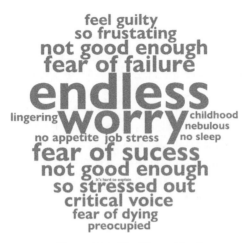

Figure 17.1: The Worry Cloud

Stage 3: Develop the ideas related to the stress responses identified that are central to the symptom. (Ask the group members to share connections and responses to their group worry cloud in various forms of verbal and/or artistic communication.)

Stage 4: Create groupings of the anxious expressions and create themes. Themes identified:

- Loss
- Silence
- Past stories
- Present stories
- Exhaustion and tiredness.

Stage 5: Construct a storyline of the anxiety themes attached to the symptom. For more structured group procedures, go in order around the circle. In our group methods example, the group is in a cohesive phase and organized enough to share ideas "popcorn style" as the inspiration comes.

One member calls out: "Endless worry!"

The next builds on that and says, "…you just linger around…"

The psychological and creative data generates material to shape into a song structure with verse, chorus, bridge, harmony, melody, and lyrics.

Stage 6: Construct the lyrics to the song that is about the symptom (initial engagement), addresses the symptom (deeper engagement), or becomes the symptom (depth and reconstructive engagement).

The group decide to sing to "Endless Worry" after generating a structure for a song.

Verse and Chorus example:

Endless Worry
You didn't make a grand entrance. You just lingered here.
In my life, and in my world, you just linger here.
I can't sleep, can't concentrate, but I have to stay awake.
In my life, in my world, you just stay.

Chorus
Endless Worry, you seem not to care.
Endless Worry, you have no weight to bear.
Endless Worry, do you have a name?
Endless Worry, please just go away!
Endless Worry, you don't belong.
Endless Worry, I need to change this song.

Method
CL-CL.
Product-led songwriting.

Techniques
The Worry Cloud: Use colorful and creative interventions to facilitate the engagement with the symptom process. Word clouds are an excellent way for this. Use the shape that the cloud ends up to guide an improvised response (movement, music, visual representations, and so on) to the creation.

> *Shape to music preferences:* Acoustic or technology/electronic tools; style/ genre of song.
> *Fill in the gaps:* Facilitate the narrative of the story. Use specific data points from the symptoms themselves such as:
> What if…
> The nervousness sounds like…and makes me feel… It does...
> Naming the symptom for projection and coping.
> Singing to the symptom.
> Dear "static"…
> Playing as the symptom for facilitating embodied and organized reparative experiences.
> Identifying musical qualities to include and guide the improvisation.
> Musical qualities of "static" are…

Intergenerational transmission
Parenting and family work vignette:
Mothering the mother, to mother
Assessment

She is quiet and friendly. She lacks the confidence to initiate speaking with the flow. She holds her baby warmly and with physical intention—rocking, regularly checking that clothes and blanket are keeping the baby warm. She has an emotional distance quality, unintentional, seemingly learned, and childhood and adulthood attachment traumas, and disorganized childhood attachment.

Preparation

Two procedures are done simultaneously: mother the mother, and mirror and hold her in the musical environment. Instruct and model for her to mother the baby with a "good enough" mothering presence. Eliminate the distal embodied proximity between mother and baby and mother and "inner critic" or "family in the head." She is in a fear-flight, depressed, no-escape state of mind.

Observation

She has a high arousal state, with flat affect. She is responsive to warmth, kindness, and works well with soft, lullaby-like work.

Procedure
GOALS

- Increase ability to relate to self and other (baby).
- Increase self-worth, self-esteem, and self-confidence.
- Reparative experiences in and out of the music.

OBJECTIVES

Example for first goal: Will be able to practice statements of productive power: I am… These are related to attaching to herself and to identity as a woman/mother, and to her baby.

Methods

CL-CL: Set intention—be aware of cultural self and other environment—and the attachment environment needed to be restored and quality of cultural presence: I'm with you, I hear you, I see you; reflexivity—agency and the context of agency for this situation; listening will be challenging, multi-sensory environments will heighten.

Technique
Improvised psychodynamic songwriting.
Mothering the mother to mother: repairing the fears to connect intimately.
Lullaby song style; simple three-note, one-chord structure for holding and containing; mirroring, matching, reflection. Lyrics structured and grounded in the intention from the CL-CL method.

Phase 1: Sing and play (guitar) to mother: I'm with you, Jenny, I see you, Jenny, I hear you, Jenny.

Use C chord, for equal frequency and resonances; middle C, E, and G below are the notes for the melody. Psychological goals: model mirroring and intimacy with the quality of presence method, eye contact, matching precisely with mother's whisper, "invisible" quality.

Phase 2: At the same time: while continuing the soft strumming on the guitar, invite the mother to sing along. Sing together. She has a soft, responsive affect and predictable musical environment. Some mirroring spontaneously happens, rocking side to side.

Phase 3: Invite the mother to sing to her baby. She sings, "I'm with you, Georgia, I see you, Georgia."

Phase 4: Continue the musical containment and ask the mother what she loves about her daughter, and build it into the improvised lullaby song structure so that the initial part becomes the chorus. Sing with the mother, so she is not alone in the experience. Allow for space and gaps to build her confidence, provide grounding vocalizations if singing in unison and with the words is too intimate. It also titrates the music experience to tailor to the mother and the baby's response while modeling.

Jenny and Georgia's Reparative and Bonding Lullaby

Verse:
I love your little hands; they are so precious.
I love your coo-ing; they make me smile.

Chorus:
I'm with you Georgia, I see you, Georgia.

Verse:
I love your little hands…

Reflect the observations of the in-session ongoing assessment and evaluation of what is observed in terms of undoing distant ways of communicating and not looking at her baby to forming intimacy and attaching while also learning to mother in a good enough way of attaching for the child to experience and learn. In time, confidence grows, and you can use various developmental musical games and interactions (Lowey, 1995) to continue to develop the reparative experience and mother–child bonding.

Research and practice

The study that I mentioned previously is represented here with significant findings and helped develop my critical improvisation framework and the CL-CL method.

The striking finding to me, related to getting people better and back to their work, families, friends, and communities, is what it takes to get the anxiety levels down. With kind permission from the journal, *The Arts and Psychotherapy,* where the study is published, see Table 17.1. The other musical-focused finding was the clear categories that lift out receptive-focused or expressive, action-oriented focused work (described in the taxonomy provided in Chapter 13).

The following table and three figures[1] are examples of the impact of the work on anxious individuals and their preferred improvisation approaches. Those with panic-related issues preferred receptive approaches and combinations of listening and playing, and individuals with fear-based and generalized anxiety disorder preferred an action-oriented, expressive vocal and instrumental approach. The other significant finding is the decrease in anxiety levels over the course of treatment, particularly by week six.

Table 17.1: Brief description of participants

Name	Brief description of participants
Tulia	34-year-old female of Italian and Irish descent. She was a full-time student. Her most reported anxiety symptom was identified as nervousness, and activated during moments of conflict in the classroom. Her most favored improvisation technique was grounding using vocalizations. Category did not change but spiked due to a conflict in the middle of treatment.

---

1   Reprinted from Zarate, R. (2016). Clinical improvisation and its effect on anxiety: A multiple single subject design. *The Arts in Psychotherapy, 48,* 46–53, with permission from Elsevier.

Deborah	35-year-old female, first generation West Indian American. She was temporarily employed and her most frequent anxiety symptom was identified as an inability to relax. Her most favored improvisation techniques were dialoguing and thematic development. Scores changed category from severe in week 1 to mild in week 12.
Sandra	22-year-old Caucasian female. She was an unemployed actor. Sandra experienced constant worries with simultaneous stomachaches in anxiety-provoking situations. Her most favored techniques were grounding, extemporizing, and amplifying. Her category changed from moderate in week 1 to mild by week 12.
Ian	Took part in intake and dropped out of the study. Scores were not used.
Trevor	27-year-old African American male who was employed full-time. He identified anxiety experience as "antsy." He reported symptoms of unable to relax, heart racing, and shock sensation, and related them to fear of losing control in his environment. He favored the technique of dialoguing with "antsy" to express of soothe the theme. Trevor's category changed from mild in week 1 to minimal by week 12.
Bruce	25-year-old Caucasian male who was employed full time. The symptoms identified were inability to relax, heart pounding, and difficulty breathing. His most favored technique was dialogue-based instrumental and vocal. Bruce's categories changed from moderate in week 1 to minimal by week 12.
Arnold	34-year-old Caucasian male and full-time student. His identified symptoms were inability to relax and fear of the worst happening. His most preferred techniques were matching, mirroring, reflecting, and dialoguing. His category changed from moderate in week 1 to mild in week 12.
Andrea	33-year-old Caucasian American female. She was unemployed and her identified anxiety symptoms were nervousness and inability to relax. Her preferred technique was grounding. His category changed from severe in week 1 to mild in week 12.
Belinda	27-year-old African American female and single mother whose identified anxiety symptom was fear of the worst happening. She responded to vocal psychotherapy methods and identified a feeling of breakthrough by the end of the study. Her category changed from moderate to minimal by the end of the study. She was unemployed at the beginning of the study and was being considered for a full-time position by the end of the study.
Cindy	26-year-old first-generation Chinese female and full-time student who identified symptoms of fears of fitting in, nervousness, and performance anxiety. Her preferred technique to use was reflecting. Her scores decreased from severe in week 1 to minimal by week 12.

Kevin	27-year-old East Indian male who was employed full-time and living in the US for 4.5 years. He identified an inability to relax as the major symptom of concern. His preferred techniques were matching, mirroring, and consistently grounding. Kevin needed to relocate due to work and did not complete the study beyond 8 weeks. His category changed from moderate to minimal by the eighth week.
Clive	33-year-old Caucasian German male who was employed full-time in US for 2 years. His identified anxiety symptoms were fear of losing control and unable to relax. His preferred technique was dialoguing. There were no changes in category but the two identified symptoms decreased in reported severity over time.
Gabbie	20-year-old Caucasian female who was employed part-time. Her identified symptom was numbness, especially in fingers, and her preferred technique was dialoguing. Her category did not change throughout the study, but she reported that her connection to the music increased and her fingers felt less numb after improvising.
Charlie	26-year-old Latin American male who was a full-time student. His identified symptoms were fear of the worst happening and fear of losing control. Charlie's preferred techniques were extemporizing, reflecting, and dialoguing. Categories did not change over time.
Mia	26-year-old Korean female who was studying for a brief time in the US. She identified extreme worry and fear of the worst happening. She could not complete the study due to moving back to Korea and completed up to week 8. Grounding and reflection were her preferred techniques. Her category did not change over time.
June	28-year-old first-generation American of Filipino parents, and full-time student. Her most frequent symptom was fear of the worst. She preferred piano improvisation and dialogue technique. Her category changed from moderate in week 1 to minimal by week 12.
Jerry	26-year-old Caucasian male who was unemployed. Multiple fearful behaviors and could not be outside alone. His mother accompanied him to sessions. He did not complete the study and stopped attending sessions at week 7. Jerry's category changed from moderate to minimal within one week and maintained that way by last session attended.

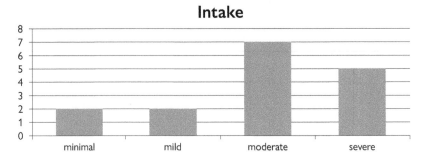

Figure 17.2: Clinical category scores at baseline

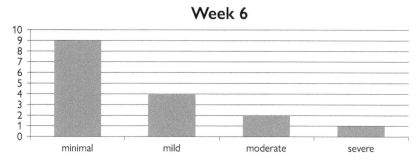

Figure 17.3: Clinical category scores at week 6

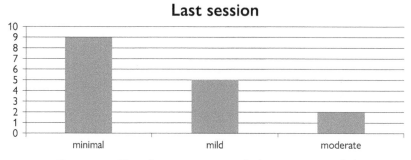

Figure 17.4: Clinical category scores at the last session attended

By the end of treatment at 12 weeks, severe symptoms were not being reported. There was an overall decrease in symptom severity, with sustained reports of minimal severity from weeks 6 to 12. This was an important finding for us to work with because it highlighted the two ways to formulate an approach for working with anxiety characteristics and led to the creation of the two-dimensional framework and taxonomy explained in Chapter 13. The change-over-time effect figures also show the swift impact of working in this way. Although the measures were for baseline, week 6, and week 12, there was also a notable difference at week 3, but it wasn't measured, just an observation. While the research is ongoing, these findings, coupled with the research offered by Erkkilä and colleagues (2019), show a collection of building areas of knowledge that certainly has a promising impact on how we perceive and achieve sustained mental health practices and healthful lives. The findings from this area of research show that music psychotherapy approaches can work swiftly and have lasting impacts beyond the treatment time frame. I hope they will resonate with the clinical community, the public, and healthcare and community policy-makers.

PART IV

APPLIED DIMENSIONS

CHAPTER 18

Collective Anxiety and Critical Improvisation: A Case Study with a Women's Rights Chorus

Groups and productive power

The community chorus case study presented in this chapter illuminates how the CL-CL method is applied in practice.

The goal of CL-CL in community-based training work is to use the four skills (see Chapter 12) to support the development of an intentional music-centered cultural context that addresses the collective impact of social and fear-based anxieties prevalent in society. As I explained in the earlier chapters, these vary in intensity and frequency of worry. Productivity and work performance, and social hostility towards gender, ability, racial, and ethnic difference are the significant areas of stress that are compounded by issues of access to healthcare, education, and healthy food and clean water.

The underlying social issues manifest in various psychological, behavioral, and emotional ways in the group context, which requires a music therapist's expertise to work through.

The case study described in this chapter is from a workshop that I co-facilitated with a colleague, Susan Firestone, an artist and art therapist who I invited to work with me on the project, and who shares an interest in girls' and women's gendered oppression. The workshop utilized clinical applications from improvisation and projective-based work with voice, narrative/song, and art materials (figurines, objects, ink, paper). In this particular workshop, the topic was girls' education rights.

The questions asked for this workshop were "How can music therapy-informed technique facilitate a deeper understanding of the piece being rehearsed?" and "Will there be any impact on aesthetic value and affect, quality of the piece, or personal insights, after engaging in the process-driven workshop?"

The following case example highlights how CL-CL was applied in practice in a training workshop setting at a community chorus group's request. While fitting my area of clinical expertise, this workshop required thoughtful planning. For instance, I researched how the group identified itself, how long it had been running, how familiar the members were with each other, the group's style and stage of development, clarity of intention of the workshop, and my role as co-facilitator. Members were familiar with working together on social justice pieces related to women's rights.

It was a voluntary, community grassroots project for women and was operated by women in the local community. This was helpful for us in planning the four-hour workshop. This workshop's topic was girls' rights to be educated, using Malala Yousafzai's story as the springboard for a dramatic narrative written by the chorus founder and director. The group consisted of six self-identified female chorus members, three self-identified women of color, and three self-identified Caucasian women. Also in the chorus were four music therapy students and two musicians from other areas of the community. While two group members were familiar with the dramatic narrative, the other four were not; it was their first encounter with the material and something that we had to consider as we planned the session. The workshop's purpose was to explore how beneficial the critical social aesthetics (CSA) approach and CL-CL method would be in eliciting responses from the members that would enhance individual, personal, and group/collective cultural and social understanding of girls' education rights. The dramatic narrative performance would use the enhanced experience to illuminate and intensify its musical aesthetic qualities. Musical data such as motifs, themes, and musical/creative reactions that emerged from the improvisational work would be reintegrated into the original piece. We hoped to learn more about the approach and method related to deconstructing the learned musical and non-musical "feminine" behaviors in this topic.

In this case, the rehearsal context was of women learning a pre-composed piece about girls' education rights. The critical improvisation framework was used with the group members to get them closer to their experience of the piece through their lived experiences as women and artists. The method (CL-CL) was used to develop the capacity for intentional, reflexive, and socially conscious lens of singing. All members were interested in exploring the method and provided consent to use their artistic work, feedback, and further education. We handed out a self-designed feedback form to chorus members before the workshop began. The purpose of the document was to gain insight into the women's usual vocal rehearsing methods and their expectations of the workshop. We offered a second reflection and feedback form after the workshop. All group members completed both forms, and all group members gave consent for feedback and material from the exploratory session to be used for educational publication purposes. The feedback about the workshop was collected and organized into tables. We analyzed the frequency of certain words in overall responses to the workshop through a qualitative software analysis tool. Visual representation of the frequency of words was placed into a word cloud, guiding future group facilitation planning and session design, and providing a deeper understanding of the method's strengths and limitations. An inductive analysis of responses was carried out to explore potential themes and categories that emerged from the workshop.

Intention: CL-CL and group warm-up
Projective techniques; narrative, play objects, and repetition/amplification

The chorus members were invited to bring their attention to their cultural and social identities and their thoughts and ideas around girls' education rights.

At the beginning of the workshop, we asked all chorus members to stand in a circle and read the piece's text (see below) without the music score. In my facilitator role, this was key because it allowed me to work with the group without the score as a barrier for process or distraction.

Using a method for collective memory from feminist qualitative researcher Frigga Haug (1980, 1999), I asked each member of the chorus to take a line from the narrative and read it aloud while standing in the circle. This technique was repeated twice as a way of amplifying the sound space and activating the skills of CL-CL: intention and reflexivity. With each reading cycle, the repetition *amplified* the relational, social complexities and social memory of the topic, and we observed and felt the impact on the group.

Malala's Song to the Taliban, music, and text by Sandra Hammond (2014) reads:

> First, you charmed us. You came into our beautiful valley; brought us food and music and friendship. But then slowly, you turned; you took away music, closed the shops, enforced a curfew. The streets were empty. You blew up our schools. I was fifteen that year. I had begun writing for the media. I spoke out. Ah! Outspoken girl. Who is this girl speaking her mind? You asked for me by name. Who is Malala, Malala, Malala!!! Who is Malala, Malala, Malala! Who is Malala?! Then you took your Colt 45 and shot me three times. One bullet went into my forehead on my left side and traveled

through my face and out into my shoulder: so much blood, so much blood, so much blood. The blood spilled onto my friends.

Fell over from the first shot, and your 2nd and 3rd bullets hit two other girls: Kainat and Shazia. I fell over. I fell over. So much blood. Then...silence. Eight days later, I opened my eyes.

Oh, where is my father? My hair is gone. Where is my family? Three days later, you threatened again to kill me and kill my father. I AM MALALA! My name means "grief-stricken." I am named for a famous Pushtun woman, a poet, and warrior, Malalai of Maiwand. My namesake was killed at 18, but I am here. I am Malala. I think so often, what I would say to you. Even if you come to kill me...I will tell you that what you are trying to do is wrong. That education is our basic right. I wish education for you and your family, for everyone. I cannot be silent. I am Malala.

Reflexivity: Shifting from verbal to vocal
Relationship to group members: Preparing for and warming up the group

It was vital for me to acknowledge to participants that we were all here to work on cultural empathy, including my ongoing journey with this work. At the beginning of every workshop I facilitate, I acknowledge that the process includes all identities and respects our similarities and differences.

In preparing for a workshop, considering the composition of the group members related to my biases and each individual's biases is vital. It supports building conversations and relationships via the group music process to address any concurrent or previous ruptures in socio-cultural experiences. As a colleague recently shared, "difference is what makes up our social fabric. Without it, we lose our vitality and human essence" (personal communication, October 29, 2018). The warm-up is grounded in an aspiration to enhance individual and group vitality, deriving from my improvisation approach and the broader creative arts therapies; for example, from critical improvisation in drama therapy and playing with race (Mayor, 2012), dance/movement therapy (Chang, 2016), and expressive arts therapies (Estrella & Forinash, 2007; Pinna-Perez & Frank, 2018).

Warm-ups are typically designed with people's stories at the center as a way to break the ice. Group members were asked to describe and sing, in a particular style, what they had for breakfast, where they shopped for food, and how they got to the store. These areas of our social life reflect the things and places we have access to and our likes and dislikes, and can move into stories of power, privilege, and oppression. The landscape becomes rich with a diversity of experience, which allows for material for process-driven workshops, such as the one described here, to develop. The stories and meanings represented on things and each other are then used in a getting-to-know-you phase that allows for discussions around the labels and the stories placed on people and groups. The warm-up concludes by asking the participants to share the insights gleaned from the experience with the larger group. The process of "airing out" and deconstructing bias, increasing relational capacity, and unpacking the cultural "knapsack" (McIntosh, 1989) is at the heart of this warm-up as it grounds expectations of how we will proceed into the music. This intentional use of creative processes encourages playfulness, which engages people to promote sharing stories that break down normalized socio-cultural and systemic barriers.

By understanding the powerful possibilities for exploring stories and relationships, the music-making and group processes can explore the skill of reflexivity. Applying reflexivity enlivens the whole therapeutic experience and activates the "dynamic forms of vitality" that Stern (2010) offers, while igniting the group's sense of empowerment, or, as I call it, "productive power." Throughout this process, it was important for me to work on my awareness of where I had power and privilege, areas of my woman identity, and how I was seen and heard by group members both in and out of the music. In my preparation for the workshop described here, I was acutely mindful of my relationship to group members as the facilitator and my professional roles in the community. I also needed to think of my own story and experience as a woman related to the major topics in this workshop—my personal story of immigration, girls' education rights, and violence against women in various social and cultural contexts. These contemplations required me to be sure that I was mindful of maintaining boundaries and using core skills of practice such as empathy, clinical psychological knowledge, musical knowledge, and theoretical knowledge as guiding skills to harness my reflexivity and intentions.

The power of group dynamics and the collective voice: Singing the stories of recovery and resistance

After taking a moment to digest and contemplate the material, my co-facilitator and I invited group members to respond in a three-step directive: verbally, then again vocally, and then to sing a word.

Musical countertransference as a transformational tool

I noticed that the pacing of responses was slow and became even slower, almost coming to a halt. I was curious about this because I felt that the energy had changed. This change affected me in that I began to have a felt sense of being unsure and insecure. The deeper emotions that emerged for me were being scared and even some sense of fear and terror. I wondered if this was my response or an intersectional group response coming into the music process. To monitor my reactions at that moment, I used grounding and resource-oriented breathing to reconnect to my intention related to my connections or disconnections to the group members' identities and the individual and group presence. I did not know what had emerged at this point. Still, I knew I needed to engage in listening to and observing the multisensory environment concerning the group as a whole, each individual, and other possible sub-groupings in and out of the music. It was a negotiation moment for me as I tried to decide whether to shift the group to using words or continue using vocals and music. If I moved to words, I might lose an opportunity to connect to the artistic process and give rise to material that may manifest. If I chose to be more direct and trust my skills as a facilitator, I might also be silencing voices that were not ready to be seen *or* heard, and I would be therefore causing harm. I chose to stay in the music context because I felt that this group could go deeper into the material, and move past what seemed to be some kind of struggle. I felt that, in the moment, the struggle to move forward or hold back was a real phenomenon that was emerging and that represented a familiar collective social narrative for women. I was actively engaged with the group dynamic, monitoring my personal narratives around this struggle and monitoring my skills to stay curious and open to possible group members' perceptions towards me, and vice versa. I was now operating with the sense of blockage as a sign of some form of individual, group, or collective symbol of the struggle that was alive and active in the group dynamic.

After these moments of active in-group assessment and evaluation, I decided to provide direction and assess for agreement or disagreement with that choice. I decided that I would proceed with whichever reaction represented the group's expression of what it needed the most. I embarked on the intervention that included a verbal prompt and technique of clinical pacing that used tempo as the musical component. I asked the group to continue to go around the circle singing the words, and I was directive in managing the pace, in particular. I decided to trust the intervention's artistic process and shape discourse with the change in tempo and sound intensity to also manage the avoidant-fearful stress response that seemed to be emerging. The group members were distancing themselves from the music, and their voices became softer and felt/appeared a little less confident. (This is a new technique and way of rehearsing, which also contributes to any reactions for process-driven musical activities.) At that moment, it felt as if some members were engaged, and some were not familiar with process-oriented music-making as a way of getting to know chorus material. Several members were music therapy students who were new to their studies, and I also wondered how they were internally responding to the psychodynamic approach. I increased the pace to create a steady beat and flow from person to person. This created a musical framework that could be used to engage group members and, at the same time, decrease any possible anxiety that was emerging (Gadberry, 2011) which may take the group members' focus outside the music and detach them from the process. The repetition created predictability and expectation, allowing the music to move to constructing a melodic phrase with different words such as "connected" and "recognition." Concurrently, the intervention was interrupting potential avoidance patterns.

Amplifying the musical data and cultural projections

Following several rounds of this structured improvisation, I asked the group to shift from a melodic narrative with improvised words to a sound that continued to build the emerging narrative—in essence, moving the group process along from the individual identification to the group to group member identification. Here, an exciting shift in the quality of music occurred. The words and melody improvisation had a conversation to it: a lower motif and an upper motif. The group sound that was mainly "ahhs" and "oohs" was less consonant and "aesthetically" un-pleasing, yet was "critically aesthetic" in its authenticity. The sound's texture was thick and heavy. The range became less and less free and more restrictive as if the frame was closing in on itself. While the group was making the sounds, I introduced perspectives of listening techniques so participants could broaden their means of participating and practice how to pick up certain parts of the group sound. This served as a way to re-focus and deepen the process and continue the process without the group becoming "stuck" in a repeating pattern. Transitioning between vocal and verbal in this kind of process-driven workshop is key to balancing the experience of the material. In this particular context, we addressed power, privilege, and oppression from a women's rights perspective. All members self-identified as women. As a woman facilitator, I felt it my responsibility to utilize my clinical knowledge in an informed way and be intentional and reflexive to that context as I engaged in my process of listening and responding to the artistic data that was unfolding.

As a clinician and facilitator of the CL-CL method, I found that my listening experience was expanded through a resource and recovery lens and the idea of "identities in the process." I noticed that my capacity for empathy increased, and this helped me open up the clinical-creative space that I allowed for the members' musical responses and cultural projections to emerge. Further, I observed and evaluated these things with a heightened sensory awareness. The method offered a space for acknowledgment of difference. Listening was the skill used to explore social norms and practices regarding girls' rights to be educated and the more significant social issue of violence against women. I was able to hear stories of recovery and resilience that emerged in the cultural projections.

The workshop was designed to ebb and flow between words and music, and music, art and words. The first planned transition between music and art occurred when my co-facilitator, Susan, moved the group into a projective art exercise and allowed the group to transition out of the musical processes and into verbal dialogue while maintaining the thread of the artistic material.

With my art therapy colleague's co-facilitation, the group worked with a projective activity using various objects such as feathers, small stones, scented items, rubber-based animals, and figures. The directive was to ask the group to move into pairs, pick one comfortable item, and discuss it. The second directive was to stay in the same pair, select one uncomfortable item, and discuss that item. The outcomes of these interactions are described in the following section.

Exploring different perspectives of listening: Engaging in multisensory experience with art, movement, and music
Do you only see our beauty, do you not hear our voices?

As the pairs of participants described what came up for them concerning girls' education rights, we introduced the perspectives of listening skill as a way to focus on the multisensory environment of the topic. The specific use of creative methods and techniques assisted in amplifying the group responses. It drove the ebb and flow of how the group members explored the skill of listening. For example, as focus and intention became more evident in every repeated sound or word, reflexivity and agency gained more musical expression from each individual and the group as a whole. Individual stories and experiences of being women emerged and filled the paper with words that built a narrative related to Malala's piece and her story. We asked members to describe or talk "about" the creatures or figures they had chosen. After some time, we then asked them to talk "to" their selections, thereby enhancing the opportunity to create a projective environment that would lead to improvised songwriting, voice work, and composition. For example, one of the chorus members shared the phrase: "Do you only see our beauty, and not hear our voices?" This was a question and response to how women are perceived and taught to be seen as objects of beauty but not heard or acknowledged in various cultural and social contexts.

The content deepened to themes of fear, torture, and darkness, and the element of surprise emerged in the artistic process. There was an overarching theme of comfort and discomfort, and the push and pull those figures created about the oppression of women and girls. It was a powerful and moving process to facilitate. Applying this awareness level to clinical listening in the workshop increased the depth of awareness and seemed to increase the potential for transformative possibilities.

This activity acted as an introduction to CL-CL and warming up, and focusing on these various aspects of how listening is directly related to sensing and perceiving sound and objects. It served to set up space for the transition into vocal work at the piano.

Music metaphor and cultural images using group vocal psychotherapy technique

We used the artifacts to elicit comfortable or uncomfortable reactions. Items such as feathers, scented candles, pieces of cloth, and plastic bugs and other animals were brought to the piano to continue the projective social work, creating one more transition back to music using more advanced techniques to deepen the process.

Choosing the improvisation techniques within the critical improvisation frame

Choice of technique within clinical improvisation is essential because it needs to fit the goals of the session. In this particular group, I had planned the workshop content to apply vocal psychotherapy techniques for the more profound process work.

I felt that vocal psychotherapy was an essential way to engage the group members because they were vocalists, and it was a chorus context. It is also part of my clinical background and training. I led the next section and facilitated the transition from discussing the objects to moving to the piano. The objects were placed on the piano's surface for all of us to look at and maintain a connection to the process. This practice of using objects, figures, scents, and images is used in psychodynamic-informed creative arts therapies, art therapy, expressive therapies, and vocal psychotherapy training. We began to combine art and music as we entered into group vocal work and social/cultural projection skills by eliciting the music metaphor.

In the vocal holding exercise, we followed Austin's (2008) theory and practice procedures of: a) establishing the two chords, b) singing ahh or ooh in unison, c) harmonizing, and d) grounding. The music metaphor emerged, which, in this case, was the intentional use of the sound to activate perception towards Malala and the topic of girls' right to be educated. Listening to that specific sound in this context provided room for any individual and collective anxiety *about* this topic to be explored as music. Once the vocal holding had time to evolve, free-associative singing was introduced, a technique I use in group work as a parallel to a free-floating conversation from group analytical music therapy. The technique provided a structured musical space where members could participate and contribute to a musical vocal narrative *about* the topic, now harnessing the skills of reflexivity and intention. The musical object had emerged, and the group moved into singing *to* Malala (oppressed-empowered) and then *to* the Taliban (oppressor). The phrase that appeared, which I noticed the group used as its social/cultural projection, was, "get away from me, ohhh, back away from me." We sang in a melody that involved a minor third frame supported by suspended and chromatic harmonies. At this point, the group also included musical and thematic material that oscillated between singing about the topic and the oppressor. At this point, I noticed that the group moved into singing *as* an empowered voice to the oppressor, with the initial phrase, "I have a scent of my own..." (repeated), moving to various phrases sung by individuals, such as, "I am...beautiful," " I am...strong," and " I am...un-ending." The music changed dramatically, with soft consonant structures and no soloists. All members converged and embraced the group by singing and harmonizing together. In terms of a group process, it was a moment of altruism and altruistic expressions shown for one another. I noticed that a unique musical-dynamic quality emerged at this moment. It was the repeating of phrases as each phrase evolved organically. It seemed that the role of the repetition was to create an echo effect and at the same time an amplification, or call-out to witnesses, and a sense of softness to this musical object. This process provided a shared experience where participants could resource and empower one another within a diverse group of women due to cultural projections and musical images and insights that emerged.

I decided to continue with the holding and also introduced doubling techniques (formulated initially and practiced by Joseph Moreno (2006) and adapted by Austin (2008)) into the vocal psychotherapy method as the singing-vocal narrative emerged. I doubled and amplified the content as the narrative progressed, including my responses as participant-observer. The group's music had now become a group song. The practice reflected the theory, which helped me to understand the process and the product that came out of it, both musically and psychologically. It had taken form, which was represented as a co-constructed social/cultural musical image. The participants' intensified way of listening from a reflexive ability provided access to a shared social/cultural space within the improvisation. I could see and hear that each individual was consciously and unconsciously negotiating, projecting, and exploring her feelings, opinions, and reactions in the various social roles and social oppressions with which she had lived experience, channeling them through the co-constructed music. This level of participation affected the quality of the music melodically and, in particular, harmonically. The music seemed to have become a collective representation of an image schemata system of disruption of traditional social concepts of harmony and an expression of an empowered collective group voice. Individual voices seemed to delicately float out of the harmonic pool with soft, breathy qualities and just as softly fall back into the blend. The harmony moved slowly between and around rich and full seventh to ninth harmonic structures between the keys of B-flat and G-flat majors. Hints of dissonance filled the air, with remnants from the prior dialogue and processing, but were sung with intention and noticed by the group members. The sense of empowerment and togetherness folded into the musical narrative, forming a group song.

Here are the lyrics composed out of vocal psychotherapy applied group technique:

> I might not seem much, but I have beauty inside me
> I have my own scent
> I am beautiful
> I am real. I am not just to be seen, I am to be heard
> I am alive
> We are beautiful
> We are alive
> We are un-ending
> So beautiful
> …un-ending…so beautiful…

Reflections and feedback

Obtaining feedback through some basic questions was vital in corroborating what both I and Susan had observed, felt, and experienced as facilitators. It was also essential to understand the group members' perspectives about the method and what they thought it had achieved.

Table 18.1: Pre-workshop questions and responses

What are your typical methods of rehearsal?
Primary run-through of the piece
Point out problem sections
Separate into sections
Work on individual parts
Put them together
…dive into rehearsal by warming up. Then we just work on trouble areas in music
Humming, buzzing (vibrating lips), breathing exercises [raising arms above the head expanding lungs while engaging the body]
Vocal warm-ups such as humming and scales
Focus on songs and blending with one another
What are you hoping to gain from this workshop experience?
Bonding with fellow choir members
Gain a better understanding of Malala/her mission
I hope to learn more about my voice and how it blends into the group sound (not a principal vocalist)
I am hoping to find ways to maintain focus during rehearsal in order to make the most out of the time
Relaxation, getting to know group members
Exposing myself to new music and technique. Enjoying and learning from one another
I am open to everything and so excited to learn from this experience

Table 18.2: Highlights and themes from responses to the post-workshop evaluation questions

What were the strengths of the workshop?
Feeling comfortable
Allowing outward expression of inner thoughts
Releasing inhibitions
Learning about Malala in an interactive and self-reflective setting.
I felt completely connected to every girl here, as well as to Becky, Susan, and Sandi. It was like we created a little community for a few hours
The ideas and directions were well communicated and in a way to understand

No pressure whatsoever. Made it easier for authentic responses and participation. Incorporation of movement with voice. The use of visual art to express feelings that are hard to put into words
It was creative, connecting, and strengthening truly beautiful
The times when I felt the most bonded with everyone were when we were in the circle singing however we felt, or saying however we felt. Especially when we sat down and expressed what our paintings meant to us
The group was small and invested in the work, vocal psychotherapy group work
Improvisation-attending to group
What were the limitations?
Personal shyness
I wish we had more time. I would have liked to put more of Malala's song to improvised singing
It was a little difficult to open up to some people I don't know very well. But it was still a meaningful and valuable experience
No limitations, maybe incorporate more movement
The only limitations were the ones I put on myself
The limitations were that some of us are too shy to just jump right in, but after a while, we all felt the flow and connection
Did not analyze the data in the workshop, not enough time
Were there any changes in your way of performing after the activities?
More loose, less planned, more authentic
When we sang at the end, I was less afraid of being louder. I wasn't nervous that anyone would comment if I was slightly off-pitch
I felt more open and comfortable to take a chance in what I was singing as time went on
Overall engagement increased, confidence level increased, awareness of my surroundings and the sounds other choir members were making [making harmonization easier]
Became more open and more aware of my behavior and emotions
I definitely feel more in touch with myself and the others around me. So much more than I did before
Which activity was the most impactful for you?
Painting with sticks felt very natural and organized. Felt comfortable in the silence and taking a few moments from singing/discussing
I was most moved when we stood in a tight circle and spoke/sang our reactions to the Malala song

The drawing was most impactful because it was time when I was to myself and creating something for myself rather than worrying what others would think
The reading of the Malala piece was very moving and when everyone went around giving a sound of how they felt and a word it was so moving. It was also wonderful seeing the paintings come together as they did
Building from one modality to the other music-art-objects-dialoguing-music
Sharing
Would you rehearse following this method again?
Absolutely
Definitely. We found ways for our voices to work together, and we grew closer as a group
Yes! Makes me more aware of my feelings about the Malala piece and the meaning of the music
Yes! I loved it!
I would absolutely do this again. It's very inspirational
Yes
Other comments?
Effective and therapeutic. Also time-consuming but worth it
Thank you so much for this opportunity! It was truly a "breath-taking" experience
So amazing, I loved working with you two wonderful women. It's women like you that make this world a better place
I am so thankful to have been able to come here and experience something so wonderful

As Tables 18.1 and 18.2 suggest, the chorus members noted that the music the group produced was closer to the authentic experiences the members had experienced in society, rather than how they had been "conditioned" in music through training to practice and listen to the content of the written music. Comments such as "I felt more comfortable to take a chance" and "Overall engagement and confidence increased" suggest that the method and approach brought participants closer to a sense of empowerment.

The group members integrated a level of awareness and felt sense about the topic. They were encouraged to experiment with this way of listening, which is an intentional reflexive social and cultural practice within improvisation. Comments such as "[I] became more open and more aware of my behavior and emotions" and "I definitely feel more in touch with myself and the others around me. So much more than I did before" are examples of such learning.

For group members, the use of art with music showed great value in this process. Several participants commented on how the music and art flowed between one another and how individual art-making with simple tools and techniques allowed for introspection and quiet moments of reflection about women's rights and their interactions and experiences as community artists.

For me, the work's meaning was to facilitate the integration of music experiences into a functional life-tool for clients to help them live healthier, more sustainable lives in their family systems, social circles, *and* larger economic and community contexts. Figure 18.1 shows the frequency of words used in feedback forms. It is interesting to note the number of times "group" was mentioned. One reason for the frequency of use is that the process affected group identity—that is, how members interacted with each other in and out of the music as chorus members, as women, as musicians, and as different identities that arose through this process. It was fascinating to note feedback about the level of individual investment in the group and the purpose of this process.

Active mechanisms of change

A recent scoping review that I carried out with colleagues revealed critical music therapy-specific and shared creative arts therapies change factors that contribute towards a creative arts therapies change process research agenda. Group and action-oriented learning were two of a collection that we found to show change.

Figure 18.1: Word cloud showing frequency of words used in feedback forms

A bond and team-building quality seem to be linked to the experience and perception changes among group members. The results also highlight the need for specialist expertise in team-building activities around critical topics such as women's and girls' rights. The workshop seemed to have a profound effect on the level of respect within the group. I began to explore the meaning of respect artistically afterwards, as I reflected on the approach and use of the method. It would be beneficial to explore this further as a way of understanding the meaning and purpose of respect and the opposite—disrespect—as it relates to the theory and practice of CSA and CL-CL.

Overall, the workshop's outcome suggests that members of the chorus experienced deeper insights into the cultural context. Furthermore, the relationship of cultural context to aesthetic representation and the group members' artistic identity was affected. I was also transformed through this process. For analysis and evaluation, I used the CL-CL method as an iterative here-and-now process to gain insight into how I was most affected as a facilitator, and as the assessment tool to understand the transitional moments dynamically.

Implications for theory and practice

Essentially, listening is connected to the projections that occur within the co-constructed sound-image-schemata, a part of the CL-CL method. The music, images, and themes that emerged from the case study suggest stereotypes and oppression of women and girls in social, community, and cultural contexts. Moreover, the case study suggests that clinical music therapists must account for their own experiences and identities. There is a need for critical social theory to position our creative roots and aesthetics. Using reflexivity, or self-reference, and intention could be key. There is also a need, as Maxine Greene (1998) points out, for a "dialect of freedom." This is a dialect that is not bound by the prevailing norm but is shaped and constructed through authentic relationships that acknowledge and embrace the multiplicity of difference from a reflexive cultural perspective.

This way of approaching music therapy aims to open the improvisation environment for voicing shared cultural relational experiences to generate clinical data that is valuable for social transformation.

The workshop revealed that using the Malala song to generate the initial focus was essential to shaping further necessary shifts to engage with the social material. As one group member stated, "I was most moved when we stood in a tight circle and spoke/sang our reactions to the Malala song." These techniques and skills are transferable into vocal/artistic practice and clinical practice. Group members reported an overall sense of empowerment and transformation of perceptions towards self and others. Lyrics composed from the vocal psychotherapy applied techniques, such as, "I am beautiful" and, "I am real," demonstrate this. At the same time, group members acknowledged empathy toward the lived experiences of women who have experienced oppression and acknowledged personal feelings of power, privilege, fear, and vulnerability. For example, the lyric "I may not seem much, but I have beauty inside of me" highlights the need for all therapists to implement a reflexive, intentional, gender-sensitive perspective. Expanding the method within the broader lesbian, gay, bisexual, transgender, queer or questioning, intersex, and asexual (LGBTQI) and other vulnerable and marginalized communities could be beneficial.

Applying the critical improvisation framework and the CL-CL methods increases the capacity to voice such complexities in the clinical process. Clinical listening is necessary to advance our practice. CL-CL offers an opportunity to build on what music therapists already do and deepen the ability to understand relationships from a cultural perspective.

CHAPTER 19

Critical Improvisation as Arts-Based Research Inquiry into Anxiety: Shaping Transformational Communities

The interdisciplinarian scholar, Kenneth Gergen, writes, "Scientific research is not principally a matter of revealing The Truth, but of participating in a community of meaning-makers to achieve goals by this community" (Gergen, 2009, p.238)

All communities have their own cultures, such as sexual orientation, gender identification, physical, cognitive, social, and emotional identifying of what citizenship means. I strive to generate data that supports the notion of transformative communities of practice (Wenger, 1998). From local clinical contexts to global community contexts, critical improvisation is a useful and productive tool for educating and generating new knowledge about anxiety and its meaning in society. The intersubjective psychodynamic approach and phenomenological ways of analyzing the music transfer into a phenomenological and morphological approach in research. I use the music and musical processes and subsequent artistic products as the core tool for data generation, data analysis, and data dissemination. In this chapter, I offer a systematic procedure that operationalizes the method of clinical listening-cultural listening as a means of data generation and data analysis. I also offer a suggestion on how and when the method can be considered in all stages of the research process.

A philosophical way of working is to consider the basic principle of moving away from the "rational" and "conditioned" ways of listening to music as musicians, clinicians, and researchers, and towards the intersectional quality of rational, emotional, social ways of listening to music. Engaging in this principle challenges and changes the musical social landscape that we are in, and the level of participation we have in it. It shapes an environment where stories can exist. Participants and participant researchers can experience those stories in the multidimensional and intersubjective improvisation environment. Combining the emotional and the cognitive capacities within an act of listening participation, the music can activate the intention to become open to socially constructed conditions and belief systems within the music. This allows the researcher-participant to apply a reflexive intentional participatory lens and to harness an environment where complex social issues can be acknowledged and explored.

Critical considerations of aesthetics in arts-based research (ABR)

Arts-based research has received growing attention in the music therapy literature, which is reflected in recent studies from authors such as Beer (2015), Ledger and McCaffrey (2015), and Viega (2013). These authors have also shown interest in the role of improvisation in ABR. The variety of interpretive research highlighted in these studies exemplifies that ABR can be identified as a "flexible research strategy" (Ledger & McCaffrey, 2015, p.453), rather than a specific method, paradigm, or approach. This understanding of ABR is helpful in that it frames the role and purpose of clinical improvisation in ABR and social justice. In his book, *Relational Being*, Gergen (2009) discusses this as a key component of action research. The principle of revealing truth is through researching *with* as opposed to researching *about*. This is the same when the therapist and client engage in the clinical musical encounter.

Attempts to shape theory into reflexive, clinical, cultural practices within aesthetics have emerged in music therapy literature. For example, Nechama (2009) found that emotional belonging and deep mental affinity was part of musical authenticity. These themes are questioned in the music and the therapeutic relationship when the therapist is faced with feelings of guilt and dislike of a client's music with a client who does not come from the same culture or ethnic background. In his study, Cominardi (2014) discusses the immigration crisis in Europe, particularly integrating immigrant children into the Italian education system. He also points out how expressive communication in multicultural multimedia platforms generates new possibilities of understanding *between* cultures. Although he recognizes the Western roots of the field and its focus on avant-gardes from the 20th century, he also positions the common aesthetic patterns and sense-perceptual elements of such music to be shared among all humans. He explores the cultural bridge in the trans-cultural process. More recently, authors such as McCaffrey (2013),

Viega (2016), and Viega and colleagues (2017) have begun discussions of the impact and experience of the self from critical perspectives in ABR.

Although it is a small but progressive body of literature, there is an underlying common thread amid these more recent positions and a movement towards considering a reflexive, relational, environmental, social, and integrated aspect of sense and perception. It challenges our traditional perspective of aesthetics as a "preference" or "experience of beauty" that silences and separates the cultural experiences and considers aesthetics in a social and more holistic light. This is a direction that complements a contemporary psychological, aesthetic lens, as Roald and Koppe (2014) point out:

> Instead of accepting such a dichotomy of between feeling and reason, one could assume that there are variations of knowledge connected to different psychic functions, and that the kind of experience in relation to the work of art is a variation, not in opposition to the rationale. And if one perceives the work of art as something that can be used to debate the common perceptual way of interacting with the world, then this implies that the everyday perceptual way of interaction with the works is something which can be discussed and transcended. It also implies that the established perception, sensing and affective life is normatively founded, that is, something into which one is socialized. (p.26).

Embracing such a notion of interaction and art as representation may provide an opening to how the music therapy field could integrate aesthetics into ABR and its collective body of knowledge.

Principles of the role of improvisation in ABR

- Interpretive
- Flexible
- Emergent
- Iterative
- Highly relational, embodies identity
- Harnesses imagination and musicianship/craft
- Action oriented
- Aesthetic, creative representations of socio-cultural phenomena.

Arts-based research still requires systematic procedures and processes–fidelity to the design!
A critical improvisation procedure in ABR:
Who, what, where, when, how, and why?

1. Establish topic and guiding question on a critical social issue. For example: access to healthcare and collective anxiety; women's empowerment and collective anxiety; political agendas and collective anxiety—alternative facts, altered realities.
2. Recruit for participants (e.g. design of music focus group).
3. Consider ethics and consents, as required.
4. Establish critical improvisation music therapy lab sessions—frequency, duration.

How will data be collected?

Data collection procedure interpreted from Moustakas' Heuristic Inquiry Model (1990).

Layer 1: Initial engagement.
Initial artistic reaction and response to the topic, create initial music product, improvise.

Layer 2: Immersion.
Critical improvisation lab sessions occur. Participants spend time with the piece working in the CSA and CL frame.

Layer 3: Incubation.
Time away from action, contemplation as a way of responding and dialoguing with the data.

Layer 4: Explication.
Researcher returns to the lab sessions work and adds more layers to the music, after each session, and begins the process of analysis, coding, member-checking for consensus of artistic data from specific points of interest:

- Visual, 3D art/journaling/moving/dancing and reflection, documentation.
- Multimedia musical components.
- Iterative and inductive artistic processes.

Researchers dialogue with each other, compare analysis notes, and check for patterns of musical meaning units, and themes, in the musical data ready to begin to organize into musical categories

Layer 5: Creative synthesis and composing.
All artistic data are collected after sessions. Findings are formed into an artistic product and checked once more. The piece is performed and the audience is asked to respond with narrative (action-based) (mechanism for feedback provided afterwards). Music score is finalized and published with a write-up. Performances continue, along with the iterative process of continuing to integrate new information.

Transferring findings and turning them into a musical product

- Musical data are analyzed through inductive and iterative processes.
- Musical productions are composed and created.
- Musical data are collected through inductive and iterative processes (Thomas, 2003).

Foundations of CL-CL in ABR

The method is intended to be flexible so that it affects the individual (therapist and client, or researcher and participant) in how they sense and perceive artistic information in clinical or research contexts. The same constructs are used to generate understanding of the data—music metaphor (object perception), image schemata (projections from the body onto a concept), and double intentionality (from idea to domain, such as music), all within the listening-observing-analysis experience.

Core research skills of the clinical listening-cultural listening (CL-CL) method
Reflexivity and intention

De Freitas (2008) discusses the need for interrogation of the multiplicity of reflexivity in our attempts to be completely present in arts-based research. Pre-conditioned lenses are brought into the improvisational space whether one is aware of it or not. Reflexivity and intention can be used as specific skills for researchers that support learning about working with and acknowledging the relationship between anxiety and its social implications. This overarching lens of analyzing the work aims to open up access in the improvisation environment for shared cultural relational experiences to be voiced to generate data that is valuable for social transformation.

Applying the method
Developing a guiding question
Consider your aesthetics position, as informed by culturally conditioned intentions, behind the motivation for what you want to discover.

Designing a research project
Consider including the aesthetic, theoretical process, and potential impact of CL-CL as part of the method in the arts-based data generation and data presentation procedures.

Generating the artistic data
Consider CL-CL as a method to use within the music improvisation procedures such as projective techniques, and holding, matching, and mirroring instrumentally and vocally as a means of getting as close as possible to the phenomenon of the social issues that are present in the reflexive, intentional, relational sonic environment.

Analyzing the artistic data
Consider the role and function of CL-CL within the music-centered evaluation of points of interest. Zoom in on specific moments in the improvisations, stay curious about possible levels of consciousness that are in operation, and observe in the process any past relational, intergenerational, and collective cultural experiences of anxiety.

Transferring findings
When performing or disseminating results, consider the CL-CL method as a mechanism that requires intention and reflexivity within the aesthetic environment to extract the musical material and incorporate it into the data's final presentation.

Theory and practice implications
Listening essentially is connected to the projections that occur within the co-constructed sound-image-schemata system that is part of my CL-CL method. This construct holds a potential foundation for what I mentioned before as a frame that works from inside the relational sense and perception environment within improvisation.

For example, when a group of participants is working on an intended social angle or issue through vocal or instrumental improvisation, the images and projections about that topic during improvisation will emerge and be transferred into the collective music-making to shape a musical image or object. Acknowledgment and transparency of conditioned

225

stereotypes and learned behaviors around the intended social topic can be identified about the music. In the case of anxiety, addressing stigma and access are two important areas of inquiry. That information can then be used as critical artistic data to examine further learning and insights into a social phenomenon.

CHAPTER 20

Applied Teaching in Critical Improvisation and Anxiety: Expanding the Capacity for the Practice of Music Therapy and Anxiety

I come from a constructive transformative philosophy in my teaching where I establish and sustain communities of practice in both disciplinary and interdisciplinary relational contexts (Gergen, 2009; Wenger, 1998). I operationalize didactic creative experiences that help to build responsive musical cultures within the music therapy and larger community practices (Voogd Cochrane *et al.*, 2017). Anxiety and stress are so prevalent that, as an educator in higher education, training students in advanced music therapy methods in improvisation and anxiety can be challenging. It requires careful consideration of pedagogical approach and teaching techniques. I approach it through the several lenses central to my philosophy of addressing the social, cultural, collective as it informs clinical knowledge and application. I explain how to apply the critical improvisation framework in techniques that work with specific symptoms, how to use it in collective contexts, via community music therapy approaches, and how to apply it in research methods utilizing musical and creative musical iterative and inductive processes (see Chapter 14).

I also find this approach helpful when teaching about anxiety in the community in arts and health programs and music and health contexts. The various ways fear and panic are understood and experienced in countries and cultures are vital characteristics of how clinical applications and methods can be designed and thought through. Working from these various lenses and using the approach truly allows for that to be central to the teaching and learning about anxiety as a social phenomenon and clinical disorder. There are also apparent universal truths to the chronic and debilitating impact of stress and anxiousness. The Covid-19 global pandemic has illuminated this truth in how it has crushed souls and devastated lives; how human beings share mental health and wellness needs for addressing and caring for the specific symptoms of anxiety and its comorbid companions, depression and sleeplessness.

Conceptualizing curriculum

An overarching framework that threads throughout all courses is optimal and includes improvisation-based work, critical and cultural work, and coverage of all anxiety dimensions.

For example, in year one of a two-year master's program, a theories-focused course can integrate the social architecture of anxiety and the various dimensions of anxiety present in clinical and cultural contexts. A follow-up course addressing clinical musicianship would include designing a series of classes to apply the four techniques or competencies of the method of clinical listening-cultural listening. It would go across populations, and other contexts or approaches as the educator and as each student is interested in exploring. Concurrently, clinical applications and group supervision courses will need to address how anxiety symptoms of an inability to relax, fear of the worst, and nervousness are present in clinical sites. It is also essential that, in these course contexts, the students' explorations of stress and anxiety and mental health coping skills can also be addressed in music-centered supervision that also uses the critical improvisation framework. In my opinion, coming from a trauma-informed lens, this is crucial to building insight, reflexivity, and flexibility as music therapists, particularly concerning advanced training preparations. For training programs that have the internship at the very end of the program, classroom-based learning relies heavily on the instructor's knowledge to bring real-life instances into the course. Due to the little research that specifically addresses anxiety disorders, I'm in favor of train-the-trainer contexts. This occurs in my research and learning lab for individuals interested in advancing their music therapy skills or music and health interests.

In advanced and contemporary methods courses, the now-familiar critical improvisation approach and framework can be used as an example and springboard for students to expand and develop their ideas and methods. In research courses, the critical improvisation framework involves the intervention's procedure being tested and can occur within a music-centered, arts-based context with an iterative and inductive artistic method.

Courses can be designed as special topics or an elective procedure that is wholly focused on the *dimensions of anxiety* in creative arts therapies contexts that transfer art forms used within the critical improvisation framework to those of the enrolled students, such as art therapy, dance/movement therapy, expressive arts therapies, drama therapy, and poetry/bibliotherapy. Whichever way, there is a genuine and immediate task at hand in music therapy mental health education. Sequencing and threading together the various areas of the dimensions of anxiety is vital for any training programs to consider in contemporary clinical practice, particularly in light of collective recovery processes after pandemics, war, disasters, and social injustices. These are complicated and necessary philosophical, humanistic, and existential questions for music therapy and music in healthcare education.

Syllabus design

The important questions to consider when designing a syllabus for this work are: What do I want to teach, and how will I teach it? This is always followed closely by the question of methods of assessment and learning outcomes. They need to include the various clinical domains required for certification in music therapy practice and other combined mental health, research, or clinical licenses necessary for different programs. In a typical US graduate 15-week semester, with three-hour weekly classes per course, the choices grow because there is time to shape a learning discourse that expands and deepens understanding of concepts and ideas, and to practice and build skills for individual and group music therapy contexts.

For instance, if I am focusing on the four major symptoms, which I know best, I'll set out an overview and assignments to build general knowledge and conversations about the presence and meaning of anxiety in our lives. I will consider laying out a series of classes that build on one another and address one specific symptom at a time. Class content time will include bringing in my examples and examples from students' internships and interests, in particular techniques and application methods. The same levels of presence are required for both in-person and distance-learning contexts for undergraduate, graduate, and doctorate programs. If you are interested in reading more about this topic, some of my colleagues and I wrote an article on distance learning (Sajnani *et al.*, 2019).

Teaching methods

Once I have the topics that I wish to teach and my course anatomy is designed, I then consider how I am going to teach each subject and methods of assessment and evaluation.

In the classroom

Just as in the clinical examples have shared, I transfer mindfulness practice into my classroom experience. I will begin every class rooted in a creative activity that sets the stage for a process-driven learning experience. The warm-up exercise considers several critical aspects of the student experience. First, where and when does the class occur in the weekly schedule? Is it in the middle of the week or the last class the students have before busy work or internship days?

What is the context of the week in terms of local, national, and international events? How might that impact students? This is incredibly important because of the diverse communities we live and teach in, and I make sure that everything I do is modeled around this and can be transferred into clinical group contexts.

For instance, a graduate-level music therapy course that I teach on Thursday mornings can be challenging because it is typically the last class of the week for students. It is a philosophically driven course that covers established and contemporary theories in the field and requires links between theory and practice. In the case of how I teach critical improvisation and the social architecture of anxiety, any warm-up needs to be directly related to a particular lens that complements and sets the stage for expanding the theory.

Critical improvisation and sounds of anxiety in action!

A snapshot of a class looks like this.

Carry out the creative warm-up, in a circle. Set the context and topic. Build the dynamic with a visual image and combination of breathing. Apply grounding techniques with intentional breathing, with a focus on breath, finding one's own breath and rhythm connected to current state. Analyze that connection in the action-oriented here-and-now space from the perspectives of listening to body–mind creative processes of attuning to self and other in breathing. Analyze for anxiousness, or nervousness and stay curious about any nuances about that. After some time, the warm-up will involve grounding and integrated musical-breath coping techniques that harness imaginative processes using imagery of people, places, and things, such as a calm, steady (tempo and rhythm) flow of a wave, or a pool of water that shows a self-image that the student can have agency about working the reflection as a grounding, conscious tool. The clinical relevance for this is to model how to shape a structured and grounded environment and teach a coping skill with music therapy techniques while clients are in the least anxious and calmer, usual state.

Lecture on the framework, methods and techniques, and general anxiety disorder, focusing on anxiety symptoms and the continuum of an anxious experience. Hold a brief discussion, followed by in-class assessment of learning and interests.

Teaching technique one: The prominent symptoms of general anxiety and didactic process

Split the group into four small groups—each will work with a symptom. Assign a series of questions for them to discuss. Think of the symptom of *fear of the worst happening* and ask what comes to mind. A situation, a person, a memory? Provide the directive to the whole group. Where possible, assign break-out rooms, or structure it that while one group is musically engaging, the rest of the group is in discussion about it. Ask them to consider the interpersonal roots and relational aspects of the contexts they are discussing. Move the students or trainees to pick one of the stories that came up. They must experiment with various musical components and instruments focusing on the symptom, then addressing the symptom, and then becoming the symptom.

Provide the self-report CIARA-MT assessment questionnaire (see Chapter 13) and have them fill it in. Explore the various dimensions of anxiety that each group chose in a particular situation.

For example, ask them to think about the collective context, the relational context, the power, privilege, and oppression, and the critical layers present. Further contexts may involve the intergenerational and transgenerational transmission of anxious symptoms and relational implications such as cognitive and physical functioning, vocational functioning, and so on.

Once they have explored this part, ask the students to think about playing and singing "to" the symptom. At this point, there should be a deepened musical process. The music will be taking form, and musical psychodynamics and the cultural musical images and metaphors will be activated directly related to the various dimensions and experiences of the particular symptom.

Have the small groups shape and structure their musical object and product and come back to the large group. Move straight into the presentation of their assigned symptom and the example they chose. Each group will explain and present the social, cultural, and musical themes and musical symbols that came out of the *about the symptom* improvisation. The same can be considered for the *as the symptom* improvisation.

In my experience, the typical scenarios that are chosen tend to be situations that we all encounter. Heart racing or pounding is represented with Orff bass tones and sounds like a heartbeat. However, this is done with a complete focus on the symptom and its situation, the combination of the musical creation and dynamics and music physiology, and the rich information about crucial music therapy considerations. If the tempo is very fast, the teaching moment comes by integrating change mechanism research on tempo in music therapy, and learning how to listen for the symptom and change the clinical musical discourse to ease the symptom.

Teaching technique two: The voice and anxiety

There has been a growing body of research on voice and music therapy, thanks to authors and colleagues who have led the way for that to happen, with a variety of approaches. For functional voice and vocal health in clinical teaching and practice, see Schwartz and colleagues (2018) on comprehensive and useful techniques and methods; for therapeutic songwriting, see Baker (2015), Baker and Wigram (2005), and Baker and Uhlig (2011) on in-depth descriptions of different approaches to songwriting (one method is adapted in Chapter 17); for vocal psychotherapy and improvisation-based vocal interventions, see Austin (2008) (see Chapter 16). If you are interested in learning more about voice and music therapy, these are the authors to refer to for comprehensive knowledge.

Improvisation-based teaching and learning come with significant responsibility to steer learning experiences of therapy technique that does not cross into therapy contexts. Clarity of when that happens is in the educator's hands, and that requires extensive clinical, musical experience. Working with anxiety and improvisation and voice also requires an understanding of the characteristics of the sounds of the voice and its presenting anxiety symptoms in individuals. In order to become familiar with their voice and how important the voice is in clinical work with anxiety, I ask students to partner up and explore the various contexts and sounds in which contexts impact their voice. I usually provide an example of my own. When I am nervous, and about to do a public-speaking engagement, sometimes my voice goes lower and I do not experience the expected physiological restricted airflow that produces a higher pitch, or the faster heart rate that produces a faster tempo. I go through the psychological-physiological/psychological route of stress response. The example lifts out specific items for the students to consider. The first is that everybody has a unique voice that responds physically and reacts dynamically to anxiety-provoking contexts. Schwartz and colleagues (2018) discuss that level of integration of qualities and how to understand them as the clinical voice in action. The second item to consider is that there are areas of vocal production of speaking and singing that can be a reference for anxiety's prominent symptoms (see Chapter 15 and the musical expressions of anxiety). I may also use clinical examples where patterns of sounds can be detected across anxious clients with similar symptoms, attachment systems, and stories, such as soft, barely audible singing voices that sound the opposite of their speaking voices. But I also teach students to be mindful of the whole context of a client's presenting voice and their voice's various qualities. For example, to use an IAP approach to voice and assessment, what is the inaudible voice's quality? Is it emotional? Psychological? Physical? What domains are predominantly connecting to the sound expression?

Culture and voice are also important for the students to discuss. I use the example of my Cornish accent and language with an entirely different inflection, tone, and quality to that of my accent and vocal quality that I need to have to be understood in international contexts, including my lived experience of being in the US. As Uhlig (2007) points out, the authentic voice is a necessary *rooted* part of the story of someone's anxiety.

After students have had a chance to discuss and explore, demonstrate the various contexts of their voices, and, particularly when they experience any of the general anxiety symptoms, the whole class can have a conversation about insights and new knowledge that has been acquired.

Using a workshop and lab-based approach, I provide pre-designed vignettes of anxiety contexts, split the class into several small groups, and ask them to choose a therapist, a client, and observers.

The vignettes come from a combination of clinical experience, creative arts therapies, and music therapy research on change mechanisms, clinical improvisation, and general anxiety. The students are asked to design an intervention that integrates: 1) the identified symptom that needs to be addressed; 2) the music therapy technique of holding both instrumentally and vocally. It is critical to introduce any work with anxiety and voice because it structures and contains the content without overwhelming students to the point of activating any anxiety from the students' perspectives and experiences. On the other hand, it is also essential to have the students go through a role-play-based lab to know what, how, and where the musical-based interventions activate and "voice" the symptoms. Holding is a simple and powerful improvisation technique that creates the predictability needed for neurological expectations to contain the experience. It sounds very simple, but is, in fact, incredibly difficult to accomplish because of the level of focus, presence, and musical competency required to achieve it successfully.

It also allows for new students of music therapy to have a level playing field regarding the learning of clinical vocal applications for all students. Vocal ability and capacity ranges in an inclusive classroom and it is therefore vital to set each student up for success and an expanded yet creative experience of clinical musical inquiry. I also make sure that I *hold* and *contain* the teaching space by actively engaging with each group and spending time with them. Stopping and redoing, re-trying, and moving around the assigned vignette is a helpful teaching mechanism. It allows me to do live, in-class assessments and demonstrate and explore the clinical and collective contexts of anxiety in each case example. Each time, the students can understand how they all fit together to shape the anxiety symptom's vocal presentation. For example, demonstrating technique that focuses specifically on the vocal quality in the holding intervention is critical. By having the clients and observers provide feedback to the student, they gain embodied learning that they can remember. As in my clinical approach, I also teach the students to embody and connect to the power of intention to enable focus and presence. As I explained in Part III, I use the phrase *I'm with you, I see you, I hear you* to teach this multisensory tool of holding.

After this initial technique is explored, there is time embedded into class to present and discuss verbally and vocally each group's insights and explorations, and assess the learning level. The students present and process areas of the intervention—what worked and what didn't work, or what came naturally or was more complex—alongside the social, cultural, and political implications from each case. For example, suppose a vignette includes a transgender client. In that case, their voice and the holistic considerations of their voice need to be attended to. It is important also to *listen* to what is being *said* and *felt* via the musical representation of any anxiety symptoms. At the same time as the students are discussing, I am also attending to the themes and learning that has been gained and is in need of further clarifying or expansion and validation. I will compile this in real time and shape a closing activity highlighting one or several of these points in the musical activity and wrap-up for the whole group. Sometimes it may involve a simple group vocal activity that focuses on creating one sound together, focusing on unique individual qualities of that sound for structure. Or it may include the inclusion of a word each individual offers and vocally expanded by the whole group. It works as a form of validation and also a reflection of the process. I ask the students to spend time individually reflecting by writing a free-associative narrative of what themes, symbols, and expressions they noticed come up for them, the role of the sounds, and the musical qualities of the sounds. We spend time discussing this and moving into more insight-oriented discussion to help them move towards further and deeper understanding of the presence of anxiety in individuals and in group contexts. These insights tend to also be connected to the larger community and cultural expressions of current affairs of the time, and how those impact or do not impact students' learning of the collective vocal symbols and expressions of anxiety.

Teaching technique three: Teaching improvisation-based research methods and collective anxiety

Creative arts therapies and music therapy pedagogy of improvisation and arts-based research (ABR) approaches in anxiety research require well-thought-out ontology and an epistemology firmly rooted in creativity as the change factor for the research methods used. The critical improvisation framework is what I apply to a methodology that systematically and iteratively explores the presence and meaning of anxiety in its collective and community contexts. Teaching requires intervention demonstrations at a certain point of the method to maintain the pace of learning needed in a structured semester or term and to provide a space for learning skills without the burden of overloading students within the multisensory nature of creative-based, music-centered research. My teaching ABR approach integrates all of the theoretical, worldview philosophy on collective contexts of anxiety with the applied critical improvisation framework and methods. I have found that it opens up student perspectives to the broader economic, social, and political implications of anxiety and its impact on community mental health. Performances that are the presentations of these projects' findings become transformative representations of anxiety's clinical and social consequences.

An example of a project from my music and mental health lab from 2016 called Alternative Facts gained momentum. Community leaders noticed, which led to further funding for music and environmental research on anxiety as informed by music therapy. Not only does this kind of way of teaching research allow for a data-driven artistic product to be performed (presented), it also teaches students the necessary skills to do their own transformative social and community work that goes beyond the clinic. It shapes a different kind of clinician who provides excellent clinical music therapy services to the community and is also equipped and ready to do socially relevant research. In my opinion, this is at the heart of how music therapists are unique and can have significant roles across all social sectors. It takes concepts from interpersonal reconstructive therapy (Benjamin, 2018) and applies them to research to allow for essential emergent narratives on anxiety and stress for more significant collective societal existential needs and healing. I have included an example of this method of teaching ABR below. The music therapy students worked through the systematic layers of the ABR method (see Chapter 19 for more details). During the final layer of data dissemination, I invited my colleague Nancy Beardall to collaborate on developing the established musical presentation (a three-movement piece) into a music and dance performance. The overall musical product included an artistic representation of the GAS three-part stress-response process concurrently with the collective sensed and felt presence of that stress. Teaching the method requires me to take a lead initially with the composition part, and when students get to see it applied, they have assignments in formal classes to do a small group project.

The first movement, *Onset*, was an electronic, ominous composition. The major musical categories that emerged were distortion (in an electric guitar melody that repeated on B, F#, G motif—frequently present across multiple instruments in all improvisation labs) and a (heart) pounding, ominous drum riff with scratch-based sound in the snare that instigated physiological stress responses of nervousness. The repeated and limited structure of the piece brings people to the edge of the ability to tolerate the physiological surges that it creates. It does its job to represent the onset of a stress response, but not to the point where it lasts long enough to be a trigger (the clinical component of use of music as affect regulation). It became a music-video (using Logic Audio and iMovie) representation and we integrated clippings of news reports and the sounds that associated them.

Movement two, *Moral Compass*, emerged as a ballad for piano and voice. Major musical categories that emerged were themes of loss and exhaustion but finding voice from the second improvisation lab. Qualities that reflected the vivid yet nebulousness of anxiety came through in ambiguous synthesizer sounds, melodic features from vocalizations of the group that were fragile, soft-sounding, with low pitches and limited tonal ranges in consonant frameworks. The feeling of the song reflects the sense of loss and abandonment and the fear of what is coming next, of the unknown. For me, as I was journaling and incubating with this part, the sense of loss of what truth is and what truth means was prominent. Social issues of immigration and refugee crises and *the general topic of systemic silencing mechanisms of others'* existences were prominent for me personally and as an educator. Using the artistic symbol of voice through song provided the function of clinical voice in data representation and presentation by allowing for three factors to occur: the expression of the social issue; the therapeutic and healing process; and the creative emotional expression in the channeling of the issue. The ballad is in Eb major, with musical components of sustained features between seventh, pensive-like rich, reverberating chords. See Figure 20.1 for an example of the lyrics and melody of Movement two *Moral Compass*.

Moral Compass

Rebecca Zarate

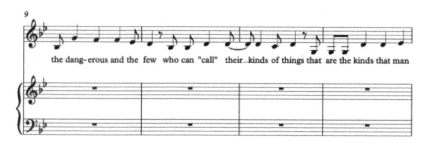

Figure 20.1: Alternative Facts: Movement two: Moral Compass

Verse 1:

Foundations of truth have lost their gain, Nobody feels the same,
Too many voices naming no names.
Caught in the cross-fire of truth,
Of the mindless and the few,
Who can control the kinds of fates,
that are the kinds that manipulate
how we communicate.

Chorus:
It's a sad song,
From a voice that doesn't belong,
in a world that's come to mean,
so many mean things. (repeat)

Verse 2:
Why is there participation in this,
When the story doesn't fit?
To them it's just a game,
To avoid and blame the shame,
On a name without no names.

Chorus:
Bridge: (Bb major)
I feel I can't breathe,
Please get me out from inside this cloud,
Reality isn't reality,
Time does not exist, but it's just a matter of time.

Verse 3:
I know it's just fake news,
But it's different when it's you, your kid, your son, your done,
Images of lost and gone, still remain…out there…
It's a mistake…
There's no escape….

Chorus:
But it's just a song, despite what's going on…
In a world that's come to mean to many mean things.

After each movement was composed, we all analyzed the musical product using an Excel spreadsheet and the micro-analysis tool of the *point of interest* (see Chapter 14), member-checked, triangulated the findings, tweaked any qualities or characteristics in the music, and reached consensus. The third movement, *Retreat-Resource-Resilience*, was a representation of recovery and social resistance processes. The major categories and symbols that emerged were a jazz framework, cohesive and attuned qualities among the group's musical motifs, and a playfulness of musical interactions between members. The music is a combination of walking bass, determined, yet light, drum riff, and improvised spoken word and dialogue between three musicians on resourcing, reconnecting, resisting, and renewing.

When the dancers responded to each movement, the symbols were transferred into that art form. Key characteristics that reflected the piece were in the physical individual movements that expressed the disenfranchised, individual and isolated, confused aspects of movement one. Dialoguing with the data of the second movement was more relational, and proximal-seeking dance moves between the dancers occurred. The process of acknowledgement of self–other entities in the experience of anxiousness about the topic was presented with fewer dancers in the space. The dancers' responses in the third movement brought everybody together, and group dance and group chorus emerged. On reflection of the final part of their movement, the dancers seemed to be responding to the driving quality of the music. They formulated the dancing into a forward-moving movement chorus structure. It evolved into a v-like shape, and the group slowly and intentionally moved towards the audience and only stopped when there was no distal experience between audience and performers. It had a protest-like, march-like symbolism and character. After the music and non-music data were aggregated, the major themes presented were: powerful, dance/movement, beautiful, and anxiety. When we performed it at an arts and health conference, the audience was asked to provide written feedback so it could be taken and reintegrated into the piece. After inductively analyzing and re-iterating the experience, emerging categories of embrace the darkness, movement, flow, embodiment and integration, and new knowledge were found.

Reflections from the educators
Reflections on critical arts-based co-teaching in music therapy and dance/movement therapy
(Originally published in a special edition for Critical Pedagogy in the Arts Therapies (blog) and co-authored by Nancy Beardall and me.)

During January 2016, I found myself in need of responding artistically and intensely to the emerging anxiety that I was feeling, seeing in my practice and on campus in our student and faculty community around the social issues that were pungent in society in the general election process. On January 22, 2018, the term "alternative facts" was introduced by one of the administration's advisors, which was a response to a mistruth. The Alternative Facts and Collective Anxiety project for my spring semester music therapy critical improvisation research lab was created. When Rebecca invited me to join her in an integrated arts social action piece, I was enthusiastic about the collaboration and shared the idea with my dance/movement therapy students. Becky had developed an outline for the project she was working on with her music therapy students entitled "Alternative Facts." It was in response to the 2016 US general election, and to the social environment that it had shaped in our community and on campus. Hostility and conflict were being experienced since the newly elected president had been in office.

In the spring semester of 2016, we pitched the idea of the topic and the final artistic product to be premiered at the Arts in Healthcare Annual Conference, hosted by Lesley University, which was accepted. We came together to work on Alternative Facts.

We wanted to provide an arena in and out of the classroom setting that educated about real-world issues and how this particular moment in time impacted the mental health of communities. Most of all, we were interested in how the emergence of alternative facts as a social construct impacted how the pursuit of truth was being manipulated and used as a divisive and avoidance mechanism. As educators and scholars, we were drawn to illuminate what we were concerned about through structured improvisations using clinical music and clinical dance processes and techniques that covered reflexive, intentional, cultural awareness and humility.

The music used to build out the performative part of the project came out of Rebecca's work with graduate music therapy students in her critical improvisation lab which focuses on anxiety from clinical, critical social and collective perspectives using clinical improvisation (Zarate, 2016a, 2016b, 2017). During this very divisive time in our country there were many people feeling isolated, unsafe, and discriminated against. This was clearly felt and experienced on campus. The music therapy students began work first, with a method of critical listening-cultural listening as a way of understanding anxiety on multiple levels, and improvised on the topic of alternative facts. Motifs from those improvisations were then transcribed and transformed into musical pieces and products, sharing feedback from analysis sessions at several points along the way from January to March. Congruence between certain motifs and phrases, instrumentation, and so on were captured in the lab and within the group so they would be integrated and added into emerging music products.

Alternative Facts was completed, and included three musical movements using a combination of technology and acoustic approaches and also reflected the anxiety process of onset-loss-resource and symptoms of nervousness, inability to relax, and fear of the worst happening. Once the music was ready, Nancy brought it to the dancers for their initial response in improvisation.

The first part (or musical movement) represented a sense of "collective anxiety," being disconnected from body and breath, feeling isolated and a lack of trust. It is a difficult state to move and remain. Observing the class was palpable in their dizzyingly individual and collective anxiety. I had the class move and take recuperative breaks while trying to embody this state.

The second part (or musical movement) of the dance/movement process revolved around the notion of "alternative facts." Students moving in duets and trios while movers representing "alternative facts" tried to split them apart and disconnect them from each other, diminishing their empowered voice. This was a challenging process but gradually an authentic collective or community began to emerge. And the third part (or musical movement) was a sense of community becoming stronger in connecting and resisting these "alternative facts." The idea that together we can resource, feeling a sense of connection between dancers against falsehoods, moving forward together, was visible and felt.

Once movement motifs and themes had emerged, we brought the students together to go over the piece. The students worked with the music and dance themes, which we felt very powerful to now observe after facilitating the process to get them there.

The performance occurred in April 2017, and was impactful on the audience and the students. The social media reach that it attained in the first hour of being posted was a testament to why we do arts-based critical social work as part of our teaching and practice as clinicians and scholars.

Working together in this way has inspired us to continue the conversation about collaboration, and specifically with regard to approaching the arts-based lab work with a more integrated approach from the initial meetings of a project. Most importantly, we were able to be in a creative process with each other and our students as artists, activists, and educators of music therapy and dance/movement therapy.

Reflections from the students

Did you find this way of learning about the presence of anxiety in society helpful?

Yes…it created deeper insights into the things (news media, politics, social media) that cause unease and worry.

I felt as though the process not only illuminated but it helped inform my relationship with these topics.

By improvising and then analysing, I could understand how these topics made me feel on an emotional/feeling sense level.

What was your most valuable part of the project/lab method of working?

What I found most valuable was the deepening of understanding I felt for my relationships with some of the "invisible" focuses that make up the fabric of social anxiety.

...engaging and learning with this emerging understanding of my (and others') relationships to these powers is what I found to be the most valuable part of this experience.

Reflections from the audience

The piece was powerful. I liked the shifts from the personal to collective and back again unified, collective way.

Powerful, beautiful confront anxiety & how to do the emotional side of responding to a crazy world.

This was very moving—so powerful—and the process so clear...to feeling–individual feeling and collective feeling. I watched and heard the collective anxiety and felt it deeply inside.

I thought the strong beat/percussion helped the drums to move the anxiety out and the body, strong.

These are just a few snapshots showing how to teach what anxiety sounds like and how to navigate a structured, simple, yet effective way for students to begin work in this area. It is also hoped that this book supports fellow colleagues in music therapy training programs who are interested in critical social arts-based research pedagogy and practice.

References

Aalbers, S., Spreen, M., Pattiselanno, K., Verboon, P., Vink, A., & van Hooren, S. (2020). Efficacy of emotion-regulating improvisational music therapy to reduce depressive symptoms in young adult students: A multiple-case study design. *The Arts in Psychotherapy, 71*. ScienceDirect. doi: 10.1016/j.aip.2020.101720.

Aalbers, S., Vink, A., Freeman, R. E., Pattiselanno, K., Spreen, M., & Hooren, S. van. (2019). Development of an improvisational music therapy intervention for young adults with depressive symptoms: An intervention mapping study. *The Arts in Psychotherapy, 65*, 1–11.

Abbassi, A. (1999). Culture and anxiety: A cross-cultural study. *Dissertation Abstracts International, 59*(11–A), 4065.

Abdulah, D. M. & Musa, D. H. (2020). Insomnia and stress of physicians during Covid-19 outbreak. *Sleep Medicine, X*, 100017, 1–7. https://doi.org/10.1016/j.sleepx.2020.100017.

Abrams, B. (2011). Understanding music as a temporal-aesthetic way of being: Implications for a general theory of music therapy. *The Arts in Psychotherapy, 38*(2), 114–119.

Adams, M., Bell, L. A., Goodman, D. J., & Joshi, K. Y. (eds). (2016). *Teaching for Diversity and Social Justice* (3rd ed.). London: Routledge.

Ahonen-Eerikäinen, H. (2007). *Group Analytical Music Therapy*. New Braunfels, TX: Barcelona.

Ahonen-Eerikäinen, H., Rippin, K., Sibille, N., & Rhea, K. (2007). "Not bad for an old 85-year-old!"—The qualitative analysis of the role of music, therapeutic benefits and group therapeutic factors of the St. Joseph's Alzheimer's adult day program music therapy group. *Canadian Journal of Music Therapy, 13*(2), 37–62.

Aigen, K. (1990). Echoes of silence. *Music Therapy, 9*(1), 44–61.

Aigen, K. (2007). In defense of beauty: A role for the aesthetic in music therapy theory: Part II. The development of aesthetic theory in music therapy. *Nordic Journal of Music Therapy, 17*(1), 3–18.

Ainsworth, M. D. S. & Wittig, B. A. (1969). Attachment and Exploratory Behavior of One-Year-Olds in a Strange Situation. In B. M. Foss (ed.), *Determinants of Infant Behavior* (Vol. 4, pp.111–136). London: Methuen.

Ainsworth, M. S. (1979). Infant–mother attachment. *American Psychologist, 34*(10), 932–937. https://doi.org/10.1037/0003-066X.34.10.932.

Akombo, D. (2007). Effects of listening to music as an intervention for pain and anxiety in bone marrow transplant patients. *Dissertation Abstracts International, 68*(1–A).

Albornoz, Y. (2016). *Artistic Music Therapy: An Individual, Group, and Social Approach*. New Braunfels, TX: Barcelona.

Albrecht, G. (2011). Chronic Environmental Change: Emerging "Psychoterratic" Syndromes. In I. Weissbecker (ed.), *Climate Change and Human Well-Being: Global Challenges and Opportunities* (pp.43–56). New York, NY: Springer.

Aldridge, D. & Fachner, J. (2006). *Altered States: Consciousness, Transcendence, Therapy and Addictions*. London: Jessica Kingsley Publishers.

Aldwin, C. (2007). *Stress, Coping, and Development: An Integrative Perspective* (2nd ed.). New York, NY: Guilford Press.

Alvin, J. (1977). The musical object as an intermediary object. *British Journal of Music Therapy, 8*(2), 7–12.

American Music Therapy Association (AMTA) Standards of Clinical Practice, Section, Mental Health 2.0 Standards II Assessment, 2.0–2.9.11. www.musictherapy.org/about/standards/#MENTAL_HEALTH.

American Psychiatric Association. (2013). *Diagnostic and Statistical Manual of Mental Disorders, 5th Edition (DSM-5)*. Washington, DC: APA.

Ansdell, G. (1991). Mapping the territory. *British Journal of Music Therapy,* 5(2), 18–27.

Ansdell, G., Davidson, J., Magee, W., Meehan, J., & Proctor, S. (2010). From "this f***ing life" to "that's better" ... in four minutes: An interdisciplinary study of music therapy's "present moments" and their potential for affect modulation. *Nordic Journal of Music Therapy,* 19(1), 3–28.

Ansdell, G. & DeNora, T. (2016). *How Music Helps in Music Therapy and Everyday Life*. London: Taylor and Francis.

Antony, M. M. & Barlow, D. H. (1996). *Emotion Theory as a Framework for Explaining Panic Attacks and Panic Disorder*. New York, NY: Guilford Press.

Antony, M. M., Orsillo, S. M., & Roemer, L. (2001). *Practitioner's Guide to Empirically Based Measures of Anxiety*. New York, NY: Kluwer Academic Publishers.

Anxiety and Depression Association of America (2017). Facts and Statistics. https://adaa.org/understanding-anxiety/facts-statistics.

Asmal, L. & Stein, D. J. (2009). Anxiety and Culture. In M. Antony (ed.), *The Oxford Handbook of Anxiety and Related Disorders* (pp.657–666). Oxford: Oxford University Press.

Au, C. (2006). The sounds of environmentally-friendly music. *Natural Life, 111,* 28–29. MAS Ultra School Edition.

Austin, D. (2008). *The Theory and Practice of Vocal Psychotherapy*. London: Jessica Kingsley Publishers.

Austin, D. S. (1996). The role of improvised music in psychodynamic music therapy with adults. *Music Therapy,* 14(1), 29–43. https://doi.org/10.1093/mt/14.1.29.

Austin, D. S. & Dvorkin, J. M. (1998). Resistance in Individual Music Therapy. In K. E. Bruscia (ed.), *The Dynamics of Music Psychotherapy* (pp.121–136). New Braunfels, TX: Barcelona.

Bachhuber, A., Hennessy, S., Cunningham, C. O., & Starrels, J. L. (2016). Increasing benzo-diazepine prescriptions and overdose mortality in the United States, 1996–2013. *American Journal of Public Health, 106*(4), 686–688.

Backer, J. & Sutton, J. (eds). (2014). *The Music in Music Therapy. Psychodynamic Music Therapy in Europe: Clinical, Theoretical, and Research Approaches*. London: Jessica Kingsley Publishers.

Baker, F. A. (2015). *Therapeutic Songwriting: Developments in Theory, Methods and Practice*. New York, NY: Palgrave Macmillan.

Baker, F. A., Rickard, N., Tamplin, J., & Roddy, C. (2015). Flow and meaningfulness as mech-anisms of change in self-concept and wellbeing following a songwriting intervention for people in the early phase of neurorehabilitation. *Frontiers in Human Neuroscience,* 9, 299. https://doi.org/10.3389/fnhum.2015.00299.

Baker, F. A. & Tamplin, J. (2006). *Music Therapy Methods in Neuro-Rehabilitation: A Clinician's Manual*. London: Jessica Kingsley Publishers.

Baker, F. A. & Uhlig, S. (2011). *Voicework in Music Therapy: Research and Practice*. London: Jessica Kingsley Publishers.

Baker, F. A. & Wigram, T. (2005). *Songwriting: Methods, Techniques, and Clinical Applications for Music Therapy Clinicians, Educators, and Students*. London: Jessica Kingsley Publishers.

Bandura, A. (1977). *Social Learning Theory*. New York, NY: General Learning Press.

Bartholomew, K. (1990). Avoidance of intimacy: An attachment perspective. *Journal of Social and Personal Relationships,* 7, 147–178.

Bartholomew, K. & Horowitz, L. M. (1991). Attachment style among young adults: A test of a four category model. *Journal of Personality and Social Psychology,* 61, 226–244.

Bartholomew, R. E. & Victor, J. S. (2004). A social-psychological theory of collective anxiety attacks: The "Mad Gasser" reexamined. *The Sociological Quarterly,* 45(2), 229–248. https://doi.org/10.1111/j.1533-8525.2004.tb00011.x.

Battles, P. (2018). Music as a Catalyst for Altered States of Consciousness and Peak Experiences in the Treatment of Depression, Anxiety, and PTSD. *Expressive Therapies Capstone Theses,* Lesley University. https://digitalcommons.lesley.edu/expressive_theses/89.

Beck, A. T., Emery, G., & Greenberg, R. L. (2005). *Anxiety Disorders and Phobias: A Cognitive Perspective* (2nd ed.). New York, NY: Basic Books.

Beck, A. T. & Steer, R. A. (1993). Beck Anxiety Inventory. *Mental Measurements Yearbook, 13*(18).

Beck, B. D., Hansen, A. M., & Gold, C. (2015). Coping with work-related stress through guided imagery and music (GIM): Randomized controlled trial. *Journal of Music Therapy, 52*, 323–352.

Beck, G. J. (2010). *Interpersonal Processes in the Anxiety Disorders: Implications for Understanding Psychopathology and Treatment.* Washington, DC: American Psychological Association. https://doi: 10.1037/12084-000.

Beer. L. (2015). From embedded to embodied: Including music in arts-based music therapy research. *Music Therapy Perspectives, 34*(1),33 -40. DOI:10.1093/mtp/miv006.

Bender, L. & Yarnell, H. (1941). An observation nursery. *American Journal of Psychiatry, 97*, 1158–1174.

Benjamin, L. S. (2018). *Interpersonal Reconstructive Therapy (IRT) for Anger, Anxiety, and Depression: It's About Broken Hearts, Not Broken Brains.* Washington, DC: American Psychological Association.

Bibb, J., Castle, D., & Newton, R. (2016). "Circuit breaking" the anxiety: Experiences of group music therapy during supported post-meal time for adults with anorexia nervosa. *Australian Journal of Music Therapy, 1.* Gale Academic OneFile.

Bissiri, K. A. (1999). *Self-Construals, Culture Change, and the Expression of Distress in Chinese and Chinese Americans (Aculturation).* (10th-B ed., Vol. 59). Dissertations International: Section B: The Sciences and Engineering.

Black, J. & Enns, G. (1997). *Better Boundaries: Owning and Treasuring Your Life.* Oakland, CA: New Harbinger.

Bolger, L. E. & McFerran, K. S. (2020). Current practices and considerations for international development music therapy: A World Federation of Music Therapy scoping project. *Voices, 20*(1). Directory of Open Access Journals. https://doi.org/10.15845/voices.v20i1.2951.

Bowlby, J. (1944). Forty-four juvenile thieves: Their characters and home life. *International Journal of Psycho-Analysis, 25*, 19–52.

Bowlby, J. (1969). *Attachment. Attachment and Loss* (2nd ed., Vol. 1). New York, NY: Basic Books.

Bowlby, J. (1973). *Separation: Anxiety & Anger. Attachment and Loss* (Vol. 2). London: Hogarth Press.

Bowlby, J. (1980). *Loss: Sadness & Depression. Attachment and Loss* (Vol. 3). London: Hogarth Press.

Bowlby, J. (1982). *Attachment. Attachment and Loss* (2nd ed., Vol. 1). New York, NY: Basic Books.

Bowlby, J. (1988). *A Secure Base: Parent-Child Attachment and Healthy Human Development.* New York, NY: Basic Books.

Bowlby, J. & Salter Ainsworth, M. D. (1976). *Child Care and the Growth of Love.* London: Penguin Books.

Bozo, O., Tunca, A., & Slimsek, Y. (2009). The effect of death anxiety and age on health-promoting behaviors: A terror-management theory perspective. *Journal of Psychology: Interisciplinary and Applied, 143*(4), 377–389.

Breen, W. E. & Kashdan, T. B. (2011). Anger suppression after imagined rejection among individuals with social anxiety. *Journal of Anxiety Disorders, 25*, 879–887.

Bressan, R. A. Q., Lucas, C., Andreoli, S. B., Araújo, C., *et al.* (2009). The posttraumatic stress disorder project in Brazil: Neuropsychological, structural and molecular neuroimaging studies in victims of urban violence. *BMC Psychiatry, 9*(30). https://doi: 10.1186/1471-244X-9-30.

Brewster, F. (2020). *The Racial Complex: A Jungian Perspective on Culture and Race.* London: Routledge.

Brodsky, W. & Sloboda, J. A. (1997). Clinical trial of a music generated vibrotactile therapeutic environment for musicians: Main effects and outcome differences between therapy subgroups. *Journal of Music Therapy, 34*, 2–32.

Brooks, D. L., Bradt, J., Eyre, L., & Dileo, C. (2010). Creative approaches for reducing burnout in medical personnel. *The Arts in Psychotherapy, 37*, 255–263. https://doi.org/10.1016/j.aip.2010.05.001.

Brown, G. P., Craske, M. G., Tata, P., Rassovsky, Y., & Tsao, J. C. I. (2000). The Anxiety Attitude and Belief Scale: Initial psychometric properties in an undergraduate sample. *Clinical Psychology and Psychotherapy, 7*, 230–239.

245

Brunt, S. D. & Johnson, H. (2013). "Click, Play and Save": The iGamelan as a tool for music-culture sustainability. *Musicology Australia, 35*(2), 221. Complementary Index.

Bruscia, K. (1987). *Improvisational Models of Music Therapy.* Springfield, IL: Charles C. Thomas.

Bruscia, K. (ed.). (1998). *The Dynamics of Music Pyschotherapy.* New Braunfels, TX: Barcelona.

Buckarov, A. V. & Knyazev, G. G. (2011). Interaction of anger with anxiety and responses to emotional facial expressions. *Personality and Individual Differences, 50*(3), 398–403.

Bunt, L. (1994). *Music Therapy: An Art Beyond Words.* London: Routledge.

Calhoun, C. (1995). *Critical Social Theory: Culture, History, and the Challenge of Difference.* Cambridge, MA: Blackwell.

Carr, C., d'Ardenne, P., Sloboda, A., Scott, C., Wang, D., & Priebe, S. (2012). Group music therapy for patients with persistent post-traumatic stress disorder—An exploratory randomized controlled trial with mixed methods evaluation. *Psychology and Psychotherapy, 85*(2), 179–202. https://doi.org/10.1111/j.2044-8341.2011.02026.x.

Cassity, M. D. & Cassity, J. E. (1991). *Multimodal Psychiatric Music Therapy for Adults, Adolescents, and Children: A Clinical Manual.* St Louis, MO: MMB Music.

Chang, M. H. (2016). Dance/movement therapists of color in the ADTA. The first 50 years. *American Journal of Dance Therapy, 38*(2), 268–278. https://doi.org/10.1007/s10465-016-9238-9.

Chang, M.-Y., Chen, C.-H., & Huang, K.-F. (2008). Effects of music therapy on psychological health of women during pregnancy. *Journal of Clinical Nursing, 17*(19), 2580–2587. doi:10.1111/j.1365-2702.2007.02064.x.

Chen, Y.-Y. (2019). Single-session improvisational group music therapy in adult inpatient psychiatry: A pilot study of the therapist's experience. *Nordic Journal of Music Therapy, 28*(2), 151–168. Academic Search Index.

Chisholm, D., Sweeny, K., Sheehan, P., Rasmussen, B., Cuijers, P., & Saxena, S. (2016). Scaling-up treatment of depression and anxiety: A global return on investment analysis. *Lancet Psychiatry, 3*, 415–424.

Chisholm, K. A. (1998). Three-year follow-up of attachment and indiscriminate friendliness in children adopted from Romanian orphanages. *Child Development, 69*, 1092–1106.

Choi, A. N., Lee, M. S., & Lim, H. J. (2008). Effects of group music intervention on depression, anxiety, and relationships in psychiatric patients: A pilot study. *The Journal of Complimentary Medicine, 14*(5), 567–570. doi:10.1089/acm.2008.0006.

Clark, I. M., Tamplin, J. D., & Baler, F. A. (2018). Community-dwelling people living with dementia and their family caregivers experience enhanced relationships and feelings of well-being following therapeutic group singing: A qualitative thematic analysis. *Frontiers in Psychology, 9*, 1332. https://doi.org/10.3389/fpsyg.2018.01332.

Clark, L. A. & Watson, D. (1991). Tripartite model of anxiety and depression: Psychometric evidence and taxonomic implications. *Journal of Abnormal Psychiatry, 100*, 316–336.

Clark, M., Isaaks-Downton, G., Wells, N., Redlin-Frazier, S., *et al.* (2006). Use of preferred music to reduce emotional distress and symptom activity during radiation therapy. *Journal of Music Therapy, 43*, 247–265. https://doi: 10.1093/jmt/43.3.247.

Clayton, S., Manning, C. M., Krygsman, K., & Speiser, M. (2017). *Mental Health and Our Changing Climate: Impacts, Implications and Guidance.* Washington, DC: American Psychological Association.

Clua, Á., Llorca-Bofí, J., & Psarra, S. (2020). Urban opportunities and conflicts around street musicians: The relationship between the configuration of public space and outdoor acoustics in Ciutat Vella, Barcelona. *Journal of Urban Design, 25*(5), 561–589.

Combs, H. & Markman, J. (2014). Anxiety disorders in primary care. *Medical Clinics of North America, 98*(5), 1007–1023. https://doi.org/10.1016/j.mcna.2014.06.003.

Comer, J., Mojtabai, M. D., & Olfson, M. (2011). National trends in the antipsychotic treatment of psychiatric outpatients with anxiety disorders. *The American Journal of Psychiatry, 68*(10), 1057–1065.

Cominardi, C. (2014). From creative process to trans-cultural process: Integrating music therapy with arts media in Italian kindergartens: A pilot study. *Australian Journal of Music Therapy, 25*, 3–14.

Congreve, W. (1703). *The Mourning Bride: A Tragedy.* Anodos.

Cook, P. R. & Smallwood, S. (2010). SOLA: Sustainable Orchestras of Laptops and Analog. *Leonardo Music Journal, 20*(1), 89. Complementary Index.

Coombes, S., Higgins, T., Gamble, K. M., Cauraug, J. H., & Janelle, C. M. (2009). Attentional control theory: Anxiety, emotional and motor planning. *Journal of Anxiety Disorders, 23*, 1072–1079. https://doi: 10.1016/j.janxdis.2009.07.009.

Crooke, A. H. D. (2018). Music technology and the hip hop beat making tradition: A history and typology of equipment for music therapy. *Voices, 18*(2). Directory of Open Access Journals. https://doi.org/10.15845/voices.v18i2.996.

Cruz, R. F. & Feder, B. (2013). *The Art and Science of Evaluation in the Arts Therapies: How Do You Know What's Working.* Springfield, IL: Charles C. Thomas.

Csikszentmihalyi, M. (1975). *Beyond Boredom and Anxiety: Experiencing Flow in Work and Play.* San Francisco, CA: Jossey-Bass.

Dassa, A., Rosenbach, M., & Gilboa, A. (2020). Towards sustainable implementation of music in daily care of people with dementia and their spouses. *The Arts in Psychotherapy, 71*, 1–8.

Dattani, S., Richie, H., & Roser, M. (2018). Mental health. *Institute for Health Metrics and Evaluation.* https://ourworldindata.org/mental-health.

Davis, M., Fallis, W. A., Campeau, S., & Kim, M. (1993). Fear-potentiated startle: A neural and pharmacological analysis. *Behavioural Brain Research, 58*(1–2), 175–198. https://doi.org/10.1016/0166-4328(93)90102-V.

de Freitas, E. (2008). Interrogating Reflexivity: Art, Research, and the Desire for Presence. In G. J. Knowles & A. L. Cole (eds), *Handbook of the Arts in Qualitative Research.* Los Angeles, CA: Sage Publications.

de Witte, M., Lindelauf, E., Moonen, X., Stams., G. J., & van Hooren, S. (2020). Music therapy interventions for stress reduction in adults with mild intellectual disabilities: Perspectives from clinical practice. *Frontiers in Pyschology, 11*, 572549. https://doi.org/10.3389/fpsyg.2020.572549.

de Witte, M., Orkibi, H., Zarate, R., Karkou, V., *et al.* (under review). From therapeutic factors to mechanisms of change in the creative arts therapies: A scoping review. *Frontiers in Psychology.*

de Witte, M., Spruit, A., van Hooren, S., Moonen, X., & Stams., G. (2020). Effects of music interventions on stress-related outcomes: A systematic review and two meta-analyses. *Health Psychology Review, 14*(2), 294–324. https://doi.org/10.1080/17437199.2019.1627897.

DeCoteau, T., Hope, D. A., & Anderson, J. (2003). Anxiety, stress, and health in Northern Plains Native Americans. *Behavior Therapy, 34*(3), 365–380. https://doi10.1016/S0005-7894(03)80006-0.

DeLoach, D. (2003). The effect of preferred music genre selection versus preferred song selection on experimentally induced anxiety levels. *Journal of Music Therapy, 40*(1), 2–12.

DeNora, T. (2004). *Empirical Musicology: Aims, Methods, Prospects.* Oxford: Oxford University Press.

Díaz de Chumaceiro, C. L. (1998). Consciously Induced Song Recall: Countertransference Implications. In K. E Bruscia (ed.), *The Dynamics of Music Psychotherapy* (pp.365–386). New Braunfels, TX: Barcelona.

DiTomasso, R. A. & Gosch, E. A. (2007). *Anxiety Disorders: A Practioner's Guide to Comparative Treatments.* New York, NY: Springer.

Dreessen, L. & Arntz, A. (1998). The impact of personality disorders on treatment outcome of anxiety disorders: Best-evidence synthesis. *Behaviour Research and Therapy, 36*(5), 483–504.

Du Rousseau, D. R., Mindlin, G., Insler, J., & Levin, I. I. (2011). Operational study to evaluate music-based neurotraining at improving sleep quality, mood and daytime function in a first responder population. *Neurotherapy, 15*, 389–398.

Elliott, D., Polman, R., & McGregor, R. (2011). Relaxing music for anxiety control. *Journal of Music Therapy, 48*, 264–288.

Elliott, E., Freitas Caton, L., & Rhyne, J. (eds). (2002). *Aesthetics in a Multicultural Age.* Oxford: Oxford University Press.

Epelde-Larrañaga, A., Ramírez, J. A. O., & Estrada-Vidal, L. I. (2020). Music as a resource against bullying and cyberbullying: Intervention in two centers in Spain. *Sustainability, 12*(5), 2057–2057. Directory of Open Access Journals. https://doi.org/10.3390/su12052057.

Erkkilä, J. (2014). Improvisational Experiences of Psychodynamic Music Therapy for People with Depression. In J. De Backer & J. Sutton (eds), *The Music in Music Therapy. Psychodynamic Music Therapy in Europe: Clinical, Theoretical and Research Approaches* (pp.260–281). London: Jessica Kingsley Publishers.

Erkkilä, J., Ala-Ruona, E., Punkanen, M., & Fachner, J. (2012). Creativity in Improvisational Pscyhodynamic Music Therapy. In D. Hargreaves, D. Miell, & R. MacDonald (eds), *Musical Imaginations: Multidisciplinary Perspectives on Creativity, Performance and Perception* (pp.414–428). Oxford: Oxford University Press.

Erkkilä, J., Brabant, O., Saarikallio, S., Ala-Ruona, E., *et al.* (2019). Enhancing the efficacy of integrative improvisational music therapy in the treatment of depression: Study protocol for a randomised controlled trial. *Trials, 20*(1), 1–13. Directory of Open Access Journals. https://doi.org/10.1186/s13063-019-3323-6.

Eschen, J. Th. (2002). *Analytical Music Therapy*. London: Jessica Kingsley Publishers.

Estrella, K. & Forinash, M. (2007). Narrative inquiry and arts-based inquiry: Multi-narrative perspectives. *Journal of Humanistic Psychology, 47*, 376–383. https://doi: 10.1177/0022167807301898.

Evans, A. (2020). Collective Psychology Project: www.collectivepsychology.org/home.

Eysenck, M. W. (1997). *Anxiety and Cognition: A Unified Theory*. Hove: Psychology Press.

Eysenck, M. W., Derakshan, N., Santos, R., & Calvo, M. G. (2007). Anxiety and cognitive performance: Attentional control theory. *Emotion, 7*, 336–353. doi: 10.1037/1528-3542.7.2.336.

Fancourt, D., & Saoirse, F. (2019). Health evidence network synthesis report 67: What is the evidence on the role of the arts in improving health and well-being? A scoping review. *World Health Organization*.

Fang, A., Asnaani, A., Gutner, C., Cook, C., Wilhelm, S., & Hofmann, S. G. (2011). Rejection sensitivity mediates the relationship between social anxiety and body dysmorphic concerns. *Journal of Anxiety Disorders, 25*, 946–949.

Feldman Barrett, L. (2017). *How Emotions Are Made. The Secret Life of the Brain*. Boston, MA: First Mariner Books.

Ferrara, L. (1984). Phenomenology as a tool for musical analysis. *The Musical Quarterly, 70*(3), 355–373.

Ferrer, A. (2007). The effect of live music on decreasing anxiety in patients undergoing chemotherapy treatment. *Journal of Music Therapy, 44*, 242–255. doi: 10.1093/jmt/44.3.242.

Fiumara, C. G. (2001). *The Mind's Affective Life*. Philadelphia, PA: Taylor and Francis.

Flores, P. J. & Porges, S. W. (2017). Group psychotherapy as a neural exercise: Bridging polyvagal theory and attachment. *International Journal of Group Psychotherapy, 67*(2), 202–222. https://doi: 10.1080/00207284.2016.1263544.

Forinash, M. (1992). A Phenomenological analysis of Nordoff-Robbins approach to music therapy: The lived experience of clinical improvisation. *Music Therapy, 11*(1), 120–141.

Forinash, M. & Gonzalez, D. (1989). A phenomenological perspective of music therapy. *Music Therapy, 8*(1), 35–46.

Foxell, R. (2015). Music in the mountains: Creating sustainable therapy programs from short-term missions. *Christian Journal for Global Health, 2*(2), 64–68. Directory of Open Access Journals. https://doi.org/10.15566/cjgh.v2i2.84.

Gadberry, A. (2011). Steady beat and state anxiety. *Journal of Music Therapy, 48*, 346–356. https://doi: 10.1093/jmt/48.3.346.

Gardstrom, S. C. & Diestelkamp, W. S. (2013). Women with addictions report reduced anxiety after group music therapy: A quasi-experimental study. *Voices, 13*(2). Directory of Open Access Journals. https://doi.org/10.15845/voices.v13i2.681.

Gergen, K. J. (2009). *Relational Being: Beyond Self and Community*. Oxford: Oxford University Press.

Gibson, C. (2019). A sound track to ecological crisis: Tracing guitars all the way back to the tree. *Popular Music, 38*(2), 183–203.

Gilbertson, S. (2013). Improvisation and meaning. *International Journal of Qualitative Studies on Health and Well-Being, 8*(1). https://doi10.3402/qhw.v8i0.20604.

Goisman, R. M., Rogers, M., Steketee, G., Warshaw, M. G., Cuneo, P., & Keller, M. B. (1993). Frequency of utilization of behavioral methods in the treatment of patients with anxiety disorders. *Journal of Clinical Psychiatry, 54*, 213–218.

Goisman, R. M., Warshaw, M. G., & Keller, M. B. (1999). Psychosocial treatment prescriptions for generalized anxiety disorder, panic disorder, and social phobia, 1991–1996. *American Journal of Insanity, 156*(11), 1819–1821.

Goldfarb, W. (1943). The effect of institutional care on adolescent personality. *Child Development, 14,* 213–223.

Gray, J. A. & McNaughton, N. (2007). *The Neuropsychology of Anxiety* (2nd ed.). Oxford: Oxford University Press.

Greene, M. (1998). *The Dialect of Freedom.* New York, NY: Teachers College Press.

Grocke, D. (2008). The effect of music therapy on anxiety in patients who are terminally ill. *Journal of Palliative Medicine, 11,* 582–590. https://doi: 10.1089/jpm.2007.0193.

Grocke, D. & Wigram, T. (2007). *Receptive Methods in Music Therapy: Techniques and Clinical Applications for Music Therapy Clinicians, Educators and Students.* London: Jessica Kingsley Publishers.

Guétin, S., Portet, F., Picot, M. C., Messaoudi, M., *et al.* (2009). Effect of music therapy on anxiety and depression in patients with Alzheimer's type dementia: Randomized, controlled study. *Dementia and Geriatric Cognitive Disorders, 28*(1), 36–46. https://doi: 10.1159/000229024.

Gutierrez, E. O. F. & Camarena, V. A. T. (2015). Music therapy in generalized anxiety disorder. *The Arts in Psychotherapy, 19.* Gale Academic OneFile. https://doi.org/10.1016/j.aip.2015.02.003.

Hadley, S. (2003). *Psychodynamic Music Therapy: Case Studies.* New Braunfels, TX: Barcelona.

Hadley, S. (2013). Dominant narratives: Complicity and the need for vigilance in the creative arts therapies. *The Arts in Psychotherapy, 40,* 373–381. https://doi: 10.1016/j.aip.2013.05.007.

Hahna, N. (2013). Towards an emancipatory practice: Incorporating feminist pedagogy in the creative arts therapies. *The Arts in Psychotherapy, 40,* 436–440. https://doi: 10.1016/j.aip.2013.05.002.

Hannibal, N. (2003). A Woman's Change from Being Nobody to Somebody: Music Therapy with a Middle-Aged, Speechless, and Self-Destructive Woman. In S. Hadley (ed.), *Psychodynamic Music Therapy: Case Studies.* New Braunfels, TX: Barcelona.

Hanser, S. B. (1999). *The New Music Therapist's Handbook.* Boston, MA: Berklee Press.

Harrison, K. (2020). Indigenous music sustainability during climate change. *Current Opinion in Environmental Sustainability.* Gale Academic OneFile. https://doi.org/10.1016/j.cosust.2020.01.003.

Hartmut, K. (2007). Zur Ästhetik der musikalischen improvisation in der musiktherapie. [The aesthetics of musical improvisation in music therapy.] *Musiktherapeutishe Umschau, 28*(1), 5–16.

Haug, F. (1980). *Beyond Female Masochism.* London: Verso.

Haug, F. (1999). *Female Sexualization: A Collective Work of Memory* (2nd ed.). London: Verso.

Hazan, C. & Shaver, P. R. (1987). Romantic love conceptualized as an attachment process. *Journal of Personality and Social Psychology, 52,* 511–524.

Heinemann, H. N. & Hesser, B. (eds). (2011). *Music as a Global Resource: Solutions for Social and Economic Issues.* www.international-iccc.org/MAGR_FINAL_2011.pdf.

Herman, J. (1992). *Trauma and Recovery.* New York, NY: Basic Books.

Hernández-Ruiz, E. (2005). Effect of music therapy on the anxiety levels and sleep patterns of abused women in shelters. *Journal of Music Therapy, 42,* 140–158. https://doi: 10.1093/jmt/42.2.140.

Heru, A. (2020). Attachment theory and object relations theory, meet neuroscience. *Clinical Psychiatry News, 48*(1), 8–10.

Hesse, E. & Main, M. (2000b). Disorganized infant, child and adult attachment: Collapse in behavioral and attentional strategies. *Journal of the American Psychoanalytic Association, 48,* 1097–1127. doi: 10.1177/00030651000480041101.

Hesser, B. (1979). Music Psychotherapy. Unpublished manuscript.

Hinshelwood, R. D. & Skogstad, W. (2000). *Observing Organizations: Anxiety, Defense and Culture in Health Care.* London: Routledge.

Hitchen, H., Magee, W. L., & Soeterik, S. (2010). Music therapy in the treatment of patients with neuro-behavioural disorders stemming from acquired brain injury. *Nordic Journal of Music Therapy, 19*(63). https://doi: 10.1080/08098130903086404.

Hood, M. M. (2014). Sustainability strategies among Balinese heritage ensembles. *Malaysian Journal of Music, 3*(2), 1–13.

Horney, K. (1992). *Our Inner Conflicts: A Constructive Theory of Neurosis*. New York, NY: W. W. Norton.

Horowitz, J. (2006). Culture-bound syndromes of anxiety disorders and mutlicultural competence. *Dissertation Abstracts International: Section B: The Sciences and Engineering, 66*(7-B), 3949.

Isenberg, C. (2015). Psychodynamic Approaches. In B. Wheeler (ed.), *Music Therapy Handbook* (pp.133–147). New York, NY: Guilford Press.

Jacobsen, S. L., McKinney, C. H., & Holck, U. (2014). Effects of a dyadic music therapy intervention on parent-child interaction, parent stress, and parent-child relationship in families with emotionally neglected children: A randomized controlled trial. *Journal of Music Therapy, 51*, 310–332. https://doi 10.1093/jmt/thu028.

James, B. (2012). The art of pianism meets science, sustainable performance: Use of arm weight. *Australian Journal of Music Education, 2*, 92–101. ERIC.

Johnson, S. M. (2019). *Attachment Theory in Practice. Emotionally Focused Therapy (EFT) with Individuals, Couples, and Families*. New York, NY: Guilford Press.

Kandel, E. R., Schwartz, J. H., & Jessell, T. M. (2010). *Principles of Neural Science*. New York, NY: McGraw-Hill.

Keller, E. F. (2010). *The Mirage of a Space Between Nature and Nurture*. Durham, NC: Duke University Press. https://doi: 10.1215/9780822392811.

Kenny, C. (2006). *Music & Life in the Field of Play: An Anthology*. New Braunfels, TX: Barcelona.

Kiesler, D. J. (1996). From communications to interpersonal theory: A personal odyssey. *Journal of Personality Assessment, 66*, 267–282. https://doi: 10.1207/s15327752jpa6602_6.

Kim, J. (2016). Psychodynamic music therapy. *Voices: A World Forum for Music Therapy, 16*(2). https://doi 10.15845/voices.v16i2.882.

Kim, S.-A. (2021). Music as an Acculturation Strategy in Culturally Informed Music Therapy. In M. Belgrave & S.-A Kim (eds), *Music Therapy in a Multicultural Context: A Handbook for Music Therapy Students and Professionals* (pp.9–42). London: Jessica Kingsley Publishers.

Kim, Y. (2008). The effect of improvisation-assisted desensitization, and music-assisted progressive muscle relaxation and imagery on reducing pianists' music performance anxiety. *Journal of Music Therapy, 45*(2), 165–191. https://doi: 10.1093/jmt/45.2.165.

Kirchner, J. M., Bloom, A. J., & Skutnick-Henley, P. (2008). The relationship between performance anxiety and flow. *Medical Problems of Performing Artists, 23*(2), 59–65.

Kohl, P. (2020). Scales of sustain and decay: Making music in deep time. *Popular Music, 39*(1), 108. Complementary Index.

Kohut, H. (1984). *How Does Analysis Cure?* Chicago, IL: University of Chicago Press.

Kossak, M. (2009). Therapeutic attunement: A transpersonal view of expressive arts therapy. *The Arts in Psychotherapy, 36*, 13–18. https://doi: 10.1016/j.aip.2008.09.003.

Kossak, M. (2015). *Attunement in Expressive Therapies*. Springfield, IL: Charles C. Thomas.

Krout, R. E. (2007). Music listening to facilitate relaxation and promote wellness: Integrated aspects of our neurophysiological responses to music. *The Arts in Psychotherapy, 34*, 134–141. https://doi: 10.1016/j.aip.2006.11.001.

LaBar, K. (2014). How anxiety is contagious. *World Economic Forum.* www.weforum.org/agenda/2014/11/how-anxiety-is-contagious.

Lai, H., Hwang, M. J., Chen, C. J., Chang, K. F., Peng, T. C., & Chang, F. M. (2008). Randomized controlled trial of music on state anxiety and physiological indices in patients undergoing root canal treatment. *Journal of Clinical Nursing, 7*(19), 2654–2660. https://doi: 10.1111/j.1365-2702.2008.02350.x.

Landis-Shack, N., Heinz, A. J., & Bonn-Miller, M. O. (2017). Music therapy for posttraumatic stress in adults: A theoretical review. *Psychomusicology, 27*(4), 334–342. https://doi.org/10.1037/pmu0000192.

Lang, P. (1971). The Application of Psychophysiological Methods to the Study of Psychotherapy and Behavior Modification. In A. E. Bergin & S. L. Garfield (eds), *Handbook of Psychotherapy and Behavior Change* (pp.75–124). New York, NY: Wiley.

Lange, W. G., Heuer, K., Langner, O., Keijers, G. P. J., Becker, E. S., & Rinck, M. (2011). Face value: Eye movements and the evaluation of facial crowds in social anxiety. *Journal of Behavior Therapy and Experimental Psychiatry, 43*(3), 355–363.

Lata, S. & Dwivedi, K. (2001). The effect of music on anxiety. *Psycho-Lingua, 31*(2), 143–146.

Lazarus, A. A. (1975). *Multimodal Behavior Therapy*. New York, NY: Springer.

Lazarus, A.A. (1989). *The Practice of Multimodal Therapy*. Baltimore, MD: Johns Hopkins University.

Lecourt, E. (1998). The Role of Aesthetics in Countertransference: A Comparison of Active Versus Receptive Music Therapy. In K. E. Bruscia (ed.), *The Dynamics of Music Pyschotherapy*. New Braunfels, TX: Barcelona.

Ledger, A., & McCaffrey, T. (2015) Performative, arts-based or arts-informed? Reflections on the development of arts-based research in music therapy. *Journal of Music Therapy, 52*(4), 441 -456.

Ledley, D. R., Huppert, J. D., Foa, E. B., Davidson, J. R. T., Keefe, F. J., & Potts, N. L. (2005). Impact of depressive symptoms on the treatment of generalized social anxiety disorder. *Depression and Anxiety, 22*, 161–167.

LeDoux, J. E. (1996). *The Emotional Brain*. New York, NY: Simon and Schuster.

Lee, C. A. (2003). *The Architecture of Aesthetic Music Therapy*. New Braunfels, TX: Barcelona.

Lee, C. A. (2016). Aesthetic Music Therapy. In J. Edwards (ed.), *The Oxford Handbook of Music Therapy* (pp.515-537). Oxford: Oxford University Press.

Lee, C. A. & Clements-Cortes, A. (2014). Applications of clinical improvisation and aesthetic music therapy in medical settings: An analysis of Debussy's "L'isle joyeuse." *Music and Medicine, 6*(2), 61–69. https://doi.org/10.47513/mmd.v6i2.181.

Lehrer, P. & Woolfolk, R. L. (1982). Self-report assessment of anxiety: Somatic, cognitive, and behavioral modalities. *Behavioral Assessment, 4*, 167–177.

Levine, P. (1996). Nature's Lessons in Healing Trauma. Unpublished PhD dissertation.

Levy, D. (1937). Primary affect hunger. *American Journal of Psychiatry, 94*, 643–652.

Lieberman, A. F., Padron, E., Van Horn, P., & Harris, W. W. (2005). Angels in the nursery: The intergenerational transmission of benevolent parental influences. *Infant Mental Health Journal, 26*(6), 504–520. https://doi: 10.1002/imhj.20071.

Lindahl Jacobson, S., Waldon, E. G., & Gattino, G. (eds). (2019). *Music Therapy Assessment*. London: Jessica Kingsley Publishers.

Lioara, P. (2015). Social and economic effects of music therapy. *Annals of the University of Bucharest, Economic and Administrative Series, 9*. Gale Academic OneFile. https://search.ebscohost.com/login.aspx?direct=true&AuthType=sso&db=edsgao&AN=edsg-cl.439271399&site=eds-live&scope=site&custid=s5702506.

Lowey, J. (2000). Music psychotherapy assessment. *Music Therapy Perspectives, 18*(1), 47–58. https://doi10.1093/mtp/18.1.47.

Lowey, J. V. (1995). The musical stages of speech: A developmental model of pre-verbal sound making though music. *Music Therapy, 13*(1), 47–73.

Lucas, A. R., Klepin, H. D., Porges, S. W., & Rejeski, W. (2018). Mindfulness-based movement: A polyvagal perspective. *Integrative Cancer Therapies, 17*(1), 5–15. https://doi10.1177/15347354166820.

Magee, J. & Davidson, J. (2004). Singing in therapy: Monitoring disease process in chronic degenerative illness. *British Journal of Music Therapy, 18*(2), 55–77.

Main, M. (1990). Cross-sectional studies of attachment organization: Recent studies, changing methodologies, and the concept of conditional strategies. *Human Development, 33*, 48–61.

Main, M. & Goldwyn, R. (1988). Adult attachment scoring and classification. Unpublished manuscript, University of California, Berkleley.

Main, M., Hesse, E., & Kaplan, N. (2005). Predictability of Attachment Behavior and Representational Processes at 1, 6, and 19 Years of Age: The Berkeley Longitudinal Study. In K. E. Grossmann, K. Grossmann, & E. Waters (eds), *Attachment from Infancy to Adulthood: The Major Longitudinal Studies* (pp.245–304). New York, NY: Guilford Press.

Main, M. & Solomon, J. (1986). Discovery of a New, Insecure-Disorganized/Disoriented Attachment Pattern. In M. Yogman & T. B. Brazelton (eds), *Affective Development in Infancy* (pp.95–124). Norwood, NJ: Ablex.

Main, M. & Solomon, J. (1990). Procedures for Identifying Infants as Disorganized/Disoriented During the Ainsworth Strange Situation. In M.T. Greenberg, D. Cicchetti & E.M. Cummings (eds), *Attachment in the Preschool Years: Theory, Research and Intervention* (pp.121–160). Chicago, IL: University of Chicago Press.

Mak, W. W. S. (2001). A culture specific model of vulnerability to psychological distress: The role of self-construals and cognitive personality styles on anxiety and depression. *Dissertation Abstracts International: Section B: The Sciences and Engineering, 62*(3-B), 1586.

Martin, L., Oepen, R., Bauer, K., Nottensteiner, A., *et al.* (2018). Creative arts interventions for stress management and prevention: A systematic review. *Behavioral Sciences, 8*(28), 1–18. https://doi.org/doi:10.3390/bs8020028.

Martin, M. A. & Orsillo, S. M. (2001). *Practitioner's Guide to Empirically Based Measures of Anxiety.* New York, NY: Plenum.

May, R. (1996). *The Meaning of Anxiety.* New York, NY: The Ronald Press.

Mayor, C. (2012). Playing with race: A theoretical framework and approach for creative arts therapies. *The Arts in Psychotherapy, 39*(3), 214–219. https://doi.org/10.1016/j.aip.2011.12.008.

McCaffrey, T. (2013). Music therapists' experience of self in clinical improvisation in music therapy: A phenomenological investigation. *The Arts in Psychotherapy, 40*(3), 306–311.

McFerran, K. (2010). *Adolescents, Music and Music Therapy. Methods and Techniques for Clinicians, Educators and Students.* London: Jessica Kingsley Publishers.

McFerran-Skewes, K. (2000). From the mouths of babes: The response of six younger, bereaved teenagers to the experience of psychodynamic group music therapy. *Australian Journal of Music Therapy, 11*, 3–22.

McIntosh, P. (1989). White privilege: Unpacking the invisible knapsack. *Peace and Freedom, July/August*, 10–12.

Merriam Webster dictionary definition of "anxiety." www.merriam-webster.com/dictionary/anxiety, accessed November 11, 2021.

Metzner, S. (2005). Following the tracks of the other: Therapeutic improvisations and the artistic perspective. *Nordic Journal of Music Therapy, 14*(2), 155–163. https://doi.org/10.1080/08098130509478136.

Metzner, S. (2016). Psychodynamic Music Therapy. In J. Edwards (ed.), *The Oxford Handbook of Music Therapy* (pp.448–471). Oxford: Oxford University Press.

Mikulincer, M., Florian, V., & Tomacz, R. (1990). Attachment styles and fear of personal death: A case study of affect regulation. *Journal of Personality and Social Psychology, 58*(2), 273–280.

Mikulincer, M. & Shaver, P. R. (2018). *Attachment in Adulthood* (2nd ed). New York, NY: Guilford Press.

Miluk-Kolasa, B., Klodecka-Rozka, J., & Stupnicki, R. (2002). The effect of music listening on perioperative anxiety levels in surgical patients. *Polish Psychological Bulletin, 33*(2), 55–60.

Mohammadi, A. Z., Shahabi, T., & Panah, F. M. (2011). An evaluation of the effect of group music therapy on stress, anxiety, and depression levels in nursing home residents. *Journal of Music Therapy, 17*(1), 55–68.

Moldavanova, A. (2016). Two narratives of intergenerational sustainability. *American Review of Public Administration, 46*(5), 526. Complementary Index.

Montello, L. (2002). *Essential Musical Intelligence.* Wheaton, IL: Quest Books.

Montello, L. (2005). *The Performance Wellness Manual.* Honesdale, PA: Innovations Press.

Montello, L. (2010). The performance wellness seminar: An integrative music therapy approach to preventing performance-related disorders in college-age musicians. *Music and Medicine, 2*(2), 109–116. https://doi: 10.1177/1943862110364231.

Moreno, J. (2006). *Citing Your Inner Music: Music Therapy and Psychodrama.* New Braunfels, TX: Barcelona.

Moustakas, C. (1990). *Heuristic Research: Design, Methodology, and Applications.* Newbury Park, CA: Sage.

Navaro-Wagner, A. (2015). The art of re-framing. *Voices: A World Forum for Music Therapy, 15*(1). https://doi: 10.15845/voices.v1i1.769.

Nechama, Y. (2009). "I am not at home with my client's music...I felt guilty about disliking it": On musical authenticity in music therapy. *Musiktherapeutische Umschau, 20*(2), 129–143.

Newham, P. (1998). *Therapeutic Voicework: Principles and Practice for the Use of Singing as a Therapy.* London: Jessica Kingsley Publishers.

Nordoff, P. & Robbins, C. (2007). *Creative Music Therapy: A Guide to Fostering Clinical Musicianship.* (2nd ed.). New Braunfels, TX: Barcelona.

Office of National Statistics. (2017). *UK Population.* www.ons.gov.uk/aboutus/transparencyandgovernance/freedomofinformationfoi/ukpopulation2017.

Okan, I. A. & Caykoylu, A. (2011). The comorbidity of anxiety disorders in bipolar I and bipolar II patients among Turkish population. *Journal of Anxiety Disorders, 25*(5), 661–667.

Olatunji, B., Cisler, J. M., & Tolin, D. F. (2010). A meta-analysis of the influence of comorbidity on treatment outcome in the anxiety disorders. *Psychology Review, 30*(6), 642–654.

Oldfied, A. (2012). Exploring Issues of Control through Interactive, Improvised Music Making: Music Therapy Diagnostic Assessment and Short Term Treatment with a Mother and Daughter in a Psychiatric Unit. In K. Brusica (ed.), *Case Examples of Music Therapy for Children with Emotional or Behavioral Problems* (pp.118–127). New Braunfels, TX: Barcelona.

Oldfield, A. (2006). *Interactive Music Therapy: A Positive Approach*. London: Jessica Kingsley Publishers.

Oliker, D. M. (2013). This is who and what they are! Exploring the need to deny it. *Psychology Today*. www.psychologytoday.com/us/blog/the-long-reach-childhood/201311/is-who-and-what-they-are.

Oliver, P. G. (2010). The DIY artist: Issues of sustainability within local music scenes. *Management Decision, 48*(9), 1422. Complementary Index.

Orman, E. K. (2004). Effect of virtual reality graded exposure on anxiety levels of performing musicians: A case study. *Journal of Music Therapy, 41*, 70–79.

Osborne, M. S. & Kenny, D. (2008). The role of sensitizing experiences in music performance anxiety in adolescent musicians. *Psychology of Music, 36*(4), 447–462.

Pacheco-Unguetti, A. P., Acosta, A., Marques, E., & Lupienez, J. (2011). Alterations of the attentional networks in patients with anxiety disorders. *Journal of Anxiety Disorders, 25*, 888–895.

Palm, M. E., Elliott, R., McKie, S., Deakin, J. F. W., & Anderson, I. M. (2010). Attenuated responses to emotional expressions in women with generalized anxiety disorder. *Psychological Medicine, 41*(5), 1009–1018. https://doi:10.1017/50033291710001455.

Passaili, V. (2012). Supporting parent-child interactions: Music therapy as an intervention for promoting mutually responsive orientation. *Journal of Music Therapy, 49*(3), 303–334.

Patel, V., Saxena, S., Lund, C., Thornicroft, G., *et al.* (2018). The Lancet Commission on global mental health and sustainable development. *The Lancet, 392*(10157), 1553–1598. https://doi.org/10.1016/S0140-6736(18)31612-X.

Pavlicevic, M. & Ansdell, G. (2004). *Community Music Therapy*. London: Jessica Kingsley Publishers.

Pearson, P. (2008). *A Brief History of Anxiety: Yours and Mine*. New York, NY: Bloomsbury.

Pender, V. B., Brandt, J. C., Mahfouz, A., & Tylim, I. (2007). Approaches to prevention of intergenerational transmission of hate, war, and violence. *The International Journal of Psychoanalysis, 88*, 507–514. https://doi: 10.1516/BX7R-1468-0207-7Q75.

Pinna-Perez, A. & Frank, F. (2018). Sleep of reason: Critical reflections on performance arts-based research as a psycho-social commentary in expressive arts therapy praxis. *Qualitative Research in Psychology, 15*(2–3), 234–246. https://doi-org.ezproxyles.flo.org/10.1080/14780887.2018.1429908.

Popa, L. (2015). The use of music therapy as a factor of sustainable development. *Procedia Economics and Finance, 32*, 1060–1065. ScienceDirect.

Porges, S. W. (2001). The polyvagal theory: Phylogenetic substrates of a social nervous system. *International Journal of Psychophysiology, 42*, 123–146.

Porges, S. W. (2017). *The Pocket Guide to the Polyvagal Theory. The Transfromative Power of Feeling Safe*. New York, NY: W. W. Norton.

Porges, S. W. & Furman, S. A. (2011). The early development of the autonomic nervous system provides a neural platform for social behavior: A polyvagal perspective. *Infant Child Development, 20*(1), 106–118. https://doi:10.1002/icd.688.

Potok, A. (2002). *A Matter of Dignity*. New York, NY: Bantam Dell.

Potvin, N., Bradt, J., & Ghetti, C. (2018). A theoretical model of resource-oriented music therapy with informal hospice caregivers during pre-bereavement. *Journal of Music Therapy, 55*(1), 27–61. https://doi.org/10.1093/jmt/thx019.

Powers, M. B., Vervliet, B., & Smits, J. A. J. (2010). Helping Exposure Succeed: Learning Theory Perspectives on Treatment Resistance and Relapse. In M. Otto & S. G. Hofmann (eds), *Avoiding Treatment Failures in the Anxiety Disorders* (pp.31–49). New York, NY: Springer Science + Business Media.

Previti, D. & Amato, P. R. (2004). Is infidelity a cause or consequence of poor marital quality? *Journal of Social and Personal Relationships, 15*(3), 93–94.

Rachman, S. (1990). *Fear and Courage* (2nd ed.). New York, NY: Freeman.

Rachman., S. & Hodgson, R. (1974). Synchrony and desynchrony in fear and avoidance. *Behavior Research and Therapy, 12*, 311–318.

Rangan, K., Chase, L. A., & Karim, S. (2012). *Why Every Company Needs a CSR Strategy and How to Build It: Working Paper.* Harvard Business School.

Ray, W. J., Molnar, C., Aikins, D., Yamasaki, A., *et al.* (2009). Startle response in generalized anxiety disorder. *Depression and Anxiety, 26*, 147–154.

Rego, S. A. (2009). Culture and Anxiety Disorders. In S. A. G. Eshun & A. R. Regan (eds), *Culture and Mental Health: Sociocultural Influences, Theory, and Practice* (pp.197–220). Hoboken, NJ: Wiley-Blackwell.

Reis, H. X. & Shaver, P. (1988). Intimacy as an Interpersonal Process. In S. W. Duck (ed.), *Handbook of Personal Relationships* (pp.367–389). New York, NY: Wiley.

Rescoria, R. A. & Wagner, A. R. (1972). A Theory of Pavlovian Conditioning: Variations in the Effectiveness of Reinforcement and Nonreinforcement. In A. H. Black & W. F. Prokasy (eds), *Classical Conditioning II: Current Theory and Research* (pp.64–99). New York, NY: Appleton-Century-Crofts.

Reynolds, C. R. & Richmond, B. O. (1978). What I think and feel: A revised measure of children's manifest anixety. *Journal of Abnormal Psychology, 6*(2), 271–280.

Rickson, D. & McFerran, K. (2014). *Creating Music Cultures in the Schools: A Perspective from Community Music Therapy.* New Braunfels, TX: Barcelona Publishers.

Rider, M. S., Floyd, J. W., & Kirkpatrick, J. (1985). The effect of music, imagery, and relaxation on adrenal corticosteroids and the re-entrainment of circadian rhythms. *Journal of Music Therapy, 22*, 46–58.

Ridley, M. (2003). *Nature Via Nurture: Genes, Experience, and What Makes Us Human.* New York, NY: HarperCollins.

Roald, T. & Koppe, S. (2014). Sense and subjectivity. Hidden potentials in psychological aesthetics. *Journal of Theoretical and Philosophical Psychology, 35*(1), 20–34.

Robarts, J. Z. (2003). The healing function of improvised songs in music therapy with a child survivor of early trauma and sexual abuse. In S. Hadley (2003). (ed.). *Psychodynamic music therapy: Case studies.*(pp. 158–200). Gilsum, NH: Barcelona.

Robarts, J. Z. (2012). The Healing Function of Improvised Songs in Music Therapy with a Child Survivor of Early Trauma and Sexual Abuse. In K. Bruscia (ed.), *Case Examples of the Use of Songs in Psychotherapy* (pp.172–202). New Braunfels, TX: Barcelona.

Robb, S. L. (2000). The effect of therapeutic music interventions on the behavior of hospitalized children in isolation: Developing a contextual support model of music therapy. *Music Therapy, 37*(2), 118–146.

Rolvsjord, R. (2010). *Resource Oriented Music Therapy in Mental Health Care.* New Braunfels, TX: Barcelona.

Royal Foundation of the Duke and Duchess of Cambridge (RFDDC) (2021). *Mental Health.* https://royalfoundation.com/mental-health.

Rubenstein, C. & Shaver, P. R. (1982). The Experience of Loneliness. In L. A. Peplau & D. Perlman (eds), *Loneliness: A Sourcebook of Current Theory, Research, and Therapy* (pp.206–223). New York, NY: Wiley.

Rugenstein, L. (1996). Wilber's Spectrum Model of Transpersonal Psychology and its application to music therapy. *Music Therapy, 14*(1), 19–28.

Ruiz-Salas, J. C. & De la Casa, L. G. (2021). Induced positive affect reduces the magnitude of the startle response and prepulse inhibition. *Journal of Psychophysiology, 35*(1), 51–60. https://doi.org/10.1027/0269-8803/a000261.

Ruokonen, I., Sepp, A., Moilanen, V., Autio, O., & Ruismaki, H. (2014). The Finnish five-string kantele: Sustainably designed for musical joy. *Journal of Teacher Education for Sustainability, 16*(1), 76–88. ERIC.

Ruud, E. (2008). Music in therapy: Increasing possibilities for action. *Music and Arts in Action, 1*(1), 46–60. Directory of Open Access Journals.

Ruud, E. (2010). *Music Therapy: A Perspective from the Humanities.* New Braunfels, TX: Barcelona.

Sacks, O. (1973). *Awakenings*. Vintage Books.

Sajnani, N., Beardall, N., Stephenson, R., Estrella, K., *et al.* (2019). Navigating the Transition to Online Education in the Arts Therapies. In R. Hougham, S. Pitruzzella, S. Scoble, & H. Weingrower (eds), *Traditions in Transition in the Arts Therapies* (pp.153–170). Plymouth: University of Plymouth Press. http://ecartepublications.co.uk/traditions-in-transition/mobile/index.html.

Sajnani, N., Marxen, E., & Zarate, R. (2017). Critical perspectives in the arts therapies: Response/ability across a continuum of practice. *The Arts in Psychotherapy, 54*, 28–37. https://doi.org/10.1016/j.aip.2017.01.007.

Salman, E., Diamond, K., Jusino, C., Sanchez-LaCay, A., & Liebowitz, M. R. (1997). *Hispanic Americans: Cultural Issues in the Treatment of Anxiety*. New York, NY: Guilford Press.

Salzman, M. (2001). Globalization, culture, and anxiety: Perspectives and predictions from terror management theory. *Journal of Social Distress & the Homeless, 10*, 337–352. https://doi: 10.1023/A:1011676025600.

Scheiby, B. (2005). An intersubjective approach to music therapy: Identification and processing of musical countertransference in a music psychotherapeutic context. *Music Therapy Perspectives, 23*, 8–17. https://doi: 10.1093/mtp/23.1.8.

Scheiby, B. B. (1998). The Role of Musical Countertransference in Analytical Music Therapy. In K. E. Bruscia (ed.), *The Dynamics of Music Pyschotherapy* (pp.213–248). New Braunfels, TX: Barcelona.

Schmid, W. (2014). A penguin on the moon: Self-organizational processes in improvisational music therapy in neurological rehabilitation. *Nordic Journal of Music Therapy, 23*(2), 152–172. Academic Search Index.

Schneck, D. J. (2015). *Basic Anatomy and Physiology for the Music Therapist*. London: Jessica Kingsley Publishers.

Schneck, D. J. & Berger, D. S. (2006). *The Music Effect: Music Physiology and Clinical Applications*. London: Jessica Kingsley Publishers.

Schore, A., Siegel, D. J., & Cozolino, L. (2021). *Interpersonal Neurobiology and Clinical Practice*. New York, NY: W. W. Norton.

Schroeder, T. & Matheson, C. (2006). Imagination and Emotion. In S. Nichols (ed.), *The Architecture of the Imagination: New Essays on Pretence, Possibility, and Fiction*. Oxford: Oxford Scholarship Online. https://doi10.1093/acprof:oso/9780199275731.003.0002.

Schwartz, E., Boyle, S. R., & Engen, R. (2018). *Functional Voice Skills for Music Therapists*. New Braunfels, TX: Barcelona.

Scruton, R. (1999). *The Aesthetics of Music*. Oxford: Oxford University Press.

Seabrook, D. (2020). Music therapy in the era of climate crisis: Evolving to meet current needs. *The Arts in Psychotherapy, 68*, 2–8. ScienceDirect.

Selye, H. (1950). Adaptive Reaction to Stress. *Psychosomatic Medicine, 12*, 149–157.

Shapiro, N. (2005). Sounds in the world: Multicultural influences in music therapy in clinical practice and training. *Music Therapy Perspectives, 23*, 29–35. https://doi: 10.1093/mtp/23.1.29.

Sharma, M. & Jagdev, T. (2012). Use of music therapy for enhancing self-esteem among academically stressed adolescents. *Pakistan Journal of Pyschological Research, 27*(1), 53–64.

Shaver, P. R. & Hazan, C. (1984). Incompatibility, Loneliness, and "Limerence." In W. Ickes (ed.), *Compatible and Incompatible Relationships* (pp.163–184). New York, NY: Springer.

Siegel, D. J. (n.d.). *Transforming Pandemic Panic into Receptive Presence and Growth" with Dr. Dan Siegel (Webinar)*. Retrieved April 1, 2021, from www.youtube.com/watch?v=qIKUYmIE_0o.

Siegel, D. J. (1999). *The Developing Mind: How Relationships and the Brain Interact to Shape Who We Are*. New York, NY: Guilford Press.

Siegel, D. J. (2020). *The Developing Mind: How Relationships and the Brain Interact to Shape Who We Are* (3rd ed.). New York, NY: Guilford Press.

Siegel, D. J. & Solomon, M. F. (2020). *Mind, Consciousness, and Well-Being*. New York, NY: W. W. Norton.

Silverman, M. J. (2010). The effect of pitch, rhythm, and familiarity on working memory and anxiety as measured by digit recall performance. *Journal of Music Therapy, 47*, 70–83. https://doi: 10.1093/jmt/47.1.70.

Sims, S. (2021). What are adaptogens and how can they help my training and performance? *Triathlete, March/April*, 32.

Singer, T. & Kimbles, S. L. (eds). (2004). *The Cultural Complex. Contemporary Jungian Perspectives on Psyche and Society*. London: Routledge.

Situmorang, D. D. B., Mulawarman, M., & Wibowo, M. E. (2018). Comparison of the effectiveness of CBT group counseling with passive vs active music therapy to reduce millennials' academic anxiety. *International Journal of Psychology and Educational Studies, 5*(3), 51–62.

Smeijsters, H. (2005). *Sounding the Self: Analogy in Improvisational Music Therapy*. New Braunfels, TX: Barcelona Publishers.

Smith, J. C. & Joyce, C. A. (2004). Mozart versus new age music: Relaxation states, stress, and ABC Relaxation Theory. *Journal of Music Therapy, 41*, 215–224. https://doi 10.1093/jmt/41.3.215.

Smith, M. (2008). The effects of a single music relaxation session on state anxiety levels of adults in a workplace. *Journal of Music Therapy, 19*, 45–66.

Sobey, K. & Woodcock, J. (1999). Psychodynamic Music Therapy: Considerations in Training. In A. Cattanach (ed.), *Process in the Arts Therapies* (pp.132–153). London: Jessica Kingsley Publishers.

Spielberger, C. D., Gorsuch, R. L., & Lushene, R. (1970). *STAI Manual*. Palo Alto, CA: Consulting Psychologists Press.

Spielberger, C. D., Gorsuch, R. L., Lushene, R., Vagg, P. R., & Jacobs, G. A. (1983). *Manual for the State-Trait Anxiety Inventory*. Palo Alto, CA: Consulting Psychologists Press.

Spitz, R. A. (1945). Hospitalism: An enquiry into the genesis of psychiatric conditions in early childhood. *The Psychoanalysis Study of the Child, 2*, 313–342.

Sroufe, A. (2000). Early relationships and the development of children. *Infant Mental Health Journal, 21*(1–2), 67–74.

Sroufe, A. & Seigel, D. (2011). The verdict is in. *Psychotherapy Networker, 35*(2), 35–39.

Stamoulis, C., Vanderwert, R. E., Zeanah, C. H., Fox, N. A., & Nelson, C. A. (2017). Neuronal networks in the developing brain are adversely modulated by early psychosocial neglect. *Journal of Neurophysiology, 118*(4), 2275–2288. https://doi: 10.1152/jn.00014.2017.

Stapleton, P. (2013). Autobiography and invention: Towards a critical understanding of identity, dialogue and resistance in improvised musics. *Contemporary Music Review, 32*(2–3), 165–174. https://doi-org.ezproxyles.flo.org/10.1080/07494467.2013.775806.

Stein, H. F. (2004). *Beneath the Crust of Culture: Psychoanalytic Anthropology and the Cultural Unconscious in American Life*. Amsterdam: Rodopi B.V.

Stern, D. N. (1985). *The Interpersonal World of the Infant: A View from Psychoanalysis and Developmental Psychology*. Cambridge, MA: Harvard University Press.

Stern, D. N. (2010). *Forms of Vitality: Exploring Dynamic Experience in Psychology, the Arts, Psychotherapy, and Development*. Oxford: Oxford University Press.

Stige, B. (2002). *Culture Centered Music Therapy*. New Braunfels, TX: Barcelona.

Sullivan, M. B., Erb, M., Schmalzl, L., Moonaz, S., Noggle Taylor, J., & Porges, S. W. (2018). Yoga Therapy and Polyvagal Theory: The convergence of traditional wisdom and contemporary neuroscience for self-regulation and resilience. *Frontiers in Human Neuroscience, 12*(67), 1–15. https://doi10.3389/fnhum.2018.00067.

Sutton, J. P. (2002). *Music, Music Therapy and Trauma: International Perspectives*. London: Jessica Kingsley Publishers.

Takriti, A. & Ahmad, T. (2000). Anxiety Disorders and Treatment in Arab-Muslim Culture. In I. Al-Issa (ed.), *Al-Junūn: Mental Illness in the Islamic World* (pp.235–252). Madison, CT: International Universities Press.

Taylor, P. A. A. (2017). The Legacy of Enough. In S. Johnson (ed.), *Seeing in the Dark: Wisdom Works by Black Women in Depth Psychology* (pp.37–54). Calabasas, CA: The Malibu Press.

Teague, A. K., Hahna, N. D., & McKinney, C. H. (2006). Group music therapy with women who have experienced intimate partner violence. *Music Therapy Perspectives, 24*, 80–86. https://doi: 10.1093/mtp/24.2.80.

Thomas, D. R. (2003). A general inductive approach for qualitative data analysis. *American Journal of Evaluation, 27*(2), 237–246.

Thornton, L. M., Dellava, J. E., Root, T. L., Lichtenstein, P., & Bulik, C. M. (2011). Anorexia nervosa and generalized anxiety disorder: Further exploration of the relation between anxiety and body mass index. *Journal of Anxiety Disorders, 25*, 727–730.

Titon, J. T. (1984). *Worlds of Music*. New York, NY: Schirmer Books.

Tone, A. (2009). *The Age of Anxiety*. New York, NY: Basic Books.

Topps, M. (2014). Slow life history strategies and slow updating of internal models: The examples of conscientiousness and obsessive-compulsive disorder. *Psychological Inquiry, 25*. https://doi.org/10.1080/1047840X.2014.916194.

Trondalen, G. (2016). *Relational Music Therapy: An Intersubjective Perspective*. New Braunfels, TX: Barcelona.

Turry, A. (2012). "Do I dare imagine?" A microanalysis of a clinically improvised song. In K. Brusica (ed.), *Case Examples of the Use of Songs in Psychotherapy* (pp.124–151). New Braunfels, TX: Barcelona.

Tyson, F. (1981). *Psychiatric Music Therapy: Origins and Development*. New York, NY: Creative Arts Rehabilitation Center.

Uhlig, S. (2007). *Authentic Voices, Authentic Singing: A Multicultural Approach to Vocal Music Therapy*. New Braunfels, TX: Barcelona.

United Nations. (n.d.). *Sustainable Development Goals*. www.un.org/sustainabledevelopment/health.

United Nations Department of Economic and Social Affairs: Population dynamics. (2017). *World Population Prospects: The 2017 Revision*. www.un.org/development/desa/publications/world-population-prospects-the-2017-revision.html.

Vaillancourt, G., Costa, D., Han, Y., & Lipski, G. (2018). An intergenerational singing group: A community music therapy qualitative research project and graduate student mentoring initiative. *Voices: A World Forum for Music Therapy, 18*(1). Directory of Open Access Journals. https://doi.org/10.15845/voices.v18i1.883.

van der Kolk, B. (2015). *The Body Keeps the Score: Brain, Mind, and Body in the Healing of Trauma*. New York, NY: Penguin Books.

Vandervoort, D. D., Divers, P. P., & Madrid, S. (1999). Ethno-culture and irrational beliefs. *Current Psychology, 18*, 287–293. https://doi: 10.1007/s12144-999-1003-5.

Viega, M. (2014). Listening in the ambient mode: Implications for music therapy practice and theory. *Voices: A World Forum for Music Therapy, 14*(2). https://doi.org/10.15845/voices.v14i2.778.

Viega, M. (2016). Science as art: Axiology as a central component in methodology and evaluation of arts-based research (ABR). *Music Therapy Perspectives, 34*(1), 4–13.

Viega, M., Zarate, R., Gilbertson, S., McCaffrey, T., Beer, L., & Woodward, A. (2017). Critical perspectives in arts based research. *Proceedings from: World Congress of Music Therapy, Tsukuba, Japan*. http://wcmt2017.com/en/proceedings/pdf/WFMT-Vol.13-1.pdf.

Voogd Cochrane, S., Chhabra, M., Jones, M. A., & Spragg, D. (eds). (2017). *Culturally Responsive Teaching and Reflection in Higher Education: Promising Practices from the Cultural Literacy Curriculum Institute*. New York, NY: Routledge.

Vuust, P. & Kringelbach, M. L. (2010). The Pleasure of Music. In M. Kringelbach & K. C. Berridge (eds), *Pleasures of the Brain* (pp.255–265). Oxford: Oxford University Press.

Wagner, D. & McGinn Hurst, S. (2018). Couples dance/movement therapy: Bringing a theoretical framework into practice. *American Journal of Dance Therapy, 40*, 18–43. https://doi.org/10.1007/s10465-018-9271-y.

Wallin, W. (2007). *Attachment in Psychotherapy*. New York, NY: Guilford Press.

Walsh Stewart, R. & Stewart, D. (2002). See Me, Hear Me, Play with Me: Working with the Trauma of Early Abandonment and Deprivation in Psychodynamic Music Therapy. In J. Sutton (ed.), *Music, Music Therapy and Trauma: International Perspectives* (pp.133–152). London: Jessica Kingsley Publishers.

Warnock, T. (2011). Voice and the self in improvised music therapy. *British Journal of Music Therapy, 25*(2), 32–27.

Weertman, A., Arntz, A., Schouten, E., & Dreessen, L. (2005). Influences of beliefs and personality disorders on treatment outcomes in anxiety patients. *Journal of Consulting Psychology, 73*(5), 936–944.

Wenger, E. (1998). *Communities of Practice: Learning, Meaning, and Identity*. Cambridge: Cambridge University Press.

Westen, D., Novotny, C. M., & Thompson-Brenner, H. (2004). The empirical status of supported psychotherapies: Assumptions, findings, and reporting in controlled clinical trials. *Psychological Bulletin, 130,* 631–663. https://doi:10.1037/0033- 2909.130.4.631.

Weymann, E. (2000). Sensitive suspense—Experiences in musical improvisation. *Journal of Music Therapy, 9*(1), 38–45. https://doi-org.ezproxyles.flo.org/10.1080/08098130009477984.

Wheeler, B. (2013). Music Therapy Assessment. In R. F. Cruz. & B. Feder (eds), *The Art and Science of Evaluation in the Arts Therapies: How Do You Know What's Working* (pp.344–382). Springfield, IL: Charles C. Thomas.

Whitehead-Pleaux, A. & Tan, X. (2016). *Cultural Intersections in Music Therapy: Music, Health, and the Person.* New Braunfels, TX: Barcelona.

Wilber, K. (2001). *No Boundary: Eastern and western approaches to personal growth.* Shambala.

Wigram, T. (1999). Assessment methods in music therapy: A humanistic or natural science framework? *Nordic Journal of Music Therapy, 8*(1), 7–25.

Wigram, T. (2004). *Improvisation: Methods and Techniques for Music Therapy Clinicans, Educators and Students.* London: Jessica Kingsley Publishers.

Wilber, K. (1977). *The Spectrum of Consciousness.* Wheaton, IL: Quest Books.

Wilber, K. (2001). *No Boundary: Eastern and Western Approaches to Personal Growth.* Boston, MA: Shambhala.

Wilkinson, I. (2001). *Anxiety in a Risk Society.* London: Routledge.

Winnicott, D. (1971). *Playing and Reality.* London: Tavistock.

Wolberg, L. (1967). *The Technique of Psychotherapy.* New York, NY: Grune & Stratton.

Wood, S. (2016). *A Matrix for Community Music Therapy Practice.* New Braunfels, TX: Barcelona.

World Health Organization. (n.d). *Global Health Observatory Data Repository.* Retrieved from https://apps.who.int/gho/data/node.main.

Wosch, T. & Wigram, T. (eds). (2007). *Microanalysis in Music Therapy: Methods, Techniques and Applications for Clinicians, Researchers, Educators and Students* (1st ed.). London: Jessica Kingsley Publishers.

Wu, S. M. (2002). Effects of music therapy on anxiety, depression and self-esteem of undergraduates. *Psychologia: An International Journal of Psychology in the Orient, 45*(2), 104–114. https://doi: 10.2117/psysoc.2002.104.

Yackle, K., Lindsay, A. S., Kaiwen, K., Sorokin, J. M., *et al.* (2017). Breathing control center neurons that promote arousal in mice. *Science, 355*(6332), 1411–1415. https://doi: 10.1126/science.aai7984.

Yalom, I. D. (1995). *The Theory and Practice of Group Psychotherapy* (4th ed.). Worcester, MA: American Psychological Association.

Yorulmaz, O., Gencoz, T., & Woody, S. (2009). OCD cognitions and symptoms in different religious contexts. *Journal of Anxiety Disorders, 23*(3), 401–406. https:// doi: 10.1016/j.janxdis.2008.11.001.

Zarafshandardaky, T. (2019). Anxiety Symptoms, Childhood Autism and Improvisational Music Therapy: A Clinical Method. In *Expressive Therapies Capstone Theses.* https://digitalcommons.lesley.edu/cgi/viewcontent.cgi?article=1143&context=expressive_theses.

Zarate, R. (2012). The Sounds of Anxiety: A Quantitative Study in Music Therapy and Anxiety. *Proquest Dissertations and Theses.*

Zarate, R. (2016a). Clinical improvisation and its effect on anxiety: A multiple single subject design. *The Arts in Psychotherapy, 48,* 46–53. https://doi: 10.1016/j.aip.2015.11.005.

Zarate, R. (2016b). The social architecture of anxiety and potential role of music therapy. *Voices, 16*(1), Directory of Open Access Journals. https://doi.org/10.15845/voices.v16i1.847.

Zarate, R. (2020). Interview with Al Jazeera. www.aljazeera.com/amp/videos/2020/3/22/coronavirus-entertainers-go-online-to-reach-locked-down-audience.

Zatorre, R., Halpern, A., Perry, D., Meyer, E., & Evans, A. (1996). Hearing in the mind's ear: A PET investigation of musical imagery and perception. *Journal of Cognitive Neuroscience, 8,* 29–46.

Subject Index

Author Index